NOV   2004

MIDLOTHIAN PUBLIC LIBRARY
3 1614 00108 7874

W9-AMN-375

MIDLOTHIAN
PUBLIC LIBRARY

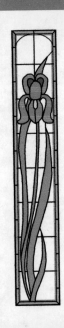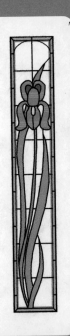

A gift to the
Midlothian Public
Library

In Memory of
Jane K. LeFever

DK COLLECTOR'S GUIDES

20TH-CENTURY GLASS

Previous page: Tiffany clear glass paperweight vase with pink, white, and green glass inclusions in the form of petals; the overall effect is of a blooming flower. *c. 1910. 6¼ in (16 cm) high* **$20,000–25,000 LN**

Riihimäki mold-blown vase, p.48

DK COLLECTOR'S GUIDES

20TH-CENTURY GLASS

JUDITH MILLER

with Frankie Leibe and Mark Hill

Photography by Graham Rae
with Andy Johnson, John McKenzie, and Heike Löwenstein

MIDLOTHIAN PUBLIC LIBRARY
14701 S. KENTON AVE.
MIDLOTHIAN, IL 60445

DK Publishing

LONDON, NEW YORK,
MUNICH, MELBOURNE, DELHI

A joint production from **DK** and
THE PRICE GUIDE COMPANY

DORLING KINDERSLEY LIMITED
Senior Editor Caroline Hunt
Senior Art Editor Mandy Earey
Editor Kathryn Wilkinson
US Editor Christine Heilman
Managing Editor Julie Oughton
Managing Art Editor Heather McCarry
Art Director Carole Ash
Category Publisher Jackie Douglas
Production Sarah Dodd
DTP Designer Mike Grigoletti
Picture Research Sarah Duncan

Sands Publishing Solutions LLP
Editors David & Sylvia Tombesi-Walton
Art Editor Simon Murrell

THE PRICE GUIDE COMPANY LIMITED
Publishing Manager Julie Brooke
Managing Editor Claire Smith
Editorial Assistant Sandra Lange
Digital Image Coordinator Ellen Spalek
Chief Consultants Dudley Browne at James D.
Julia Inc., Jeanette Hayhurst, Mark Hill
Chief Contributor John Wainwright

While every care has been taken in the
compilation of this guide, neither the authors nor
the publishers accept any liability for any financial
or other loss incurred by reliance placed on the
information contained in *DK Collector's Guides:
20th-Century Glass*.

First American Edition, 2004

Published in the United States by
DK Publishing, Inc.
375 Hudson Street
New York, New York 10014

The Price Guide Company (UK) Ltd
info@thepriceguidecompany.com

04 05 06 07 08 09 10 9 8 7 6 5 4 3 2 1

Copyright © Judith Miller and
Dorling Kindersley Limited 2004

All rights reserved under International and
Pan-American Copyright Conventions. No part
of this publication may be reproduced, stored in a
retrieval system, or transmitted in any form or by
any means, electronic, mechanical, photocopying,
recording or otherwise, without the prior written
permission of the copyright owner. Published in
Great Britain by Dorling Kindersley Limited.

A Cataloging-in-Publication record for this book
is available from the Library of Congress.

ISBN 0-7566-0525-3

Color reproduction by Colourscan, Singapore
Printed and bound in China by L. Rex Printing Co. Ltd

Discover more at
www.dk.com

Contents

Blown & Cased Glass   18

Murano sommerso vase, p.34

Burgun, Schverer & Cie vase, p.81

Pressed & Molded Glass   84

748.2

Steuben Blue Aurene bowl, p.123

Blenko Tangerine bottle, p.70

Symphony by Lino Tagliapietra, p.218

How to use this book

DK Collector's Guides: 20th-Century Glass is divided into six chapters: blown and cased; pressed; iridescent; enameled, painted, and stained; engraved and cut; and contemporary and studio. The chapters open with an introduction that discusses the technical processes and historical developments of each type of glass. Here you'll also find a list of handy collectors' tips. Each chapter contains profiles of the most important glass designers and factories from the United States, Great Britain, and Europe, as well as examples of their work. Sidebars provide an at-a-glance list of the key dates for each designer or factory, and "Closer Look" boxes highlight pieces of interest. Every item is briefly and concisely described, given an up-to-date price, and, where possible, dated.

Key Dates
A timeline of important dates in the history of each designer and factory.

Designer Information
Gives a fascinating insight into the career and history of the glass designer or factory. Also highlights the particular characteristics of their work, and offers advice on what to look for when collecting.

A Closer Look
Selects, annotates, and highlights the features that make the piece stand out as an icon of glass design.

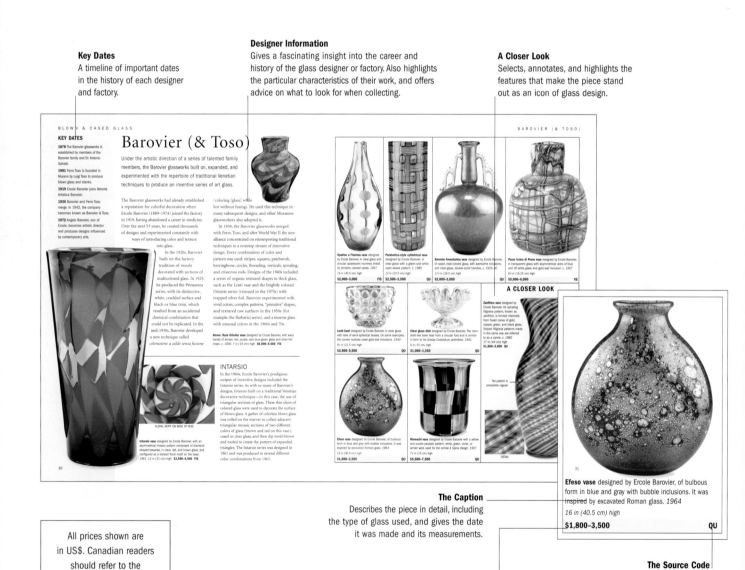

All prices shown are in US$. Canadian readers should refer to the latest currency conversion rates at http://finance.yahoo.com

The Caption
Describes the piece in detail, including the type of glass used, and gives the date it was made and its measurements.

The Price Guide
All prices are shown in ranges to give you a ballpark figure. If the piece is in a museum and no price is available, the letters NPA will be used. The last chapter uses price bands; a key can be found on p.189.

The Source Code
With the exception of museum pieces, most items in the book were specially photographed at an auction house, dealer, antique market, or private collection. Each source is credited here. See pp.229-232 for full listings.

Foreword

Twenty years ago I started collecting Monart glass—partly out of nostalgia for my Scottish homeland, and partly because, while everyone insisted it was kitsch, I found the idea of a family of Spanish glassmakers working in central Scotland producing very un-Scottish glass rather romantic.

Today, my collection is on display in my sitting room, where the morning sun hits the aventurine inclusions and makes them sparkle to life. It always reminds me why we collect things—the thrill of seeing and living with the things we love.

Having become intrigued by glass, I wanted to know more about it. From Emile Gallé to Louis Comfort Tiffany, Whitefriars to Holmegaard, the very diversity of the subject is exciting in itself. As American glass maestro Dale Chihuly says, "People for centuries have been fascinated with glass. It's the most magical of materials." We love glass because of its fragility combined with its strength, its ability to encapsulate the design of the times and be practical yet decorative. Glass is simply a conduit for light—the greatness of a Tiffany lamp is the moment it is illuminated and the shade takes on a new dimension.

Great glass is down to the maker, not the system or the technique. The wonderful thing about working on this book has been the opportunity to witness at first hand the dramatic work of glass maestros in one of the homes of glassmaking—Murano, Italy. We were able to experience the drama of creation, the sheer thrill of a man working with and against the molten gather to create a work of art. The knowledge that at any moment the glass may shatter makes you hold your breath. The vision the glass maestro has for the piece he is working on may be more than the glass will allow him to do.

Of course, the more you learn about a subject like glass, the more there is to know. To marvel at the cameo techniques developed by Gallé, to delight in the iridescent finish that Tiffany employed, to understand the inspirations of Geoffrey Baxter is to start a long journey of discovery. A contemporary glass maestro can take an ancient technique such as murrines and use it to make something essentially of today.

That is why 20th-century glass is so inspiring.

Baldwin & Guggisberg vase, p.192

Judith Miller.

7

The Art of Glass

Magic and mystery shroud glass, in terms of both how it is made and how it first came to be made. From sand, one of the most common materials found on earth, springs a fountain of forms in a kaleidoscope of colors via the skilled hand of the glassmaster, the burning furnace, and the experience of centuries.

Nobody truly knows how or why glass was first made, but its inherent beauty and ability to be transformed into a plethora of shapes made it instantly highly prized. Although the earliest known glass items are beads from Mesopotamia dating from c. 2500 BC, it was the Egyptians and Romans who truly blew life into the medium, making jewelry, jugs, vases, and flasks, many of which continue to inspire glassmakers today. The blown Roman flask on the left, for example, was made using processes similar to those that allowed the creation of the modern goblet on the right.

To make glass, sand and other simple ingredients are heated in a furnace at a very high temperature until they reach a near-liquid state. A "gather" is made by twisting a steel rod into the molten glass and drawing it out like melted chocolate.

Roman translucent blown glass jar with two handles and a ribbed body. The body has a good level of iridescence from being buried in the ground for centuries. AD 200–400 4½ in (11.5 cm) high **$1,500–2,000 ANA**

Colored glass rods are selected and melted on to the outside of a molten gather of clear glass. The resulting gather, with its coat of different-colored stripes, is then spun rapidly and stretched by the glassmaster and his assistant until it is long and thin, giving the colored twists seen in the final piece. This *zanfirico* rod is cut into sections and the pieces melted together to form the bowl and the foot, which are worked separately in the furnace and with tools. The dolphin is made by dripping molten glass on to the foot and shaping it. At the end, all the pieces are assembled.

One or more other furnaces are then used to heat the piece as it is worked. Tools and techniques have remained largely unchanged through the centuries and are surprisingly simple, mainly comprising tongs and scissors. Their effectiveness comes from the skill of the user.

The historic development of glassmaking can be traced to the countries surrounding the Mediterranean, and glassmaking on the Venetian island of Murano, in particular, dates back to the 11th century. Although glass design has changed over the centuries, historic styles continue to be a strong influence. The style of the goblet on the right is traditional, dating back to before the 19th century, but it was made in 2004. As well as acting as an example of Venetian design, the goblet is also an outlet for the Muranese maestro to display his virtuosity. The tradition of glassmaking on Murano still continues, albeit on a smaller scale. Many of today's leading glass artists, including Richard Marquis and Dale Chihuly, have studied or worked on the island, and even more have been influenced by its extraordinary output.

Zanfirico **goblet** of traditional form with dolphin-shaped ornamental stem with gold foil inclusions, made by Andrea Zilio and signed on the base. *2004. 10½ in (27 cm) high* **$400–600 VET**

Murano Styles

Although many historic Muranese techniques are used today in the same way they always have, some have been updated and are used in the modern idiom by avant-garde artists with an eye for the past.

One such technique is the murrine. A design is built up on the surface of a piece of glass using small colored tiles, or tesserae, usually only an inch or so in diameter, similar to a Roman mosaic. The tesserae are made in a process similar to the *zanfirico*

Large tapering vase by W.A. Hunting with layers of colored glass, murrines, and trails of glass. *c. 198*. *14¾ in (37 cm) high* **$1,500–2,000 FIS**

rods on the previous pages, where a design is created using colored glass powder melted onto and inside a gather, which is then pulled and extruded into a long, thin cane, and cut, this time into small tiles, to reveal the pattern inside.

The desirability value of a piece incorporating murrines is largely dependent on who made it and the design, complexity, and success of the murrines

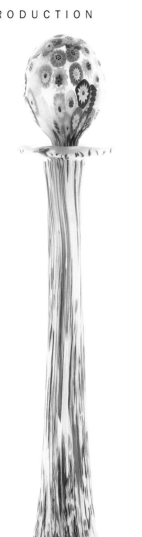

Venetian revival *millefiori* perfume bottle made at the Fratelli Toso factory. The murrine-covered body has an attenuated neck. *c. 1910. 11 in (28 cm) high* **$600–800 AL**

As he has done since the 1930s, glassmaster Vittorio Ferro creates a mosaic pattern by laying out glass murrines on a board. A hot gather of glass is rolled over them, picking them up, and the whole mass is inserted in the furnace to melt the murrines and bond them to each other and to the core. The body is then blown into a hollow form that is refined with tools. The neck is opened out with tongs and a glass foot is applied to the base.

themselves. For example, the Roman murrines depicting miniature portraits are highly complex, rare, and valuable. The same is true of murrines today: the more complex and pictorial the murrine, the more sought-after the piece. The most familiar type of murrine, as seen on the bottle on the left and on paperweights around the world, is in the form of a small, almost geometric, flower. These are arranged in colorful patterns and are often known as *millefiori*, meaning "a thousand flowers."

Typical features of the Venetian style, murrines have been used for centuries, and pieces in the traditional style are still made today. However, glass designers such as Venetian Vittorio Ferro and a number of 20th-century makers, such as Richard Marquis, Sabine Lintzen, Jesse Taj, and David Sobel have reinterpreted the style and brought it up to date. Some use strong, contrasting colors typical of the design revolution of the 1950s and 60s, but sparse, randomly placed murrines can also be found, while others favor modern motifs taken from contemporary society, such as cartoon characters.

Murrine footed vase by Vittorio Ferro featuring his trademark black internal striations; signed. *2004. 9½ in (24 cm) high* **$1,000–1,500 VET**

Cased Creations

As is becoming clear, craftsman-produced glass is never simply made, which explains its cost and desirability. Examine a piece and you may notice that it has more than one layer, each one applied over the other. But great care must be taken by the craftsman, because if the temperature of the core is too different from the new layer, the piece will fail. This technique—known as casing—is used in glassmaking the world over.

At its most basic, a clear glass casing houses a colored, internal design, which it can reflect and refract, creating a clever optical effect. Even on comparatively simple mold-blown glass, a clear glass casing, especially at the foot, can "lift" a piece, particularly when contrasted against strongly colored glass. Add a contrasting color to the casing and a different effect is gained, as exemplified by the *sommerso*, or submerged, work designed by Flavio Poli—considered the leading proponent of the style—from the 1930s onward.

Casing does not purely concern the reflective abilities of glass, nor simply afford the opportunity to contrast one color against another. Motifs such as trailed internal air bubbles or images can be captured between the layers, as seen

Rolling Stone vase designed and made by Anthony Stern, using images from original pictures taken by Stern in the 1960s. *2004 8½ in (21.5 cm) high* **$1,200–1,800 ASG**

The glassmaster's assistant starts by taking a molten gather of orange glass and rolling it in gold foil, bonding the foil to the gather. This is then inserted into a metal bucket-shaped mold with a series of internal protrusions, giving the glass shape and leaving rows of indentations. Applying a layer of molten glass over the top of the cooling gather traps air bubbles inside the piece. The outer layer is then worked toward the bottom of the vase while it is still malleable, and the piece is blown and worked into shape using a range of tools. After the rim has been pulled into the desired shape, the piece is left to cool.

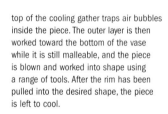

in both the vase to the right and Anthony Stern's Rolling Stone vase (*left*), where Stern has trapped photographic images of rock star Mick Jagger between layers of clear glass and superimposed against a core of opaque white glass.

The casing glass is as close to a liquid as possible when it is taken from the furnace. This allows it to be massaged into position on the piece using wooden paddles or, incredibly, a simple wad of wet newspaper, which becomes the only barrier between the glassmaker's hand and the molten glass. At this point, the glass is so hot that its true color cannot be seen, and it takes experience to understand the colors that lie beneath the orange-red heat and that will only be revealed when the fully formed glass is allowed to cool.

There is no single factor responsible for great glass. It is made by a combination of factors, including the experience and skill of those handling it, the furnace, the design, and the material itself. Glass is demanding and as such is rarely handled by a single person, but more often by a small team centered around an experienced glassmaster.

Sommerso **cased glass vase** by Andrea Zilio, with trails of trapped air bubbles and gold leaf inclusions; signed on the base. *2004. 18½ in (47 cm) high* **$500–700 ANF**

Blown Forms

To watch glass being made is akin to watching a silent ballet. No words are spoken, yet each member of the team works intuitively with the others, always in the right place and always under the silent but implicit guidance of the maestro. White-hot molten glass is brought to and from the furnace, tools are passed, and the piece is reheated, worked, reheated, and worked again.

At the epicenter lies the glass itself. Each member of the team, but especially the maestro, must focus on and understand the glass at every stage. The risk of error is high, and to succeed the glass must be treated with care and attention, but mostly respect. Failure to control the molten mass at every point will result in the piece being lost, the near-liquid form vanishing as it warps and flows under the pull of gravity.

There are also other factors working against the makers. These include the heat of the furnaces, the heat of the glass, and its weight. Together with the steel rod

Mantle vase of oval form with transparent band of colored strands and elongated cylindrical neck. Designed and made by Paul Cunningham (US). *c. 2003. 11½ in (29 cm) high* **$2,500–4,000 AGW**

A colored molten glass spiral is applied over a cone-shaped gather, which will provide the colors of the end piece. The piece is then blown on a supporting bench to give a hollow form. When the top is being worked on, a rod is "glued" to the base with molten glass. After casing, the final form is created by massaging the glass with a wad of wet newspaper.

upon which the gather is mounted, the glass can weigh in excess of 20 lb (9 kg) and, where possible, floor stands are used to bear the weight. Time is a further and significant enemy. The glass can be formed successfully only when it has reached a certain temperature, meaning that the gather can only be manipulated for a short time before being pushed back into the furnace and reheated without losing the latest changes. When out of the furnace, it must be turned, swung, or spun quickly and constantly to prevent gravity from weighing down on it, ruining the carefully worked form. All too often, the maestro and his team must struggle to regain control, the strain of concentration showing on their faces as they go through motions practiced and refined over centuries.

When the maestro is satisfied and considers the piece finished, the glass must rest, cooling slowly in an oven for many days before emerging in its true colors.

Left: Contour bowl designed and made by Bob Crooks, of free-blown form with a flared and undulating rim with colored glass striations. It is signed on the base. *2000 21½ in (54.5 cm) longest* **$1,000–1,800 CG**

Aurora cased stone form vase by Peter Layton, with orange and blue spiraling decoration and heavy clear glass casing reflecting the internal pattern. *2004 9¼ in (23.5 cm) high* **$700–900 PL**

The Greats

Throughout the 20th century, great glassmakers have changed the way we see glass, using a combination of traditional techniques and groundbreaking ideas. Many of them have overlapped so that several trends occur simultaneously. In the early 1900s, Emile Gallé in France took the cameo glass techniques that had been rediscovered the century before and used his mastery of them to take glass to a new level. At the same time, Louis Comfort Tiffany in the United States and the Loetz glassmakers in Austria were inspired to copy the iridescent Roman glass being discovered in new excavations. American glass manufacturer Steuben is often wrongly accused of copying Tiffany. In fact, under the directorship of Frederick Carder, it was among the most innovative glass factories of the pre-war years.

French glassmaker René Lalique took pressed and mold-blown glass and turned it into a work of art, rather than a utilitarian product, inspiring other makers to follow suit. From lamps and vases to hood ornaments and the hundreds of perfume bottles he designed, Lalique's work sums up the spirit of the Art Deco period. Scandinavian factories such as Orrefors and Holmegaard and glassmakers such as Edvard Hald and Simon Gate took complex trapped-air and engraving techniques to new levels of execution.

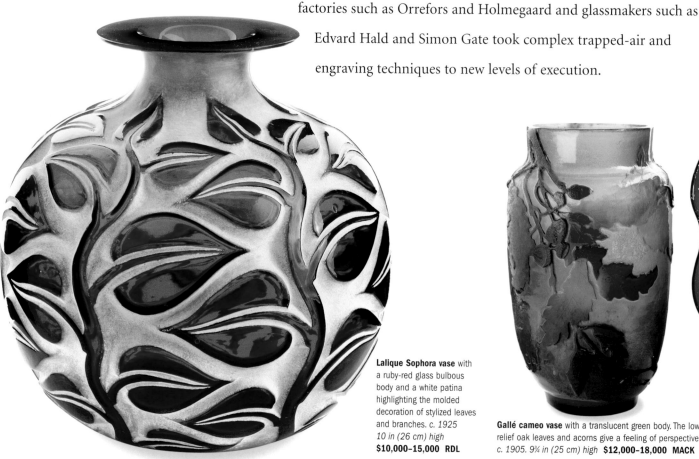

Loetz iridescent vase in the form of a tulip, overlaid with a curling leaf flowing up from the base. *1900–10. 9½ in (24 cm) high*
$70,000–100,000 LN

Lalique Sophora vase with a ruby-red glass bulbous body and a white patina highlighting the molded decoration of stylized leaves and branches. *c. 1925 10 in (26 cm) high*
$10,000–15,000 RDL

Gallé cameo vase with a translucent green body. The low-relief oak leaves and acorns give a feeling of perspective. *c. 1905. 9¾ in (25 cm) high* **$12,000–18,000 MACK**

Rare Tiffany Favrile paperweight vase with trailing murrine decoration in the form of leaves and flowers. *c. 1910. 10½ in (26.5 cm) high* **$50,000–90,000 MACK**

Rare Steuben crystal quartz glass bottle-shaped vase by Frederick Carder, with applied acid-etched flowers and leaves. *1930–32 11½ in (29 cm) high* **$9,000–12,000 TDC**

Kraka vase designed by Sven Palmqvist for Orrefors, with internal net design in blue and green glass, cased in clear glass. *1960s 6 in (15.5 cm) high* **$1,000–1,200 JH**

Pezzato bottle designed by Fulvio Bianconi for Venini. The exterior is covered with irregularly sized, multicolored glass rectangles. *1951 14¼ in (36.5 cm) high* **$8,000–12,000 QU**

After World War II, glassmakers started to look at their craft in a different way, translating the inventive optimism into imaginative forms and designs. In Italy, Murano reemerged as a center of the glass world. Maestros and designers such as Paolo Venini, Dino Martens, and Fulvio Bianconi took centuries-old techniques, injected them with bold colors, and used them to make the latest design shapes.

American designer Dale Chihuly was inspired by a pile of Navajo baskets to create a range of glass sculptures. His chandeliers also show that by questioning how glass should be used, a new art form can be made. Like the medium itself, a glassmaster is never static, and the maestros of today are constantly changing and diversifying. Time will show us who the greats of the 21st century will be.

Chrome orange Persian set by Dale Chihuly. *2001. 27½ in (70 cm) wide* **$50,000–70,000 EVD**

Venini vase designed by Fulvio Bianconi, of shouldered form with red and blue *pietina* bands over clear glass. Signed on the base. *1951. 9½ in (24 cm) high*
$3,000–5,000 FIS

Blown & Cased Glass

The ancient technique of glass-blowing was gradually adapted and refined over the centuries and remained the dominant way of making glass until the 19th century. The magical process of transforming a bubble of glass into a vessel or sculptural shape demanded great skill but also offered the virtuoso glass-blower and imaginative designer unparalleled freedom and spontaneity of expression. In the 20th century, Scandinavian and Italian glassmakers in particular took blown and cased glass to new heights. Where Scandinavian designers explored organic but elegant, harmonious forms and muted complementary colors, highly individualistic Italian designers celebrated color, applying it in dramatic and bold combinations and ever more inventive patterns to an equally broad range of blown and cased forms.

EARLY DEVELOPMENTS

In the 1st century BC, a technique that would revolutionize glass production was discovered: glass-blowing. The basic technique involved collecting a blob, or gather, of hot or molten glass on the end of a long hollow pipe (the blowing iron) and then blowing into it to inflate the glass to the required shape and size.

FREE-BLOWING

This apparently simple technique demanded speed, coordination, and control. It was often carried out by a team led by a master glass-blower. In the 20th century, master glass-blowers came into their own, as designers explored the plastic quality of glass in the organic, free-blown, clear glass sculptural and asymmetrical shapes that formed the core of the Scandinavian style. These included the extended "swung out" shapes created by swinging the molten glass downward on the end of the blowing iron.

MOLD-BLOWING

At its most basic, blowing glass into a mold allows serial repetition of form with an economy of time and skill. The glassmaker blows the molten gather into a preformed mold to create the shape, pattern, or both. Where the gather is blown into a mold with a relief or intaglio pattern, the design is felt on

the inside of the vessel. Some glass with molded patterns is then reblown to enlarge or distort the design. This technique was popular in the 1920s and 30s, with British glassworks creating optic-molded glass in many colors and patterns.

In the 1960s and 70s, mold-blowing came to the fore for fashionable ranges such as the textured glass designed by the Scandinavian glassworks, notably Finnish Iittala (*see p.49*), and in Great Britain by Geoffrey Baxter for Whitefriars (*see p.55*). Mold-blowing was used for the increasingly complex variations on the geometrical cylinder shapes that developed as part of the 1960s Pop Art style. When the glass was turned during the mold-blowing, it created a wonderfully smooth surface. Turned mold-blown glass was a technique associated with the monochrome, minimalist style of the Scandinavian glassworks.

CASED GLASS AND OVERLAY GLASS

In cased glass, an outer layer of glass is blown into a mold and other layers of different colored glass are then blown inside it and fused through heating. Developed in the 1800s, this technique was used to stunning effect by Bohemian glassmakers, and in the 1900s, Italian glassmakers developed it further to create the unique *sommerso* glass (*see p.34*).

In the ancient technique of overlay glass, the main gather of glass is dipped into molten glass of another color to coat it with a thin layer.

In the 20th century, cased glass was combined with color and trailing, cutting, engraving, acid-etching, sandblasting, and trapped air bubbles in an increasingly sophisticated range of trailblazing techniques such as Graal, Ariel (*see p.177*), Ravenna (*see p.178*), and Kraka glass.

Sommerso vase designed by Vicke Lindstrand for Kosta, of tapering cylindrical form, with internal green and blue glass with trails in a net pattern heavily cased in clear glass. It is signed on the base. *c. 1955*
11 in (28 cm) high **$900–1,200 BONBAY**

COLLECTORS' TIPS

Perfect condition is vital; on clear glass, even a scratch will reduce value.
Check vases in particular for rough-textured internal lime deposits.
Cased glass may be cracked; hold the piece up to the light to check for damage.
Venini glass is usually marked; many other Italian factories used paper labels that are now missing.
1950s and 60s mold-blown glass is increasingly sought-after for retro interiors.

Steuben jade green glass water jug. The body has a moulded swirl pattern and an applied cream glass handle. *c. 1930s*
9¼ in (23 cm) high **$320–360 JDJ**

Red mold-blown vase with cased foot, designed by Tamara Aladin for Riihimäki. It has a typically shaped body with horizontal ribbing. *1970s*
8 in (20 cm) high **$50–100 MHT**

A cased *sommerso* vase is inserted into the furnace to heat the rim so that it can be shaped. A rod is attached to the base to allow this to be done, and removed when the piece is finished.

THE USE OF COLOR

At its simplest, colored glass can be blown from a gather of single glass; multicolored glass can be blown from two or more colors combined in a molten state. Italian glassmakers in particular combined blowing with dazzling multicolored decoration, often in bold, contrasting hues. Many of the reworked traditional techniques involved blowing a molten gather and then rolling it on a marver (a special flat surface or table) to collect decorations such as colored tesserae, murrines (slices of decorative colored glass canes), gold and silver leaf, and fine preformed white and colored glass canes before shaping.

A simpler version of this cased and colored marvering technique was used by many British glassworks in the interwar years to produce ranges such as Monart art glass (*see p.56*) and the work it inspired, such as the Whitefriars Cloudy range.

Louis Comfort Tiffany's Paperweight vases (*see right*), also used decoration trapped between two layers of transparent colored glass. The inner layer was sometimes lustered or decorated with reactive glass flower-shapes that changed color when reheated. Alternatively, embedded *millefiori* canes were used to create flowerlike effects.

Rare Tiffany cameo carved Paperweight vase with white flower and green leaf vine design on an amber and yellow background. It is delicately inlaid with different colors and then engraved. *c. 1910 7 in (18 cm) high* **$30,000–50,000 LN**

Tapering vase designed by Dino Martens for Aureliano Toso. The body is covered with sections of colored glass and cased in clear glass. It has its original factory label. *c. 1950. 12 in (30.5 cm) high* **$2,500–5,000 FIS**

Large free-blown glass vase made at Hartley Wood of Sunderland. The baluster body is decorated with swirls of red, yellow, blue, and green glass. *1930s. 13½ in (34 cm) high* **$350–500 GC**

MURANO

The small island of Murano, in the Venetian lagoon, is virtually synonymous with Italian glass and home to many major Italian glassworks. In the 13th century, many glassworks on the Venetian mainland were forced to relocate to Murano to protect the city from the risk of fire from the glass furnaces. Great secrecy surrounded the Venetian supremacy in glassmaking and members of the city's glassmaking guild were forbidden to travel or divulge their secrets. From about the mid-15th century through to the 17th century, Venice became the leading glassmaking center of the world, as the virtuoso Muranese glass-blowers produced glass of matchless quality.

During the 18th and 19th centuries, the Venetian star waned, as the new lead crystal glass, well suited to cutting and engraving, came to the fore. By the beginning of the 20th century, production in the Murano glassworks was largely confined to glass in conservative, historical styles. However, as the century progressed, Italian glassmakers sought the help of artists, architects, and sculptors to revive many of the traditional Venetian decorating techniques and bring them once more to the forefront of glass design.

Sommerso vase designed by Flavio Poli for Seguso Vetri d'Arte, of tapering cylindrical form in blue and green, clear cased glass. *c. 1960* 9½ in (24 cm) high **$600–900 QU**

THE 1920S AND 30S

Strong family traditions of glassmaking had produced a highly skilled workforce, whose specialty remained hot techniques such as blown glass and lampworking, almost to the exclusion of cold techniques such as cutting and engraving. This expertise, combined with a predilection for bright colors, original forms, and an individualistic approach to life and design, created the exuberant, colorful, and stylish Murano glass.

Italian glassworks collaborated with artists who had trained as painters, sculptors, and architects. The skilled Murano glassmakers were able to interpret their imaginative designs. In the 1920s and 30s, the Venini glassworks (*see pp.24–25*) was at the forefront of the renaissance of Murano glass with the aid of such leading designers as Carlo Scarpa (1906–78), who introduced many of the innovative decorative techniques that brought the company, and Italian glass, international acclaim.

FROM THE 1940S TO THE 1960S

Italian design came into its own in the postwar years with a range of colorful designs in both glass and plastic, materials that share the same malleable qualities. Once again, fine artists were commissioned for designs in the organic "new look" shapes, transferring their skills from canvas to glass, combining bright vibrant color and abstract decoration with a confidence and flair

KEY STYLES

Delicate thinly blown shapes with ruffled or pleated edges.
Pitcher, bottle, and decanter shapes and tall attenuated bottles and decanters.
Thickly blown vases of simple form but with elaborate colored decoration.
Sommerso cased glass, typically in restrained Scandinavian shapes, with strong contrasting color combinations.
Free-blown small glass animals in a variety of types of glass and decoration.

Oriente jug with slender neck and applied handle, designed by Dino Martens for Aureliano Toso with painterly yellow, blue, red, white, and black glass, gold aventurine inclusions, and one black-and-white star-shaped murrine. *c. 1955. 13½ in (34 cm) high* **$1,500–2,000 QU**

MURANO *aux Venitiens*.

XLI

St Bernard

S. Maria

S. Cypriano

S. Michel

S. Giacomo

Golfe de Venise

that characterized the Italian style. Where the major glassworks such as Barovier (*see p.30*) and Salviati (*see p.28*) led, smaller workshops swiftly followed, freely "borrowing" new techniques and designs and adapting them for a range of decorative glass such as ashtrays, glass animals and figures, and ornaments for the tourist trade.

DECORATIVE TECHNIQUES

In the 20th century, Italian glassworkers revived and reworked traditional Venetian decorating techniques, often making witty reference to

historical styles. These included the use of lampwork details, the multifarious use of colored glass canes for various types of filigrana glass (for example, *zanfirico*, *see p.31*), mosaics, murrine, tesserae, and *sommerso* cased and colored glass (*see p.34*). These were used in various combinations, along with other demanding techniques, to create an almost endless series of brightly colored designs that captured the spirit of postwar optimism but acknowledged the debt to the long tradition of Muranese glassmaking.

Stellato murrine ovoid vase designed by Ermanno Toso for Fratelli Toso, with multicolored starlike surface decoration and with paper factory label. *c. 1960. 8½ in (21.5 cm) high* **$3,000–5,000 QU**

Contemporary goblet in a historic Muranese style, with pink latticework body applied with glass daisies. The knop and lid finial are decorated with applied mythical creatures. The design demonstrates the virtuosity of Muranese glassmasters. *c. 2000 17 in (43 cm) high* **$7,000–10,000 ANF**

KEY FEATURES

1921 Paolo Venini and Giacomo Cappellin (1887–1968) set up Vetri Soffiati Muranesi Cappellin-Venini & C. in Murano.

1925 The partnership dissolves, and Venini sets up his own glassworks employing Napoleone Martinuzzi (1892–1977) as artistic director.

1933 Carlo Scarpa begins an influential collaboration with Venini.

1948 Fulvio Bianconi's designs attract critical acclaim at the Venice Biennale Design Fair.

1951 Venini glass triumphs at the Triennale Design Fair in Milan.

1959 Paolo Venini dies and his widow and son-in-law take over the company.

Venini

Trained as a lawyer, Paolo Venini went on to establish a glassworks that became the leading name in Italian glass and spearheaded the renaissance of Murano art glass and the development of the Italian style.

Paolo Venini (1895–1959) looked to artist-designers—painters, sculptors, and architects—to help him realize his passion for glass and intuitive understanding of its huge design potential. The early collaboration with painter Vittorio Zecchin (1878–1947) resulted in a range of beautiful, thinly blown, transparent colored forms in historical styles such as the acclaimed Veronese vase.

As artistic director from 1925, the sculptor Napoleone Martinuzzi initiated radical changes in Venini's design, with a move toward more sculptural shapes, such as free-blown small animal sculptures and large plant

shapes, and technical developments, including *pulegoso* (bubbly) glass. Martinuzzi's successor, architect and painter Tommaso Buzzi (1900–1981), contributed a range of designs, including formal shapes with applied decoration, and cased organic forms (some with gold-foil inclusions), as did Swedish designer Tyra Lundgren (1897–1979).

NEW INVENTIONS

The arrival of architect Carlo Scarpa (1906–1978) signaled a particularly productive period for Venini in the 1930s and 40s. As artistic director from 1934 to 1947, Scarpa introduced a dazzling array of decorative techniques that became

Above: Occhi vase by Carlo Scarpa, designed c. 1960 and still made today. The square section clear glass body is overlaid with a mosaic pattern of murrines. *8½ in (22 cm) high* **$1,500–2,000 FIS**

FULVIO BIANCONI

Trained as a graphic designer, Fulvio Bianconi (1915–1996) became one of the most inventive designers of Italian glass. His often witty and playful experiments with form and color included trailed glass for Cenedese, figures for Seguso Vetri d'Arte, and rectangular sparsely decorated vases for Vistosi. But it was probably his numerous designs for Venini that brought him most critical acclaim.

Bianconi began working for Venini around 1946 with designs that included a delightful series of small figures in regional costumes. From 1950 he designed a host of multicolored patterns such as *pezzato* (patchwork, *see left*) and stripes—the Fasce Orrizontale and Fasce Verticali series (*see right*).

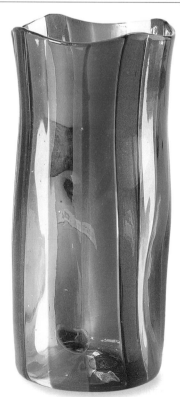

Pezzato vase designed by Fulvio Bianconi. The clear glass body is overlaid with multicolored squares of glass, or tesserae, in the Paris colorway. It is signed on the base. *c. 1950 8¼ in (20.5 cm) high* **$5,000–9,000 FIS**

Fasce Verticali glass vase by Fulvio Bianconi. Vertical strips of colored glass are used with clear glass to form the walls. Its form and lip are uneven; signed. *c. 1950 9¾ in (24.5 cm) high* **$6,000–8,000 HERR**

HANDKERCHIEF VASES

The Venini Handkerchief (Fazzoletto) vase
is one of the icons of postwar Italian glass.
It was a collaborative venture between Paolo
Venini and Fulvio Bianconi, who developed the
design in 1948–49. A huge success, it was made
in a wide variety of sizes, colors, decoration,
and types of glass. The naturalistic folds and
the delicate shape have been widely copied and
widely faked. Authentic versions have the acid-
etched Venini Murano mark (which has also been
faked), but also an inimitable delicacy and quality.

Fazzoletto vase designed by Fulvio Bianconi
for Venini, in the typical form of a "falling"
handkerchief. It has cobalt-blue spots on
pink ground and is signed with an acid
stamp "Venini Murano Italia." *c. 1950*
6¼ in (15.5 cm) high **$2,000–3,000 QU**

EXPERIMENTS AND SUCCESSES

*Both Paolo Venini, and the designers with
whom he collaborated, experimented with
the plastic nature of glass, and sought new
or reworked historical ways of decorating
it. The Italian tradition of small independent
workshops "borrowing" freely from one
another created the perfect environment
for Venini's ongoing experiments with form,
color, and technique.*

TESSERAE TESSUTO

In the years before his death in 1959, Paolo
Venini experimented with a new type of lead-
free stained glass window. The technique
involved fusing colored tesserae onto clear
glass. Venini showed the stained glass design
above at the Milan Triennale Fair of 1957.

Venini hallmarks. These included the *sommerso*
technique (*see p.34*), *corroso* glass with its
distinctive matt, slightly iridescent surface,
battuto glass with a textured surface rather like
hammered metal, the spiraling stripes of the
mezza filigrana glass, *tessuto* glass (named after
the fabric effect created by finely striped canes),
lattimo glass with its opaque milk-white color,
and many others.

Fulvio Bianconi (*see opposite*)
and Gio Ponti (*see p.27*) also
contributed new techniques
and designs at this fruitful
period, when the brilliant colors,
organic shapes, and virtuoso
decoration of Italian art glass
offered a popular alternative
to understated and restrained
Scandinavian glass.

Venini himself was also
designing, collaborating
with Bianconi on the
Handkerchief vase (*see
above*), and developing
the *sommerso* Inciso series
through an adaptation of
designs by Bianconi and
Scarpa. The smooth outer
layer of the vessels was cut
with a pattern of shallow

incisions that diffused the color and created a
distinctive surface effect. For other designs,
Venini reworked the use of tesserae and mosaics
(the plaid Scozzese designs) in a typically Italian
juxtaposition of bright contrasting colors.

THE NEXT GENERATION

The tradition of collaboration with artist-
designers continued after Paolo
Venini's death in 1959. Tobia
Scarpa, Carlo Scarpa's son, worked
with the company from 1959 to
1960 adapting existing techniques
as well as developing the Occhi
vases (*see opposite*), named after
the little clear glass "eyes" set
in opaque colored glass. The
distinguished Finnish sculptor
and designer Tapio Wirkkala
also collaborated with Venini
between about 1966 and
1972, making full use
of the range of Italian
decorative techniques
available to him.

Inciso vase by Paolo Venini. The
colored core is cased in clear glass
that has been incised all over with very
fine lines on the outer surface. *c. 1955*
8¼ in (21 cm) high **$1,500–2,000 HERR**

MILAN TRIENNALE 1951 DESIGN FAIR

The 1951 Milan Triennale was a turning
point for Fulvio Bianconi. He enjoyed a
huge critical success with several ranges he
had designed for Venini and subsequently
became a freelance designer, working for
a number of prestigious Italian glassworks.

Spherical vase designed by Carlo Scarpa. The body is overlaid with foil inclusions that split into fragments when the piece was blown. *c. 1950*
4¼ in (10.5 cm) high

$900–1,200   **HERR**

Mezza Filigrana bowl designed by Carlo Scarpa; the clear glass has an internal spiraling pattern of white glass threads. *c. 1935*
6¾ in (17 cm) wide

$700–1,000   **QU**

Tessuto vase designed by Carlo Scarpa in 1940 and made up of two halves, each with fine vertical colored glass threads. *c. 1980*
13 in (33 cm) high

$900–1,200   **HERR**

Mezza Filigrana vase designed by Carlo Scarpa with an internal spiraling pattern of fine white glass threads; signed. *c. 1940*
16¼ in (41 cm) high

$3,500–4,500   **QU**

Vetro Corroso vase by Carlo Scarpa for Venini, the exterior of which has been corroded with acid, giving an uneven translucent effect. *c. 1935*
8¼ in (21 cm) high

$3,500–5,000   **QU**

Rectangular Sommerso a Bollicine vase designed by Carlo Scarpa, with inverted corners, internal gold foil inclusions, and random bubbles. *c. 1935*
4¾ in (12 cm) high

$2,000–4,000   **QU**

Pulegoso vase by Napoleone Martinuzzi, of ovoid form with short neck; it has a translucent and rough surface with small bubbles. *c. 1925*
10 in (25 cm) high

$8,000–10,000   **QU**

Inciso footed bowl designed by Paolo Venini, with gold foil inclusions, a flared rim, and exterior surface incised with a series of very fine lines; signed with an acid stamp. *c. 1950*
10 in (25.5 cm) wide

$2,000–3,000   **BK**

Ovoid glass vase by Napoleone Martinizzi, with flared rim and foot; the exterior of the body has applied vertical ribs. *c. 1925*
10 in (25.5 cm) high

$2,000–3,000   **QU**

Leaf-shaped dish designed by Tyra Lundgren. The slightly iridescent body of clear glass has internal blue stripes; signed with an acid stamp "Venini Murano made in Italy." *c. 1940*

8½ in (22 cm) long

$1,500–2,000   QU

Bowl with pulled rim designed by Tommaso Buzzi, with opaque white glass interior and orange glass exterior cased in clear glass and with gold foil inclusions. *c. 1940*

6 in (15 cm) wide

$60–90   BMN

Table lamp base designed by Massimo Vignelli. The tapering cylindrical base has internal horizontal bands. *c. 1950*

14 in (36 cm) high

$1,500–2,000   BK

Veronese vase designed by Vittorio Zecchin. The body has a flared neck and is mounted on a spherical stem with domed foot. *c. 1950*

22 in (55 cm) high

$400–600   HERR

Gio Ponti

A trained architect, Gio Ponti (1891–1979) also designed ceramics, glass, and furniture. In the 1940s, he began designing glass for Venini. Many of Gio Ponti's designs made use of intense colors in a Mediterranean palette of turquoise, red, green, ultramarine, and gold. His *A Canne* series of decanters, vases, and tumblers used bright colors that were combined in bicolored or multicolored stripes. Some of his carafes and bottles show the influence of the human form on his designs, such as the *Bottiglie Crinoline*, which has crystal glass frills applied to the blown glass to represent the layers of a lady's petticoat. He also designed a range of decanters inspired by the paintings of the Italian still-life artist Giorgio Morandi.

A Canne **vase** designed by Gio Ponti. The flared beaker form has a wavy rim and is decorated with multicolored vertical canes. *1955*

11½ in (29.5 cm) high

$5,000–7,000   QU

Attenuated bottle by Gio Ponti. It is formed in green glass with a lower half formed in opaque white glass cased in red. *1946–50*

11¼ in (29 cm) high

$400–600   HERR

Salviati

From its early beginnings as a mosaic workshop, Salviati went on to commission designs from leading Italian painters and international designers, who created a range of mosaics, art glass, lighting, and glass sculpture.

In the 1930s, Salviati, then run by the Camerino family, was associated with some of the leading Italian painters and designers. Mosaics remained an important part of the company's production, and designs for them were provided by, among others, Futurist painter Gino Severino (1883–1966) and Dino Martens (*see p.35*). Martens designed both mosaics and vessels, with exaggerated lips, rims, and handles that made reference to traditional Venetian glass vessels.

The 1950s were dominated by the designs of another well-known painter, Luciano Gaspari (b. 1913). He joined Salviati in 1950 and designed both domestic and art glass. Gaspari's unusual composite art-glass forms became increasingly

exaggerated in the 1950s, reaching a peak in the tall, attenuated forms of the Pinnacolo vases, with their characteristic colored underlays. By the 1960s, his forms became less exaggerated and the color less formal, as seen in the Sasso range of vases.

Salviati continued working with designers from artistic backgrounds. In the 1970s, these included American architects, who helped build a reputation for glass sculpture, and, in the 1980s, the German fashion designer Heinz Oestergaard and, once again, Luciano Gaspari.

Above: Heavily cased amber and green *sommerso* glass pear table decoration by Salviati & Co. Signed "salviati Et c. MADE IN ITALY." *c. 1965. 7½ in (19 cm) high* **$300–500 VZ**

Decorative vessel designed by Heinz Oestergaard, with a spherical body and inverted conical dish. *1985*
11½ in (29 cm) high
$800–1,200 **QU**

Sasso vase designed by Luciano Gaspari. The clear glass body is of teardrop form, overlaid with trails of red, dark purple, blue, and yellow. Signed. *c. 1960*
11½ in (29 cm) high
$1,500–2,000 **QU**

Honey-yellow glass jug designed by Dino Martens, with the rim pulled into an elongated spout and handle. *c. 1935*
15 in (38 cm) high
$700–1,000 **QU**

AVEM

The founders of AVEM were accomplished glass-blowers and men of vision. Producing both their own designs and those commissioned from Italian painters, they created a distinctive range of technically and artistically refined colored art glass.

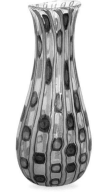

KEY DATES

1932 A group of glass-blowers set up Arte Vetraria Muranese (AVEM) on the island of Murano in Venice.

1934 AVEM builds on its success at the 1932 Venice Biennale with a range of vessels in bubbled glass and dark glass.

1936 Emilio Nason (1891–1959), one of the founders of AVEM, begins designing small glass sculptures of animals and people.

1952 Giorgio Ferro (b.1931) becomes artistic director and creates an acclaimed range of glass for the Venice Biennale.

1955 Anzolo Fuga (1914-98) begins working for the company as a freelance designer.

The combination of technical expertise and collaboration with leading artists paid off from the beginning, when the painter Vittorio Zecchin (1878–1947) received acclaim for his technically demanding wine glasses in the Venice Biennale of 1932—the year in which AVEM was founded.

Designs by the founders of AVEM also shaped the company's style from the 1930s until the 1950s. Emilio Nason specialized in small sculptural figures and animals, while Giulio Radi designed a range of dramatic patterned glass, incorporating gold leaf, murrines, and experimental iridescent finishes.

In the 1950s, Giorgio Ferro, who had trained as a painter, designed vases and pitchers in fashionable organic asymmetrical shapes influenced by contemporary sculpture, with multiple necks and handles and a distinctive iridescent finish. Dino Martens (*see p.35*) combined organic shape with *zanfirico* canes and other vibrant designs that reinterpreted traditional Venetian decorating techniques, as did Anzolo Fuga. A graphic artist turned glassmaker, Fuga had produced flat colored glass in his own studio and adapted the technique for a series of vases, often using vertical colored rods and murrines.

Above: Oval vase with open rim designed by Anzolo Fuga, in clear glass with internal bubbles and yellow canes. *c. 1960* *16½ in (42 cm) high* **$3,000–4,000 HERR**

Flattened double-gourd-shaped vase in graduated clear, purple, and gold glass. Designed by Giorgio Ferro. *c. 1950* *12½ in (32 cm) high* **$1,800–3,500** HERR

Organic-shaped vase designed by Dino Martens, with two branchlike openings, of clear glass, murrines, and white *filigrana*. Zanfirico rods are arranged vertically. *c. 1950* *14 in (35.5 cm) high* **$3,000–4,000** HERR

A canne cased vase designed by Anzolo Fuga, composed of clear glass with vertically placed colored canes and a central band of blue and black concentric-circle murrines. *c. 1960* *9¾ in (25 cm) high* **$3,000–4,000** FIS

KEY DATES

1878 The Barovier glassworks is established by members of the Barovier family and Dr. Antonio Salviati.

1901 Ferro Toso is founded in Murano by Luigi Toso to produce blown glass and blanks.

1919 Ercole Barovier joins Vetreria Artistica Barovier.

1936 Barovier and Ferro Toso merge. In 1942, the company becomes known as Barovier & Toso.

1972 Angelo Barovier, son of Ercole, becomes artistic director and produces designs influenced by contemporary arts.

Barovier (& Toso)

Under the artistic direction of a series of talented family members, the Barovier glassworks built on, expanded, and experimented with the repertoire of traditional Venetian techniques to produce an inventive series of art glass.

The Barovier glassworks had already established a reputation for colorful decoration when Ercole Barovier (1889–1974) joined the factory in 1919, having abandoned a career in medicine. Over the next 53 years, he created thousands of designs and experimented constantly with ways of introducing color and texture into glass.

In the 1920s, Barovier built on the factory tradition of vessels decorated with sections of multicolored glass. In 1929, he produced the Primavera series, with its distinctive, white, crackled surface and black or blue trim, which resulted from an accidental chemical combination that could not be replicated. In the mid-1930s, Barovier developed a new technique called *colorazione a caldo senza fusione*

(coloring [glass] while hot without fusing). He used this technique in many subsequent designs, and other Muranese glassworkers also adopted it.

In 1936, the Barovier glassworks merged with Ferro Toso, and after World War II the new alliance concentrated on reinterpreting traditional techniques in a nonstop stream of innovative design. Every combination of color and pattern was used: stripes, squares, patchwork, herringbone, circles, threading, verticals, spiraling, and crisscross rods. Designs of the 1940s included a series of organic textured shapes in thick glass, such as the Lenti vase and the brightly colored Oriente series (reissued in the 1970s) with trapped silver foil. Barovier experimented with vivid colors, complex patterns, "primitive" shapes, and textured raw surfaces in the 1950s (for example, the Barbarici series), and a tesserae glass with unusual colors in the 1960s and 70s.

Above: Rare Oriente vase designed by Ercole Barovier, with wavy bands of amber, red, purple, and blue-green glass and silver-foil inlays. c. 1940. 7 in (18 cm) high **$8,000–9,500 FIS**

FLORAL MOTIF ON BASE OF VASE

Intarsio vase designed by Ercole Barovier, with an asymmetrical mosaic pattern composed of diamond-shaped tesserae, in clear, red, and brown glass, and configured as a stylized floral motif on the base. *1961. 12 in (31 cm) high* **$3,500–4,500 FIS**

INTARSIO

In the 1960s, Ercole Barovier's prodigious output of inventive designs included the Intarsio series. As with so many of Barovier's designs, Intarsio built on a traditional Venetian decorative technique—in this case, the use of triangular sections of glass. These thin slices of colored glass were used to decorate the surface of blown glass. A gather of colorless blown glass was rolled on the marver to collect adjacent triangular mosaic sections of two different colors of glass (brown and red on this vase), cased in clear glass, and then dip mold-blown and tooled to create the pattern of expanded triangles. The Intarsio series was designed in 1961 and was produced in several different color combinations from 1963.

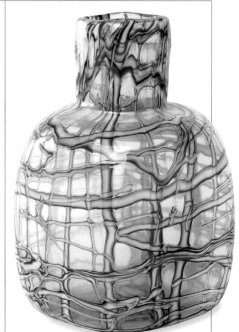

Opalino a Fiamma vase designed by Ercole Barovier, in clear glass with circular opalescent murrines linked by similarly colored canes. *1957*

16 in (40.5 cm) high

$2,000–3,000   **FIS**

Parabolico-style cylindrical vase designed by Ercole Barovier, in clear glass with a green-and-white open-weave pattern. *c. 1980*

13 in (33.5 cm) high

$2,500–3,500   **QU**

Barovier Avventurina vase designed by Ercole Barovier, of cased, rosé-colored glass, with aventurine inclusions, and clear-glass, double-scroll handles. *c. 1929–30*

11½ in (29.5 cm) high

$2,000–3,000   **QU**

Pezzo Unico di Prova vase designed by Ercole Barovier, in transparent glass with asymmetrical veins of blue and off-white glass and gold-leaf inclusion. *c. 1957*

6¼ in (16.25 cm) high

$5,000–6,000   **VS**

Lenti bowl designed by Ercole Barovier, in clear glass with rows of semi-spherical bosses. On some examples, the convex nodules cover gold-leaf inclusions. *1940*

8½ in (21.5 cm) high

$3,500–5,500   **QU**

Clear glass dish designed by Ercole Barovier. The clam-shell-like bowl rises from a circular foot and is similar in form to his Grosse Costolature jardinières. *1942*

6 in (15 cm) high

$1,000–1,350   **QU**

A CLOSER LOOK

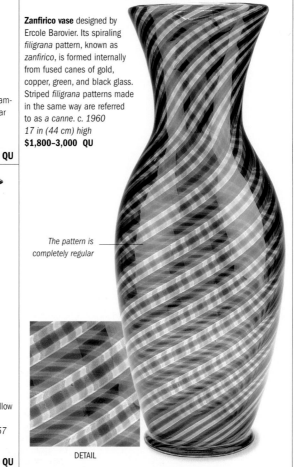

Zanfirico vase designed by Ercole Barovier. Its spiraling *filigrana* pattern, known as *zanfirico*, is formed internally from fused canes of gold, copper, green, and black glass. Striped *filigrana* patterns made in the same way are referred to as *a canne*. *c. 1960*

17 in (44 cm) high

$1,800–3,000 QU

The pattern is completely regular

DETAIL

Efeso vase designed by Ercole Barovier, of bulbous form in blue and gray with bubble inclusions. It was inspired by excavated Roman glass. *1964*

16 in (40.5 cm) high

$1,800–3,500   **QU**

Moreschi vase designed by Ercole Barovier with a yellow and purple *pezzato* pattern; white, green, violet, or amber were used for the similar A Spina design. *1957*

7½ in (19 cm) high

$5,500–7,500   **QU**

Seguso Vetri d'Arte

The winning combination of an inspirational designer and a supremely skillful glass-blower brought Seguso Vetri d'Arte early success in the 1930s, which was consolidated by major prizes and a worldwide reputation in the 1940s and 50s.

KEY DATES

1933 Former employees of the Barovier glassworks set up Artistica Vetreria e Soffieria Barovier Seguso e Ferro in Murano to produce lighting fixtures, and domestic and art glass, mainly in historical styles.

1934 Archimede Seguso becomes the factory's master glass-blower.

1934 Flavio Poli is appointed artistic director and begins a fruitful collaboration with Archimede Seguso.

1937 The glassworks begins to trade as Seguso Vetri d'Arte.

1942 Archimede Seguso leaves to set up his own glassworks.

1954 Flavio Poli's *sommerso* designs win the Compasso d'Oro.

1992 Production is discontinued.

In the 1930s, Archimede Seguso (1909–99) used his exceptional glass-blowing skills to interpret Flavio Poli's (1900–84) sculptural designs for small-scale glass animals and figures and large-scale glass panels such as *I Segni dello Zodiaco* (The Signs of the Zodiac) and *La Mescita* (The Wineshop), both 1936. In the same year, Poli launched his cased Bullicante range, combining clear bubbled glass with colored underlay.

However, Seguso Vetri d'Arte is probably best known for Flavio Poli's outstanding *sommerso* art glass, designed in the 1940s and produced in the 1950s. The now highly prized organic shell-shaped Conchiglie vases, the elliptical Valva, and the Siderale or Astrale vases, with their colored concentric rings, brought Poli international acclaim, status, and awards. The restrained and harmonious color combinations and elegant, understated forms of the Valve vases in particular are much closer in style to Scandinavian glass than to typically exuberant Murano pieces.

Mario Pinzoni (1927–93), Poli's assistant and artistic director after Poli left in 1963, continued the *sommerso* designs. His pieces, however, are less sophisticated, with fewer colors, and are more modestly priced.

Above: Flat oval-shaped vase by Archimede Seguso, with vertical spiraled ribbing. Made of pink opalescent glass with fine aventurine inclusions. *c. 1955. 10½ in (27 cm) high* **$3,600–4,500 QU**

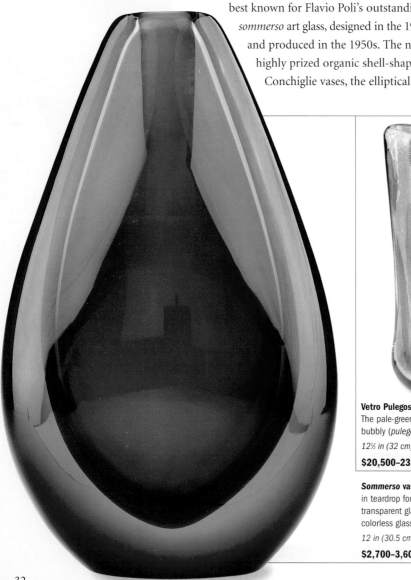

Vetro Pulegoso vase by Archimede Seguso. The pale-green inner layer has a froth of bubbly (*pulegoso*) clear glass. *c. 1948*
12½ in (32 cm) high
$20,500–23,800   **QU**

Sommerso vase designed by Flavio Poli, in teardrop form with blue and green transparent glass cased within clear, colorless glass. *c. 1960*
12 in (30.5 cm) high
$2,700–3,600   **QU**

Polveri glass vase by Archimede Seguso, of twisted organic form with graduated bands of coral-red and violet-brown. Infused throughout with fine gold-foil particles. *c. 1950*
15 in (38.5 cm) high
$7,200–8,100   **VS**

Fratelli Toso

Fratelli Toso was among the leading Murano glassworks to revive traditional Venetian decorating techniques, giving them new life and applications in the 20th century, in a series of vibrantly colorful art glass designs.

KEY DATES

1854 Six brothers from the Toso dynasty of glass-blowers set up the Vetreria Fratelli Toso glassworks in Murano to make lighting and tableware.

1912 The company exhibits glass plates and vases by German jewelry designer Hans Stoltenberg Lerche at the Venice Biennale.

1924 Ermanno Toso joins the Fratelli Toso glassworks.

1936 Ermanno Toso becomes marketing and artistic director of the company and pioneers the company's new modern style.

1973 Rosanna Toso, whose designs for Fratelli include colorless glass, becomes artistic director.

1982 Fratelli Toso closes.

In the early 1900s, Fratelli Toso used a variety of traditional techniques for its main production of elaborate glass in the Italian Art Nouveau style. Modern designs, such as those by Hans Stoltenberg Lerche, were produced only for exhibitions. From the 1920s, the range of modern designs increased alongside the traditional Toso glass made primarily for export to the United States.

When Ermanno Toso became artistic director, he pioneered the factory's contemporary art glass. In the 1950s he designed lightweight, finely blown pieces that employed a modern interpretation of *filigrana* and *murrine* techniques, as well as a series of delicate *millefili* vases made entirely of fused colored glass canes. In 1953, the company launched the first Stellato series of mosaic glass with colorful star-shaped patterns designed by painter Pollio Perelda (1915–84). In the late 1950s, Ermanno Toso developed the Nerox range, named after the nero oxide used to create the black background that formed a dramatic contrast to the scattered mosaic sections in strong colors.

In the 1960s, Ermanno's son Renato (b. 1940) continued the tradition of brightly colored glass but also explored the use of clear colorless glass.

Above: Classical-shaped vase of squat, baluster form with twin C-scroll handles, decorated with amber and white tesserae on a clear glass ground. *c. 1910. 4 in (10 cm) high*
$650–710 QU

Farfalle (butterflies) vase designed by Pollio Perelda, with asymmetric *pezzato*-style pattern and bright colors. *c. 1960*
14¼ in (36.5 cm) high
$11,100–12,800 QU

Margherita e Kiku vase designed by Ermanno Toso, of bulbous form with polychrome daisy and chrysanthemum motif murrines blown to a *millefiori* pattern. *1960*
8½ in (22 cm) high
$6,800–7,650 QU

Stellato vase designed by Pollio Perelda. The clear glass features blown, star-shaped murrine decoration in red, pink, orange, light and dark blue, green, and black. *1953*
11 in (28.5 cm) high
$5,100–6,000 FIS

Murano Designs

Vibrant, contrasting colors and exuberant, often eccentric shapes are the hallmarks of postwar Murano glass. Vases, pitchers, bowls, decanters, animal figures, and ashtrays were produced in quantity, often for the tourist trade. The *sommerso* technique perfected by Venini in 1934 was soon taken up by many smaller Murano workshops. The colored halo effect was created by casing the main color with a thin layer of another color and then a layer of clear glass. Price is usually determined by name: a well-known factory or designer will command a premium, but many small workshops produced their own more modestly priced versions.

Sommerso glass ashtray with a bulbous, bowl-like body rising to a square-cut rim. The blue and green center is inside clear glass. *1950s*

4¼ in (10.5 cm) wide

$80–120   **P&I**

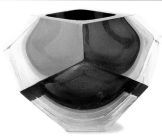

Sommerso glass ashtray with an amber, oval center bowl in a layer of yellow glass and an octagonal outer layer of clear glass. *1960s*

4 in (10 cm) high

$200–250   **DTC**

Pair of *sommerso* swans with cobalt-blue centers and air bubbles in clear glass. Standing on rocky, air-bubbled clear-glass plinths. *1950s*

7¾ in (19 cm) high

$180–200   **AG**

Rare Vetreria Vistosi *pulcino* (chick) designed by Alessandro Pianon, with a burnt-orange body encased in clear, textured glass, and with murrine eyes and copper legs. *1961–62*

8½ in (22 cm) high

$4,000–5,000   **QU**

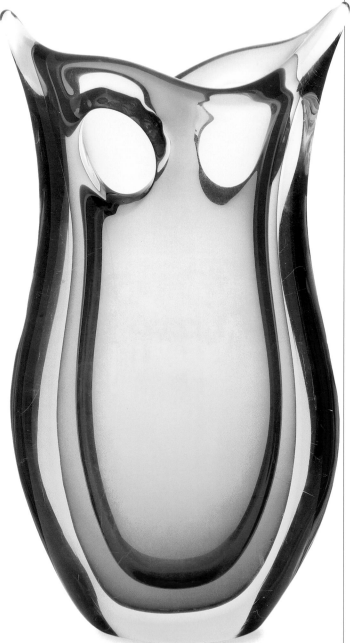

Triple-cased *sommerso* vase in the form of a stylized owl, in graduated shades of green, amber, and red glass, cased in clear glass. *1950s*

10½ in (27 cm) high

$100–150   **TGM**

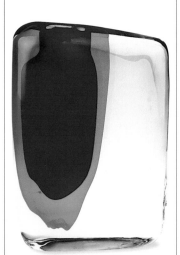

Vetreria Gino Cenedese *sommerso* vase designed by Antonio da Ros, with clear-cased bands of purple and cherry-red glass. *1960*

8¾ in (22.5 cm) high

$2,200–2,800   **QU**

Triple-cased *sommerso* vase of organic free-form design, the inner layers in shades of pink, purple, and pale blue glass. *1950s*

11 in (28 cm) high

$200–260   **PC**

Twin-handled amphora vase designed by Napoleone Martinuzzi for Zecchin-Martinuzzi Vetri Artistici e Mosaici. The piece is in cased iridescent white and opalescent green glass. *c. 1935*

7½ in (19.5 cm) high

$6,800–7,500   QU

Twin-handled amphora-like vase of bulbous, footed form. The body is colored with mottled reddish-brown enamels and aventurine inclusions, and the foot with violet enamel. *1925*

6½ in (17 cm) high

$700–850   QU

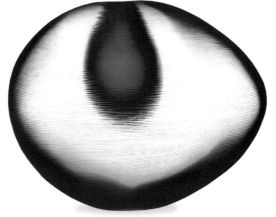

Vetro Pesante *sommerso* **vase** by Alfredo Barbini. The teardrop center is in cherry-red glass; the thick oval casing in smoked clear glass and with *inciso* decoration. *c. 1962*

6¾ in (17.25 cm) high

$3,500–4,000   QU

Saluti *sommerso* **glass vase** of *solifleur* form, designed by Luciano Gaspari. In amethyst and turquoise blue, encased in clear glass. *1960s*

13½ in (35 cm) high

$150–200   P&I

Dino Martens

Italian painter Dino Martens (1894–1970) played a major role in establishing the reputation of 20th-century Murano glass. He relished working in the new medium and created a stir at the 1948 Venice Biennale, using traditional Venetian glass-making techniques like painting, with glass as his canvas. The colorful, exuberant vessels reflected his personality. For Salviati, Martens designed a range of vessels with elaborate handles and spouts that made playful and irreverent reference to the Venetian serpent-stemmed drinking vessels. For Aureliano Toso, he designed witty and colorful abstract pieces that combined a wide variety of decorating techniques.

Dino Martens Oriente tumbler-shaped vase designed for Aureliano Toso, with irregularly shaped bands of vivid, polychrome enamel coloring and aventurine inclusions. *1952*

11 in (28 cm) high

$5,500–6,000   FIS

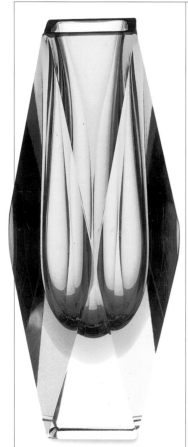

Heart-shaped red and yellow *sommerso* cased vase made on Murano and with the remains of the original foil factory label. *1950s*

4½ in (11.5 cm) high

$80–120   **AG**

Yellow *sommerso* cased vase made on Murano, with diamond-shaped, facet-cut sides adding optical interest when viewed. *1960s*

6½ in (16 cm) high

$60–90   **TGM**

Rectangular navy blue *sommerso* cased vase made on Murano and clearly showing the "halo" effect associated with the technique around the deep blue interior. *1960s*

5¾ in (14.5 cm) high

$70–100   **TGM**

Unsigned Murano flattened oval-shaped vase with blue and yellow canes arranged in a tartan pattern and cased in clear glass. *Late 20th century*

9½ in (24 cm) high

$200–300   **TA**

Large Murano glass table lamp attributed to Cenedese, with a spiraling colored glass ribbon internal design heavily cased in clear glass. *c. 1960*

18½ in (47 cm) high

$400–500   **MHT**

Opaque green Opaline mold-blown vase made by Fratelli Ferro of Murano, with original foil factory labels on the reverse. *1960s*

8¼ in (21 cm) high

$50–70   **MHC**

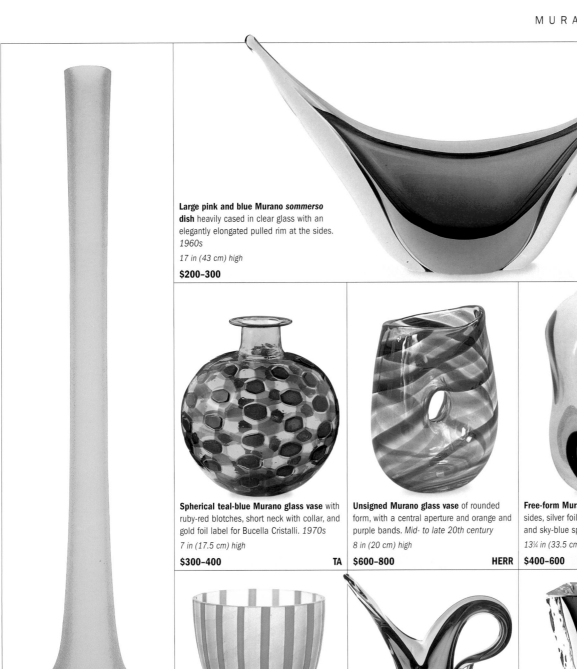

Large pink and blue Murano *sommerso* **dish** heavily cased in clear glass with an elegantly elongated pulled rim at the sides. *1960s*

17 in (43 cm) high

$200–300

V

Spherical teal-blue Murano glass vase with ruby-red blotches, short neck with collar, and gold foil label for Bucella Cristalli. *1970s*

7 in (17.5 cm) high

$300–400　　　　TA

Unsigned Murano glass vase of rounded form, with a central aperture and orange and purple bands. *Mid- to late 20th century*

8 in (20 cm) high

$600–800　　　　HERR

Free-form Murano glass vase with bulging sides, silver foil inclusions, and deep-purple and sky-blue spots. *Mid- to late 20th century*

13¾ in (33.5 cm) high

$400–600　　　　HERR

Tall frosted yellow Murano glass vase by Carlo Moretti, with a spherical body and long cylindrical neck. *Mid- to late 20th century*

17½ in (44.5 cm) high

$80–120　　　　GC

Opaque Murano glass vase of hour-glass form with striped decoration using vertical orange-red canes. With maker's label. *1960s*

12 in (30.5 cm) high

$70–100　　　　GAZE

Sommerso **Murano vase** of decanter form, heavily cased in clear glass, with the rim pulled into a spout and handle. *1950s*

8½ in (21.5 cm) high

$100–150　　　　PC

Amethyst *sommerso* **Murano vase** cased in clear glass. The form of the colored glass echoes the form of the vase. *c. 1970*

7 in (18 cm) high

$100–150　　　　P&I

Paperweights & Spheres

The desirability and manufacture of paperweights has continued unabated from their origins in mid-19th-century France, with an ever-expanding range in both traditional and modern styles. Related art forms, such as the sphere, have also begun to grow in prominence.

The United States and Britain are the centers of modern paperweight design. From the 1930s, Paul Ysart was one of the earliest designers, initially working for Monart and Caithness Glass Ltd. (*see p.56*), before running his own company in the 1970s. Many of his weights are in the traditional manner, with "setups" of *millefiori* rods. The highly complex lampwork designs of legendary American glass artist Paul Stankard show his love for his native New Jersey countryside.

Other makers to look for include American Ken Rosenfeld, who has focused on paperweights since 1984, and William Manson of Scotland (est. 1997). Colin Terris continued making paperweights at Caithness after Ysart left, and their abstract

designs and limited editions, particularly from the 1960s and 70s, are highly desirable. Scottish factories Perthshire, founded by the Drysdale family in 1968, and Selkirk are also notable, as is John Deacons. Look for signature canes, usually featuring the initials of the designer.

The newly emerging sphere movement is partly derived from the creation of paperweights, with many artists working across the forms, and is considered more of a sculptural art form. Leaders include Paul Stankard and Mark Matthews. Inspiration often comes from nature as well as contemporary life and culture. Jesse Taj and David Sobel combine contemporary motifs with traditional techniques, such as murrines.

Ovoid cased paperweight vase with internal lamp-work garden scenes by Chris Heilman. *2000. 8½ in (21.5 cm) high* **$900–1,500 JDJ**

Ovoid paperweight with a lamp-worked, three-dimensional dragon, by Milon Townsend. *1998. 5½ in (14 cm) high* **$900–1,500 JDJ**

Hummingbird with Flowers glass sphere by Jesse Taj. Signed "Taj03". *2003 1¼ in (3 cm) wide* **£100–200 BGL**

Siberian Tiger glass sphere by Mark Matthews, from the Animal Skin series inspired by animal pelts in the Smithsonian Collection. *1998. 2¾ in (7 cm) wide* **$700–1,000 BGL**

School of Fish glass sphere by Cathy Richardson, the internal design of fish amid seaweed over three layers of glass. Signed. *2003. 2 in (5 cm) wide* **$180–250 BGL**

Cat in the Hat glass sphere by Jesse Taj, with design murrines manipulated with a torch. *2003. 1½ in (4 cm) wide* **$250–350 BGL**

Joe Cool glass sphere by Harry Besett and painted by artist Ken Leslie. *2001 2 in (5 cm) wide* **$600–800 BGL**

Monarch Ladybug & Floral lampwork paperweight by Ken Rosenfeld, signed. *2003. 2½ in (6.5 cm) wide* **$500–550 BGL**

Floral with Berries & Moss glass sphere by Paul Stankard with torchwork techniques; signed. *2003. 3½ in (9 cm)* **$5,000–7,000 BGL**

Pansy with Gold Bee paperweight by Charles Kaziun, signed with a golden "K." *1970s 1¾ in (4.5 cm) wide* **$1,500–1,800 BGL**

Densely packed multicolored millefiori glass sphere by Douglas Sweet, signed. *2003. 2 in (5 cm) wide* **$180–360 BGL**

Perthshire paperweight, with millefiori canes surrounding a floral cane with butterfly, signed. *c. 1970s. 2¾ in (7 cm) wide* **$400–600 WKA**

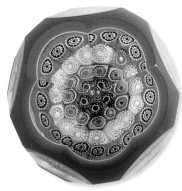

World Marble glass sphere by Geoffrey Beetem, with different layers of glass for each element and dichroic glass. Signed and numbered. *2003. 3½ in (9 cm) wide* **$1,500–2,000 BGL**

Overlaid paperweight with four millefiori rings and faceted top and sides. *Early 20th century 2½ in (6.5 cm) wide* **$100–150 CHEF**

KEY FACTORIES

Flygsfors glassworks, Sweden (est. 1888); closed 1979.

Holmegaard, Denmark (est. 1825); now part of Royal Scandinavia.

Iittala glassworks, Finland (est. 1881); still active.

Karhula glassworks, Finland (est. 1899), merged with Iittala.

Kosta Glasbruk, Sweden (est. 1742); now part of Royal Scandinavia.

Nuutajärvi glassworks, Finland (est. 1793), now marketed as Iittala glass.

Orrefors Glasbruk (Glassworks), Sweden (est. 1898); still active.

Riihimäki glassworks, Finland (est. 1910); closed 1990.

SCANDINAVIAN BLOWN & CASED

Style and function, harmony and elegance were the keywords of the Scandinavian style that came to the fore and was so influential in the mid-20th century. The clarity and quality of the glass and the virtuoso skills of the glass-blowers were put at the service of a range of highly talented designers, many of whom had trained as fine artists or sculptors. They explored the plastic quality of glass, creating deceptively simple free-blown sculptural forms that were in fact highly sophisticated, often incorporating elements of asymmetry and subtle coloring.

Most Scandinavian glassworks and designers espoused the democratic aim of making good design available for all, and created stylish ranges of mold-blown tableware that shared many of the features found in the more exclusive art glass.

THE NATURAL LANDSCAPE
Scandinavian designers looked to their rugged, often harsh, natural landscape for inspiration. It influenced both the organic forms of such well-known Finnish

designers as architect Alvar Aalto in the 1930s and Tapio Wirkkala and Timo Sarpaneva in the 1940s and 1950s. The textures of ice, frost, bark, and lichen became an integral part of blown sculptures, art glass, and tableware, while the foaming rivers and rapids were echoed in the cased glass with random and linear bubbled designs. The cool palette of the forest, water, and skies was echoed in the restrained, often muted colors that were used primarily to delineate the form rather than as a celebration in their own right.

FREE-BLOWN FORMS
The organic "new look" was interpreted by Scandinavian designers in a range of free-blown elegant shapes or fluid, plastic pulled forms, often in clear glass or in subdued monochromatic colors. The Swedish giants Orrefors (*see p.44*) and Kosta (*see p.42*) in particular exploited the refractive and reflective qualities of glass in their optical-blown clear or transparent colored glass to create the rippling effect of water.

The blown, thick-walled, clear-cased colored glass that epitomized the Scandinavian style was imitated and adapted worldwide. Again, the use of color was very restrained—a single

Sydan vase designed by Timo Sarpaneva for Iittala, of cylindrical form with conically indented base and heavy clear glass casing over the blue glass body. *c. 1955*
8 in (20.5 cm) high **$150–200 BONBAY**

KEY STYLES

Thick-walled, clear and colored cased glass.
Clear free-blown asymmetrical and organic shapes.
Mold-blown colored cylindrical and bottle-shaped vases.
Mold-blown tableware.

Clear glass vase designed by Vicke Lindstrand for Kosta, of ovoid form and randomly decorated with pale blue, red, and amethyst internal threads. Signed on the base "Kosta LH 1089." *c. 1960*
7 in (17.5 cm) high
$500–700 MHT

Many Scandinavian designers of the period were inspired by the remarkable natural landscape that surrounded them, from the deep colors of the forest and the cool colors of frozen lakes and rushing water, to the varied textures of bark, ice, snow, and rock.

Below: Pine green geometric vase designed by Tamara Aladin for Riihimäen Lasi Oy, with original "Lasi" label showing how such vases came to be nicknamed "Lasi" vases. *1960s. 8 in (20 cm) high* **$80–120 MHT**

color, often very muted, or internal spirals of color to emphasize the form and set off the clear glass.

MOLD-BLOWN GLASS

The Pop Art movement of the 1960s celebrated color—the brighter, the better—and, Scandinavian designers responded with mold-blown tableware and vases in a variety of bright colors, either transparent, opaque, or a color combined with a white internal casing. The free-blown organic shapes of the 1950s were replaced by the more geometric and cylindrical mold-blown shapes of the 1960s. The Riihimäki glassworks, Kaj Franck at Nuutajärvi (*see p.49*), and Timo Sarpaneva and Tapio Wirkkala at Iittala used these angular forms in ranges of stylish, aesthetically pleasing, but affordable tableware and vases. These are now avidly collected for retro interiors.

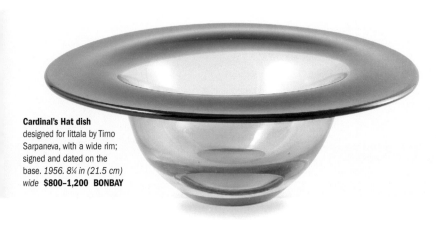

Cardinal's Hat dish designed for Iittala by Timo Sarpaneva, with a wide rim; signed and dated on the base. *1956. 8¼ in (21.5 cm) wide* **$800–1,200 BONBAY**

KEY DATES

1742 Anders Koskull and Georg Bogislaus Stael von Holstein found Kosta Glasbruk in Smaland, Sweden.

1864 Glass-blowers from Kosta found Boda glassworks.

1929 Elis Bergh is appointed art director at Kosta.

1950 Vicke Lindstrand joins Kosta as chief designer and art director.

1964 Kosta, Boda, and Åfors make an alliance; Erik Rosen is director.

1990 Kosta, Boda, and Åfors merge with Orrefors to form Orrefors Kosta Boda.

1997 Orrefors Kosta Boda becomes part of Royal Scandinavia.

Kosta Boda

From the 1920s, a succession of highly talented designers turned around the fortunes of the ailing Kosta glassworks and gained international renown for the company, Swedish glass, and Scandinavian design.

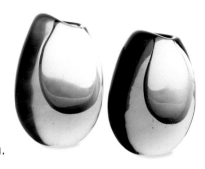

Kosta's renaissance began with Elis Bergh (1881–1954), who was the company's art director from 1929. It was given a further boost when designer Vicke Lindstrand (1904–83) joined the company in 1950. He subsequently produced a huge body of designs, for both art glass and domestic ware. Lindstrand's heavy, blown, clear-cased pieces came to epitomize the Scandinavian style that enjoyed such success in the 1950s. Shapes tended to be simple and thick-walled, with curvilinear organic forms, relying on the clarity and quality of the clear glass and subtle use of color for effect. Internal decoration included spiraled and vertical stripes, threading, and the trapped-air Graal and Ariel techniques (*see p.177*) that were initially exclusive to Orrefors and Kosta. Many designs incorporated patterns of internal bubbles. Any obvious distortion or misalignment may mean that the piece was originally a second.

At the same time, sculptor Erik Höglund (1932–2001) redefined the image of the Boda glassworks with his radical new designs for blown glass in a collaboration that lasted from 1953 to 1973.

Venini-trained Mona Morales-Schildt (1908–99) joined Kosta in 1958, introducing a southern European influence that showed in her Ventana range of vases with thick, clear casing over color and optical cutting. Five years later, Bertil Vallien (b. 1938), who had studied in the United States, joined Åfors and created a series of designs—mostly in clear glass—that earned him a place in the pantheon of 20th-century Swedish glass designers.

Above: Two Dark Magic gray-cased vases designed by Vicke Lindstrand, each signed on the base "Kosta LH 1605." *1950s. 5 in (12.5 cm) high* **$500–550 each MHT**

VICKE LINDSTRAND

The talents of Swedish designer Vicke Lindstrand were matched only by his versatility. He was a sculptor and draftsman, an avid musician—he played the church organ—and had worked as a newspaper editor and book illustrator before turning his talents to designing glass, ceramics, and textiles. At Orrefors and Kosta, his rich artistic background made him equally at home with figurative and abstract designs, unique studio pieces, domestic glassware, and sculpture, creating both small-scale pieces and huge complex structures for public spaces.

Blown and cut cased glass vase designed by Mona Morales-Schildt. The base is engraved "Kosta Mona Schildt 0-29." Morales-Schildt had trained at Venini on Murano. *c. 1955 9 in (23 cm) high* **$250–350 FRE**

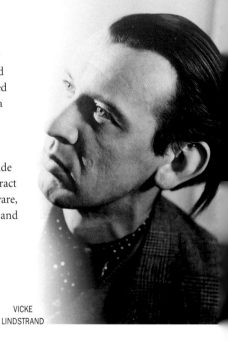

VICKE LINDSTRAND

Triform clear cased-glass dish with internal swirling strands emanating from the center. Designed by Vicke Lindstrand and signed "Kosta LH 1386." *c. 1960*

6¼ in (16 cm) wide

$200–400   **MHT**

Large internally ribbed optic blue vase designed by Elis Bergh and signed on the base "B473." Similar to examples by Whitefriars. *1930s*

10½ in (26.5 cm) high

$180–240   **MHT**

Cased oval vase with alternating bands of cream and amethyst strands, designed by Vicke Lindstrand. Signed on the base "KOSTA LH 1260." *c. 1960*

6¼ in (16 cm) high

$400–600

MHT

Small Moonshine cased bowl designed by Vicke Lindstrand and signed "Kosta LH 1316/90." *1950s*

3 in (7.5 cm) high

$120–180   **MHT**

A CLOSER LOOK

Orange hanging Sun Catcher designed by Erik Höglund for Boda. With impressed abstract animals and two holes at the top for hanging. Signed "H866/F." *1950s.* 11¾ in (30 cm) wide

$150–180 MHT

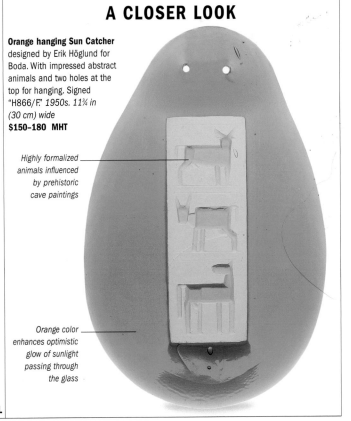

Highly formalized animals influenced by prehistoric cave paintings

Orange color enhances optimistic glow of sunlight passing through the glass

Free-blown rose-colored glass bottle by Kjell Engman. Signed "K.Engman" on the base. *1980s*

15 in (38 cm) high

$100–150   **GAZE**

Cased vase with heavy clear base with trapped air bubble. Designed by Vicke Lindstrand; signed on the base. *1950s–60s*

9 in (23 cm) high

$300–400   **MHT**

Tall, waisted, cased vase with internal alternating amethyst and white glass rods. Designed by Vicke Lindstrand. *c. 1960*

12¼ in (31 cm) high

$180–250   **GORL**

Orrefors

The superb quality of the blown and cased glass by Swedish glassmakers Orrefors helped establish the pre-eminence of the Scandinavian style in the 1950s and 60s. The long tradition of glass-blowing in Sweden had built up a skilled workforce that, along with talented designers, produced a range of deceptively simple sculptural and organic shapes that showed off the quality of Orrefors glass. Any damage is immediately apparent, since the pieces depend on perfect surface condition for appeal and value. All Orrefors glass is clearly marked and extensively documented. Work by Ingeborg Lundin (1921–92) and Sven Palmqvist (1906–84) commands a premium.

Apple blown and cased spherical vase in green. This is Ingeborg Lundin's most famous design. Signed "Orrefors Expo D 32-57 Ingeborg Lundin." *1957*

14½ in (37 cm) high

$3,500–5,000   BK

Blown gray and clear cased glass vase with a heavy base; designed by Sven Palmqvist. *1950s–60s*

6¾ in (17.5 cm) high

$120–150   MHT

Large Expo blown and spun blue glass charger designed by Sven Palmqvist. Engraved on the base "Orrefors Expo PM 243-62 Sven Palmqvist." *1962*

20½ in (52 cm) wide

$700–900   FRE

Shouldered cased-glass vase in smoky dark-grey and clear glass with a heavy base. *1950s*

6¾ in (17.5 cm) high

$30–60   **BMN**

Pop glass designed by Gunnar Cyrén who pioneered bright colors at Orrefors. Signed "Orrefors Expo B 553-67 Gunnar Cyrén." *1967*

8 in (20.5 cm) high

$1,500–2,000   **BK**

Red blown glass bowl with a gentle curve and a strong, resonating color. Signed on the base. *1950s*

8½ in (21.5 cm) wide

$30–70   **GORL**

Small opalescent blown glass vase with an organic, wavy rim. Signed on the base "Orrefors Tal 3090/1." *1960s*

2¼ in (6 cm) high

$60–90   **TGM**

Small thick-walled clear glass dish that has been blown then worked on a wheel. Designed by Ingeborg Lundin; signed "Orrefors D 3658/511." *1950s–60s*

7 in (17.5 cm) high

$70–100   **MHT**

Selena dish with a typically organic and elegant curving shape and strong color. Designed by Sven Palmqvist; signed "Orrefors Pu 3092/31." *1950s*

6 in (15.5 cm) wide

$90–120   **MHT**

Tulpanglas designed by Nils Landberg— one of the most notable and elegant designs of 1950s Scandinavian glass. *c. 1955*

NPA   **V&A**

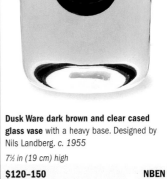

Dusk Ware dark brown and clear cased glass vase with a heavy base. Designed by Nils Landberg. *c. 1955*

7½ in (19 cm) high

$120–150   **NBEN**

KEY DATES

1825 The aristocratic Dammeskiold-Samsø family builds a glassworks on the Danish island of Zealand.

1927 Architect Jacob E. Bang joins Holmegaard and designs a range of tableware that determines the style of Danish glass between the wars.

1965 Holmegaard merges with Kastrup to supplement Holmegaard's production.

1985 Holmegaard becomes part of the Royal Copenhagen Group, and in 1997 part of Royal Scandinavia.

Holmegaard

The story of the Holmegaard glassworks is the story of 20th-century Danish domestic and art glass, which was shaped by a series of talented designers who brought the company international recognition.

With his range of tableware in sober shapes and colors, Jacob Bang (1899–1965) established Holmegaard's place in the modern glass pantheon in the interwar years. After World War II, that role fell to Per Lütken.

During the 1950s, Lütken explored the supremely plastic nature of glass with a range of flowing, organic, free-blown designs, such as the famous series of Beak vases and heart-shaped Minuet vases, mostly in smoky gray, aqua blue, and a range of soft, clear greens. Although he was not a glass technician, Lütken had an intimate understanding of the glass-blower's art and developed several new techniques, such as "self-blowing," pin-blowing, and "swung-out" glass.

In the 1960s, the Holmegaard designs reflected the trend toward increasingly angular and geometric shapes and the bright colors associated with Pop Art with such ranges as Lütken's cased and mold-blown Carnaby series. The mass-produced Carnaby shapes varied and became increasingly complex in larger sizes. The Gullvase series designed in 1962 by Otto Brauer was based on a Lütken design of 1958. However, these vases were made in both transparent and cased (more popular, especially in red) brightly colored glass and were part of the trend for inexpensive but stylish accessories for modern interiors; this remains their appeal today.

Michael Bang (b.1924) continued the popular mass-produced Holmegaard ranges with his Palet tableware series (1968–76). The distinctive mold-blown shapes were made in a base layer of white glass cased in a bright color, giving the pieces a fashionably bright plastic-like appearance.

Above: Heart-shaped, asymmetrical, blown, aqua-colored vase designed by Per Lütken. The piece is typical of his organic, budlike designs and use of cool colors. *1950s. 7¼ in (18 cm) high* **$500–600 EOH**

PER LÜTKEN

The name of Per Lütken (1916–98) is virtually synonymous with Danish glass. Lütken originally trained as a painter at the School of Arts and Crafts in Copenhagen and designed his first piece of art glass for the Danish Handicraft exhibition in Stockholm in 1942. During his 56-year career at Holmegaard, he created an extraordinarily broad and inventive range of designs—from one-off sculptural art glass, to mass-produced table and domestic ware—constantly reinventing himself, as well as adapting and discovering new techniques. Lütken was a generous deeply respected designer and acknowledged the skill of the glassmakers who executed his pieces, recording their names alongside his design sketches.

Double-waisted, red cased Carnaby mold-blown vase with white interior and flared rim. Designed by Michael Bang for Kastrup & Holmegaard. *1960s. 12 in (30 cm) high* **$700–900 EOH**

Per Lütken cased, tapering cylindrical vase in light green. The color becomes deeper and stronger where the glass is thicker. *1959–60 11½ in (29 cm) high* **$150–200 GC**

Opaque white glass bowl from the Atlantis range by Michael Bang, with gray free-form veining. *c. 1980*

3 in (7.5 cm) high

$30–50   **MHT**

Smoky glass bowl with asymmetric flaring form and rim, designed by Per Lütken. The base is engraved "Holmegaard PL." *1950s*

9½ in (24 cm) wide

$150–200   **FRE**

Kingfisher-blue mold-blown vase with an angular lip; thought to be by Holmegaard. *1960s*

15½ in (39.5 cm) high

$150–200   **GC**

Cylindrical blue glass vase by Per Lütken. The heavy base is signed "Holmegaard" and "PL." *1950s–60s*

12 in (30.5 cm) high

$100–150   **GC**

Tapering, cased smoky-gray vase with heavy base, designed by Per Lütken. Signed and dated. *1960*

5½ in (13.5 cm) high

$70–100   **TGM**

Purple vertically flanged vase of triform section, designed by Per Lütken. *1955*

10¼ in (26 cm) high

$200–300   **GC**

Brown-tinged cased-glass vase by Per Lütken, signed with his monogram on the base. *1950s*

8¾ in (22 cm) high

$60–90   **GC**

Three red cased, mold-blown Gulvases with white interiors, designed by Otto Brauer in 1962. Based on a 1958 design by Per Lütken. *1970s*

Large: 19¾ in (50 cm) high; medium: 17¾ in (45 cm); small: 13¾ in (35 cm)

Large: $1,200–1,500; medium: $900–1,100; small: $700–900   EOH

Large mold-blown cased bottle with a white glass interior and matching spherical stopper. *1960s*

21¾ in (55 cm) high

$1,000–1,500   **EOH**

Waisted, mold-blown cased vase with a white interior, from Per Lütken's Carnaby range. *1960s*

8 in (20 cm) high

$200–300   **EOH**

Mold-blown red cased vase with white interior. From the Palet range by Michael Bang. *1968–76.*

6½ in (16 cm) high

$300–400   **EOH**

Riihimäki

KEY DATES

1910 Riihimäki Joint Stock Co. is founded in Riihimäki, Finland.

1927 Riihimäki buys Kaukalahti glassworks and becomes the largest glassworks in Finland.

1933 Riihimäki holds a design competition that results in a collaboration with the architect and designer Alvar Aalto.

1946 Helena Tynell joins the company, the first of the trio of women designers who dominate production for some 20 years.

1990 Riihimäki factory closes.

Riihimäki's quest for good, modern design began in the 1920s, when the factory began to hold design competitions and started fruitful collaborations with a series of highly talented women designers.

In the 1950s and 1960s, Riihimäki produced a range of innovative, useful, affordable mold-blown glass. The designs, textures, and colors incorporated in the pieces epitomized the style of the period and make them increasingly popular today.

The design trio of Helena Tynell (b. 1918), Nanny Still (b. 1926), and Tamara Aladin (b. 1932) dominated during the 1950s and 60s, with their mold-blown designs for both tableware and art glass. These pieces were mass-produced and widely available, so aim to buy them in perfect condition.

Tynell designed a very successful series of textured vases in a variety of shapes, and many of Nanny Still's cylindrical designs for brightly colored, angular, mass-produced vases, such as her cylindrical bottle vases, had a long production run and are readily found today. Tamara Aladin's contribution included mold-blown cased vases, typically with undulating forms and bright colors. She produced both textured designs and a series with a smooth surface formed by turning the glass during blowing.

Above: Pair of Lasi vases by Tamara Aladin, of mold-blown, angular form, with flanges in blue-green and olive-green glass. *1960s. 11 in (28 cm) high* **$100–120 each MHT**

Mold-blown vase by Helena Tynell, of geometric form with curvaceous, S-scroll sides—echoed in the pattern on the front—and an angular rim and base. In ruby-red cased glass. *c. 1975* *8¼ in (21 cm) high*
$200–250 **MHT**

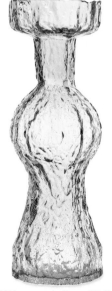

Mold-blown vase by Nanny Still. The hour-glass-figure form is in yellow glass with a heavily textured surface. *1970s* *8¼ in (21 cm) high*
$50–85 **MHT**

Fossil-range vase by Helen Tynell. The mold-blown, textured body is in shades of aqua-blue glass. *1960s–70s* *6¼ in (16 cm) high*
$120–150 **GC**

Two Timalasi vases by Nanny Still. Their angular red and green cased-glass bodies have molded knops. *1970s* *7 in (18 cm) high*
$100–120 each **MHT**

Karhula-Iittala

In the 1950s and 60s, some of the major glass designers of the 20th century helped bring Iittala and its native Finland to the forefront of glass design, sweeping the board at several prestigious Milan Triennales.

KEY DATES

1881 Swedish glass-blower Petter Magnus Abrahamsson establishes the Iittala glassworks in Finland.

1917 Iittala is acquired by A. Ahlstrom Oy, which had acquired the Karhula glassworks (est. 1899) in 1915.

1936/7 Alvar Aalto wins the invitation-only design competition with designs that included the now-iconic Savoy vase.

1946 Tapio Wirkkala designs the Kantarelli vase, which comes to symbolize 1950s Finnish glass.

1951 Wirkkala wins the Grand Prix at the Milan Triennale, which Timo Sarpaneva wins three years later.

1988 Iittala merges with Nuutajarvi Finnish glassworks to form Iittala-Nuutajarvi Oy.

The Finnish architect Alvar Aalto initiated Iittala's range of internationally famous modern designs with the Savoy vase, designed in 1936. The originals were blown in bottle glass in wooden molds, creating a softer finish than the post-1954 versions blown in metal molds.

After World War II, production of hand-blown glass transferred from the Karhula glassworks to Iittala. Iittala abandoned its traditional glassware and in the 1950s and 60s became an international design force, thanks largely to the designers Tapio Wirkkala (1915–85) and Timo Sarpaneva (b. 1926). They created many award-winning designs, both one-of-a-kind sculptures and tableware, and with both smooth and textured surfaces. Their textured designs reflected the harsh climate and rugged surfaces—ice, bark, wood—of the Finnish landscape. The tableware and art-glass ranges were produced mainly in gray or clear glass, in one-of-a-kind versions or more affordable series.

Wirkkala and Sarpaneva both experimented with molds. Wirkkala's Lichen vase was blown in a mold lined with plate; Sarpaneva's textured Festivo (1967) and Finlandia (1964) series were blown into wooden molds. The hot glass charred the surface, ensuring a unique finish for each piece.

Above: Mold-blown vase by Tapio Wirkkala in deep-red glass encased in sand-blasted and acid-textured clear glass with three embossed squares on one side. *c. 1955. 7 in (18 cm) high* **$500–650 BONBAY**

Savoy, or Aalto, vase by Alvar Aalto, of undulating, slightly flared, free-form section. Mold-blown in deep-green tinted glass. *c. 1936*
6 in (15.25 cm) high
$1,000–1,500 BONBAY

Multiple-flange glass candlestick with an irregular, barklike pattern, from the Festivo tableware range by Timo Sarpaneva. *1968*
8½ in (21.5 cm) high
$70–100 MHT

Finlandia bark-pattern vase by Timo Sarpaneva. The blistered surface was produced by the wooden mold into which it was blown, which was charred by the hot glass after each usage. *1964*
6½ in (17 cm) high
$170–250 TGM

Scandinavian Blown & Cased

The Scandinavian style of the 1950s and 60s was created by talented designers who moved freely between different media, factories, and countries. In Sweden, Paul Kedelv (b. 1917) worked at Orrefors and Nuutajärvi in Finland before joining Flygsfors; Bengt Edenfalk (b. 1924) designed for Skruf glassworks before joining Kosta. Edvard Strömberg (1872–1946) was manager at Orrefors and Kosta before founding the Strömbergshyttan glassworks with wife Gerda (1879–1960). In Norway, Jacob Bang (1899–1965) and Willi Johansson (1921–93) worked for Holmegaard and Hadeland, respectively.

Rectangular green mold-blown vase with abstract textured shapes inspired by the textures of bark and ice. Made by Ruda of Sweden. *c. 1965*

7 in (17.5 cm) high

$70–100　　　　　　　　**MHT**

Hexagonal mold-blown clear glass vase with textured exterior. Designed by Bengt Edenfalk for Skruf glassworks; signed "skruf edenfalk." *c. 1975*

8¼ in (21 cm) high

$120–180　　　　　　　　**MHT**

Opaque white opaline glass and pitcher with a bound cane band and four similar glasses, designed by Jacob E. Bang for Kastrup. *1960*

Pitcher: 8¾ in (22 cm) high

$400–500　　　　　　　　**EOH**

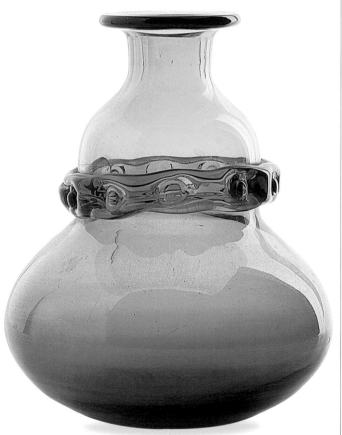

Shouldered mold-blown orange glass vase designed by Willy Johansson for Hadeland of Norway. Signed on the base "Hadeland 60 WJ." *1960*

6½ in (16.5 cm) high

$120–180　　　　　　　　**MHT**

Mold-blown green glass vase designed by John Orwar Lake for Ekenas of Sweden. It has an applied glass band impressed with circular shapes. *1950s*

5½ in (14 cm) high

$70–100　　　　　　　　**MHC**

Slender cased-glass vase with a layer of trapped air bubbles over a rose-colored glass core. Designed by Gunnel Nyman for Nuutajärvi Notsjö; signed "G.Nyman Notsjo 1947."

12½ in (31.5 cm) high

$300–400 DN

Thick-walled, heavy, elliptical vase in clear glass, made at Strömbergshyttan. The clarity of the glass is typically Scandinavian. *1960s*

7 in (18 cm) high

$400–600 EOH

Two ice buckets made by Strömbergshyttan of Sweden, with Danish sterling-silver handles. The icelike design and appearance reflects their use. *1960s*

Large: 6 in (15 cm) high; small: 4¾ in (12 cm) high

Large: $1,800–2,000; small: $1,200–1,500 EOH

Light-brown glass vase with a wavy rim, designed by Edvard Strömberg for Strömbergshyttan. *1930s*

10½ in (27 cm) high

$300–400 GC

Tapering, mold-blown vase in yellow ocher designed by Paul Kedelv for Flygsfors. Kedelv worked for Flygsfors between 1949 and 1956. *1950s*

3½ in (9 cm) high

$70–100 GC

Kaj Franck

A modest, self-effacing man, Kaj Franck (1911–89) nevertheless acquired an international reputation and played a key role in establishing the 20th-century design idiom in his native Finland. He originally trained as a furniture designer in Helsinki before becoming a freelance designer of lighting and textiles. His success as a textile designer led to his appointment as head of design at the Arabia ceramics factory, which in turn brought him offers of work from the Iittala glassworks. Franck was a restrained and practical designer who believed the role of design was to make products that served people rather than the designer's ego. This philosophy underpinned his work in a variety of media.

Kaj Franck blue cased tapering vase with a heavy, clear glass base. Designed for Nuutajärvi Notsjö of Finland. Original label on the rim. *1950s*

12 in (30 cm) high

$500–600 JH

KEY DATES

1834 James Powell acquires a glassworks in Whitefriars, London.

1873 Harry James Powell, James's grandson, joins Whitefriars and establishes the company's reputation for innovation.

1923 The glassworks relocates to Wealdstone, Middlesex.

1954 Geoffrey Baxter (*see p.55*) joins Whitefriars and helps create the modern glass range.

1963 James Powell & Sons officially becomes known as Whitefriars Glassworks.

1980 Whitefriars Glassworks closes.

Powell & Whitefriars

Whitefriars' reputation for technical and artistic innovation began in the 19th century, and in the 20th century it was one of the first glassworks to embrace modern glass design and produce a range with a truly British character.

The interwar years were a period of reassessment for Whitefriars. The factory relocated from central London to the leafy suburbs of Wealdstone, and Barnaby Powell (1891–1939), great-grandson of the founder, became chief designer.

During the 1920s and 30s, Whitefriars developed its colored glass, with a popular range of blown optic-molded vases, bowls, and lamp bases in the clear transparent Whitefriars palette, and a series of vases with ribbon trailing and applied strap decoration. The Cloudy range of colored cased-glass bowls and vases with internal bubbles was popular then and now—especially the rare two-color versions and the brilliant Sanctuary blue. The company also developed a range of unique exclusive blown and cut transparent colored glass, with designs by William Wilson.

By the late 1930s, more modern organic shapes, influenced by the Scandinavian style, were being designed by James Hogan (1883–1948), and these prepared the way for the more overtly modern Whitefriars postwar ranges.

POSTWAR DESIGNS

The two major designers to develop Whitefriars' postwar identity were William Wilson (1914–72), chief designer and managing director, and Geoffrey Baxter, who continued the trend for organic forms. Wilson's designs included bubbled glass, and in 1964 he introduced the Knobbly

Above: Banjo mold-blown vase in meadow green, with a textured surface. It is pattern number 9681 and was designed by Geoffrey Baxter. *c. 1970. 12½ in (32 cm) high* **$2,500–3,500 GC**

HARRY POWELL

Chemist, designer, glass technologist, art lover, and historical glass enthusiast, Harry Powell (1853–1922), grandson of the founder of Whitefriars, was the archetypal Renaissance man. He joined the company in 1873, and over the next 46 years he made an unparalleled contribution to its technological and artistic development, creating new colors, new decorative techniques, and new designs, many influenced by his passion for historical glass. His inspiration and sources for his Glasses With Histories series ranged from museums to historical paintings, in particular the Dutch masters, which he saw on a visit to Amsterdam's Rijksmuseum in 1910.

Peacock Studio range tall cylindrical vase designed by Peter Wheeler. It has silver nitrate–based random applied trails, making each piece unique. *1969. 9½ in (24 cm) high* **$1,300–1,600 TCS**

DETAIL OF STILL LIFE BY GERRIT WILLEMZ-HEDA

MASTERING COMPLICATED TECHNIQUES

Geoffrey Baxter's range of two-tone cased and colored vases and bowls, which was developed in the 1960s, sometimes posed technical problems. Some color combinations were incompatible because of the different rates at which colors expanded and contracted. The blue and green shown here in the Aquamarine vase was a particularly problematic marriage. This combination almost always failed; the vases broke while cooling and had to be discarded. To date, only about five successful versions of this vase are known, which makes it extremely rare and correspondingly sought-after and expensive.

Aquamarine cased mold-blown vase designed by Geoffrey Baxter, comprising blue and green colored layers of glass. Only around five examples are known to exist. *c. 1955. 3¾ in (9.5 cm) high* **$1,500–2,000 GC**

BOLD COLORS

Colored glass was a Whitefriars specialty. The company's early expertise in stained glass translated into the brilliant swirling colors of the 1930s Streaky range, the vivid hues of the Cloudy range, and Geoffrey Baxter's textured ranges. Certain colors have become collecting niches—such as Sanctuary blue and the vivid tangerine and purple that epitomize the 1960s Pop Art style.

1951 FESTIVAL OF BRITAIN

The Festival of Britain, held on London's South Bank in the summer of 1951, was a showcase for the best in modern British postwar design. The selection committee invited Whitefriars to take part and show its range of glass; this was a real tribute to the company's policy of constant experiment with techniques and design.

range, the first step toward the newly fashionable textured glass. The free-blown knobbly surfaces were created by tooling the molten surface, and the resulting vases were made both in cased colored glass and clear crystal with internal coloring. However, it was the designs of Geoffrey Baxter that really established the new Whitefriars look. His interest in and knowledge of Scandinavian glass was reflected in several designs. These included free-blown bowls and vases, with pulled and indented rims and "swung-out" forms; blown and cased bubbled glass in organic forms, with unusually strong colors for Whitefriars; blown and cased, thick, smooth-walled vessels in a new range of colors (vivid greens, blues, and reds); thin-blown, turn-molded glass in angular shapes; and textured, cased, colored glass, which is probably now his best-known range.

Baxter experimented with numerous ways to produce texture—lining the molds with tree bark, bricks, copper wire, and nail heads—to create now-celebrated and quintessentially 1960s designs such as the Bark vases (which are available in various sizes and colors). Other Baxter designs include the Banjo vase, and, most popular, the so-called Drunken Bricklayer vase, with its distinctive asymmetrical shape.

IDENTIFYING WHITEFRIARS GLASS

Whitefriars glass was unmarked and unsigned, and only a very few pieces still retain the original paper labels with the image of the White Friar. However, the influential exhibition of Whitefriars glass held in 1995 at the Museum of London has generated some excellent, thoroughly documented, and comprehensive reference books and catalogs. These provide details of the company's distinctive color ranges, as well as its designs— from the early historical glass, through to the Scandinavian-inspired ranges of the 1950s and 60s, and the studio glass of the 1970s. The years in which colors were introduced or phased out is an invaluable aid in dating Whitefriars glass, and in distinguishing early versions of ranges that were produced for many years.

Drunken Bricklayer vase in tangerine, with a textured surface. Designed by Geoffrey Baxter; pattern number 9673. *c. 1970 8¼ in (21 cm) high* **$250–400 GAZE**

THE INFLUENCE OF THE STUDIO MOVEMENT

In Great Britain, the studio movement of the late 1960s gathered momentum at the Royal College of Art in London, where young glassmakers were taught a new hot-glass technique that allowed them to work as independent studio artists rather than in an established glassworks. The factories responded with their own studio ranges. At Whitefriars, Geoffrey Baxter experimented with unique studio vases, while Peter Wheeler developed the expensive Peacock Studio range shown opposite.

Whitefriars streaky tumbler vase in blue and red, designed by Marriott Powell. Shown in the 1938 catalog. *1930s*

7 in (17.5 cm) high

$100–150 NBEN

Whitefriars wave-ribbed mold-blown tumbler vase in sea green, designed by Marriott Powell. *1920s–70s*

8¼ in (20.5 cm) high

$100–150 JH

Powell amber Ribbon Ware, conical-shaped, footed glass bowl with applied spiraling trails. Pattern number 8901; designed by Barnaby Powell. *1930s*

10½ in (26.5 cm) wide

$150–200 NBEN

Whitefriars Antique, sanctuary-blue brick-shaped vase with the Whitefriars label showing the logo used by the factory. *c. 1955*

9 in (23 cm) long

$250–350 TCS

Whitefriars threaded-trail vase in pale sapphire blue. Pattern number 8894, designed by Barnaby Powell. *1930s*

8¼ in (20.5 cm) high

$300–600 GC

Whitefriars Knobbly mold-blown vase with internal streaked decoration. Pattern number 9612, designed by Harry Dyer. *c. 1964*

9½ in (24 cm) high

$60–90 GAZE

Good, Better, Best

Geoffrey Baxter's 1967 Textured range was immediately popular and continues to be highly desirable among collectors today. Consider size and rarity of form, as well as color.

$60–90

With a barklike surface texture, this **small cylindrical vase** designed by Baxter in 1966 and produced until 1980 is commonly found. *1967–80. 7½ in (19 cm) high* NBEN

$300–400

With a geometrically shaped textured design formed by wire inside the mold, this **Totem Pole vase** designed by Baxter is more desirable. *c. 1965. 10½ in (26 cm) high* GC

$300–500

One of Baxter's most recognizable and desirable designs, this **Drunken Bricklayer vase** is in the rarer pewter color. *1966–77 8½ in (21.5 cm) high* JH

Geoffrey Baxter

A graduate of the Royal College of Art, Geoffrey Baxter (1922–95) was one of the pioneers of postwar modern British glass design. He joined Whitefriars in 1954 and immediately introduced designs for organic cased vases with a contemporary Scandinavian feel but a distinctly British character. Baxter drew inspiration from the most familiar objects. Walks through local woods inspired his experiments with homemade molds, and in 1967 his ingenuity, curiosity, and determination resulted in the bark-lined molds that launched the now-iconic Whitefriars textured vases (*see Good, Better, Best box, opposite*).

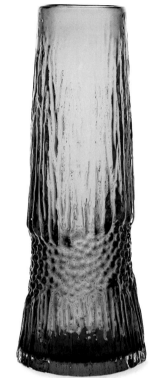

Rare Vesuvius Kingfisher mold-blown cased vase in blue with a textured surface. Designed by Geoffrey Baxter; model number 9825. *c. 1975*

12 in (30 cm) high

$1,800–2,500　　　　　GC

Whitefriars clear cased green vase with internal bubbled decoration and a pulled rim. Designed by Geoffrey Baxter. *1950s*

8 in (20 cm) high

$60–100　　　　　NBEN

Whitefriars Arctic Blue cased mold-blown vase designed by Geoffrey Baxter. *c. 1960.*

6¼ in (15.5 cm) high

$30–50　　　　　GC

Whitefriars Swungout willow-and-clear-glass cased vase also known as the Mutton or Long John vase. Designed by Geoffrey Baxter. *c. 1960*

15¾ in (40 cm) high

$1,000–1,500　　　　　GC

Whitefriars kingfisher-blue clear cased vase with a green ribbon trail. Pattern number 9706, designed by Geoffrey Baxter *c. 1970*

9 in (23 cm) high

$150–200　　　　　NBEN

KEY DATES

1921 Spanish glass-blower Salvador Ysart and his son Paul join John Moncrieff glassworks in Perth, Scotland.

1924 Moncrieff launches Monart art glass, using a combination of Moncrieff and Ysart for the name.

1947 Salvador Ysart and his sons Vincent and Augustine set up Ysart Bros. glassworks in Perth and launch Vasart art glass, combining their initials for the range's name.

1956 Ysart Bros. becomes Vasart Glass.

1961 Production of Monart art glass ceases.

1965 Vasart Glass becomes Strathearn Glass.

1980 Strathearn Glass is acquired by Stuart and renamed Stuart Strathearn Ltd.

Monart, Vasart & Strathearn

The Ysart dynasty of Spanish glassworkers was largely responsible for distinctive blown and cased colored art glass with swirling decoration produced by various Scottish glassworks from 1924 until the 1980s.

The distinctive Monart range was developed by Salvador Ysart and his sons. Together they made some 300 shapes for vases, bowls, and lidded jars.

The simple, often Asian-inspired shapes focused attention on the rich and subtle palettes, dramatic color combinations, and swirling internal decoration designed by Salvador Ysart. The basic technique involved sandwiching small shards of colored glass between two layers of clear glass. The colored glass could be manipulated, using various tools, to create the swirling patterns. The more sophisticated, and sought-after pieces had an extra layer of external decoration, or crackled effects.

Salvador Ysart and his sons used the same technique for their subsequent ranges of Vasart and Strathearn glass, although these are generally more limited in range of patterns and colors. Monart's original paper labels are often missing; Strathearn pieces have an impressed mark on the base.

Above: Monart small glass vase of shouldered cylindrical form, with mottled green, black, and red crushed enamels and aventurine inclusions. *c. 1924–61. 5¼ in (13 cm) high* **$180–220 NBEN**

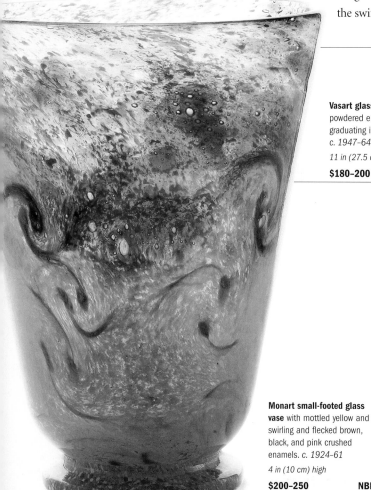

Vasart glass bowl with flared rim and powdered enamel inclusions in mottled white, graduating into swirling pink around the rim. *c. 1947–64*

11 in (27.5 cm) high

$180–200

NBEN

Monart small-footed glass vase with mottled yellow and swirling and flecked brown, black, and pink crushed enamels. *c. 1924–61*

4 in (10 cm) high

$200–250   NBEN

Strathearn vase with thick, clear-glass casing over inner-glass body, decorated with powdered enamels. *c. 1965–late 1970s*

8¼ in (21 cm) high

$100–150   AOY

Vasart glass vase of oval form, with powdered-enamel decoration in the form of S-scrolls on a mottled, two-tone pink ground. *c. 1947–64*

9¾ in (25 cm) high

$1,800–2,800   NBEN

King's Lynn & Wedgwood

Ronald Stennett-Willson established King's Lynn Glass to produce English glass with the modern, clean lines and clear colors associated with the Scandinavian style. Many of his designs were produced by Wedgwood.

KEY DATES

1967 Ronald Stennett-Willson sets up King's Lynn Glass in King's Lynn, Norfolk, England. The successful Sandringham range is launched.

1969 Wedgwood Group acquires King's Lynn Glass. King's Lynn becomes Wedgwood Glass and is marked with an acid-etched Wedgwood Glass mark.

1982 Wedgwood acquires a 50 per cent share in Dartington Glass and Frank Thrower begins designing for King's Lynn.

1986 Wedgwood merges with Waterford Crystal.

1992 King's Lynn factory closes.

Stennett-Willson had already established a considerable reputation as an industrial glass designer when he set up his glassworks in 1967. He employed glassmakers from Sweden and Austria to help create the modern style. His stemware and candlesticks—some with hollow "straw" stems (Sandringham and Brancaster ranges), and the popular, strongly colored Sheringham candlesticks with decorative multi-disc stems— exemplify the exciting new designs that attracted public attention. They epitomized the cylindrical shape that became so popular in the 1960s.

Technically, the designs were very demanding— the nine-disc Sheringham candlestick involved gathering 21 pieces of glass— and very vulnerable, which accounts for their popularity today.

Stennett-Willson's commitment to modern design also informed his pieces for Wedgwood. His mold-blown vases had fashionable textured surfaces or smooth, thick walls and internal decoration, typically in muted colors.

Above: Wedgwood Brancaster glass candlestick No. RSW 16–2, in graduated tones of light blue, designed by Ronald Stennett-Wilson. *Early 1970s. 8 in (20.25 cm) high* **$100–120 MHT**

Wedgwood vase No. RSW110 designed by Ronald Stennett-Willson with cased, variegated hardstone-like coloring made by rolling the gather in polychrome enamels. *c. 1968–70*

5¼ in (13 cm) high

$100–150 **GC**

King's Lynn glass vase in pale amber. Its craterlike surface was designed by Ronald Stennett-Wilson to mark the moon landing. *1969 10 in (26 cm) high*

$150–200 **GC**

Three Wedgwood Sheringham candlesticks designed by Ronald Stennett-Wilson, two in amethyst and clear glass with five-flange stems, and one in dark blue with nine flanges. *c. 1969*

Tallest: 14 in (36 cm) high

$350–500 each **GC**

KEY DATES

1824 Robert Lucas Chance acquires British Crown Glass Company in Smethwick, West Midlands, England.

1832 Robert is joined by his brother William, and the company becomes known as Chance Brothers.

1945 Chance is taken over by Pilkington Brothers of Lancashire.

1951 Chance launches the Fiesta range of domestic glass.

1981 Factory closes.

Chance

In 1851, Chance supplied glass for the Crystal Palace, home to the Great Exhibition in London. A century later, it launched a range of tableware that captured the spirit of 20th-century postwar Britain.

Although also known for its blown glass, Chance's expertise with sheet glass reached its pinnacle with the popular and inexpensive Fiesta range, launched in 1951 and produced for more than 30 years. The mass-production technique involved cutting the thin sheet glass to shape and decorating it before it was "sag-bended" to shape in the kiln. The Fiesta range of new contemporary-shaped bowls and trays had transfer-printed and screen-printed patterns that were regularly updated to follow fashion. As with any mass-produced glassware, condition determines value, and the screen-printing and gilded edges must be perfect.

Designs reflected the style of the times—from the science-inspired motifs of the 1950s, such as

Margaret Casson's Night Sky (1957), to the brightly colored floral patterns of the 1960s, and the textured Fiesta ware introduced in 1970. The first full Fiesta tableware set, launched in 1955, included the giraffe carafe with its "modern" angled lip (*see below left*).

Chance produced its own version of one of the contemporary Italian signature designs of the time—the handkerchief vase—from the 1950s until the 1970s. Unlike the handcrafted Venini originals, the Chance versions were mass-produced in a variety of printed patterns in several colorways.

Above: Handkerchief vase inspired by similar, handcrafted vessels made by Venini. This example has a rare black-and-white "psychedelic" pattern. *1960s. 4 in (10 cm) high* **$80–120 MHT**

Fiesta-range dish with a dove-gray Night Sky pattern designed by Margaret Casson and inspired by diagrams of stellar formations. *c. 1957*

8¼ in (21 cm) wide

$50–70 MHT

Handkerchief vase with a printed red-and-white polka-dot pattern. These vases were introduced in the 1950s, but this example is later. *1960s*

4 in (10 cm) high

$70–100 MHT

Fiesta-range Giraffe carafe with a delicate screen-printed Calypto pattern in dove gray, designed by Michael Harris and based on eucalyptus leaves and flowers. *c. 1959*

11½ in (29.25 cm) high

$150–200 MHT

Fiesta-range plate with wavy body and screen-printed floral decoration. Introduced in 1951 at the Ideal Home Exhibition, London, the Fiesta range remained in production for 30 years. *1960s*

9½ in (24 cm) wide

$60–80 MHT

Mdina & Isle of Wight

The colors and textures of Malta inspired the art glass that Michael Harris produced there, and they continued to dominate the palette of the early pieces he designed for his glassworks on the Isle of Wight.

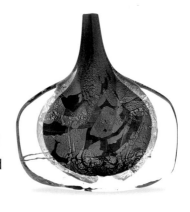

KEY DATES

1969 Michael Harris establishes Mdina Glass on the island of Malta to make studio-type glass.

1972 Harris leaves Malta and returns to Britain to set up Isle of Wight Glass. Eric Dobson takes over Mdina Glass.

1979 Isle of Wight Glass launches Azurene art glass, designed by Michael Harris and William Walker, which won a Design Council Award.

1981 Joseph Said takes over Mdina Glass.

1994 Michael Harris dies. His wife and two sons remain with the company.

With the help of two experienced Italian glassblowers from the Whitefriars glassworks (*see pp.54-57*), Michael Harris set up his own factory on Malta, training local apprentices to produce studio-type glass. The early (pre-1972)—and now most collectible—blown shapes were lively but at times rather unrefined. The chunky glass bowls, vases, decanters, jugs, and goblets were decorated with the distinctive Mdina color combinations of the 1970s: blue/green and ocher/gold.

The colors and shapes of early Isle of Wight glass were similar to Mdina glass, but the shapes, like the attenuated bottle below, tend to be more finely blown. Harris continued to draw on the colors and abstract patterns of nature as he gradually expanded decorative techniques. The Aurene range (1974–79) included iridescent effects and was followed by Azurene, launched in 1979, with internal surface decoration of fragmented gold and silver leaf. Azurene is still produced today and is the hallmark range of Isle of Wight glass.

Above: Large Black Azurene Isle of Wight vase by Michael Harris and Richard Walker, with gold- and silver-leaf decoration. *c. 1980. 9½ in (24 cm) high* **$250–350 PC**

Tortoiseshell Isle of Wight vase with bands and swirls of brown-gold coloring originally developed at Mdina. *1972–79*
9¼ in (23.5 cm) high
$70–100 **PC**

Blue Aurene Isle of Wight bottle vase, with the severely attenuated form, subtly colored streaks, and speckled effects typical of the Aurene range. *1974–79*
14¾ in (38 cm) high
$150–200 **PC**

Unsigned Mdina goblet intended for display. The bowl and knop are in blue-green glass, the base and stem in clear glass. *Early 1970s*
7½ in (19 cm) high
$150–200 **MHC**

Mdina bottle-shaped vase in blue and green glass. Designed by Michael Harris, its aquatic pattern and hue are characteristically inspired by the colors of the Maltese coastline. *Early 1970s*
9 in (23 cm) high
$60–100 **MHT**

British Blown & Cased

The success of Monart glass (*see p.56*) prompted many other British factories to produce blown colored art glass in the 1920s and 1930s. Nazeing glass (est. 1928) and the high-quality Gray-Stan pieces (1926–36) were very similar to Monart. The vibrant colors of Hartley-Wood (est. 1836) glass reflected the company's expertise in stained glass, while H.G. Richardson (est. *c*. 1850) used optic molding and the subtle colors adopted by most British manufacturers.

By the 1960s, the fashionable Scandinavian style influenced production, as seen in Caithness Glass turn mold-blown glass. It also informed Frank Thrower's designs for Dartington Glass.

Caithness Glass lamp base designed by Domhnall O'Broin and made by blowing a heather-colored gather cased in clear glass into a mold. *c. 1967*

10 in (25.5 cm) high

$80–120   **GC**

Small Caithness Glass vase with a thin, flared rim, tapering body, and heavy base, made by mold-blowing a twilight-blue gather cased in clear glass. *c. 1965*

5 in (12.75 cm) high

$50–70   **MHT**

Richardson bubble vase in pale pink graduating into deep purple. From 1930 to the mid-60s, Thomas Webb & Sons marketed a number of pieces as Richardson. *c. 1930–50*

8¾ in (21 cm) high

$200–250   **GC**

Oval glass vase by Hartley, Wood & Co. of Sunderland. The streaky colored glass—here, blue, yellow, green, and black—was originally developed for stained-glass work. *1930s*

9½ in (24 cm) high

$200–255   **GC**

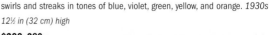

Club-shaped glass vase by Hartley, Wood & Co. of Sunderland, stained with ethereal, wispy swirls and streaks in tones of blue, violet, green, yellow, and orange. *1930s*

12½ in (32 cm) high

$200–280   **GC**

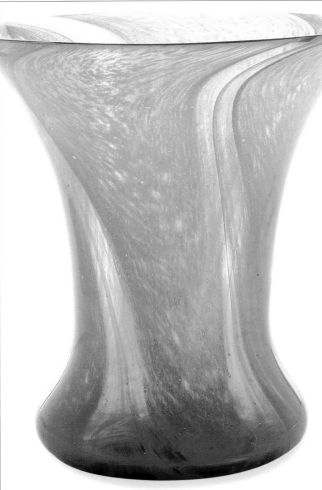

Tumbler-shaped Cloud vase by Nazeing Glassworks, with opaque, mottled coloring in deep sky blue. Other colors used included Sherwood green. *Mid- to late 1930s*

8¼ in (21 cm) high

$180–250   **GC**

Shouldered oval vase by Gray-Stan, with a two-tone electric-blue and pastel-yellow powder-enameled gather encased in clear glass. *1930s*

8½ in (22 cm) high

$1,000,1,500   **L&T**

Footed Cloud-range bowl with flared rim, by Nazeing Glassworks. Its opaque, mottled finish is produced from powdered Sherwood-green enamel. *Mid- to late 1930s*

4¾ in (12 cm) high

$120–180   **GC**

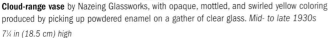

Cloud-range vase by Nazeing Glassworks, with opaque, mottled, and swirled yellow coloring produced by picking up powdered enamel on a gather of clear glass. *Mid- to late 1930s*

7¼ in (18.5 cm) high

$180–220   **NBEN**

Frank Thrower

Although the name Frank Thrower (1932–87) is now virtually synonymous with Dartington Glass, Thrower originally worked as a salesman for Wuidart & Co., a company that imported Scandinavian glass into Britain. Here he developed his drawing skills and his passion for Scandinavian glass alongside the designer Ronald Stennett-Willson. In the 1960s, he traveled in Finland and Sweden before joining Dartington Glass as co-director and chief designer in 1967. He produced some 500 designs for Dartington. His pieces reflect two widely different influences—Scandinavian design and 18th-century English glass—but have a distinct personality that combines simplicity and good proportions.

Frank Thrower Greek Key vase (one of a pair), designed for Dartington Glass. Its cubelike, textured body and round, flaring neck and rim are mold-blown. *1960s*

3½ in (9 cm) high

$180–220 (the pair)   **MHT**

Frank Thrower candle holders designed for Dartington Glass, both with a saucerlike drip pan. The taller is in kingfisher turquoise, the shorter in clear glass. *1969*

Tallest: 7¼ in (18.5 cm) high

$40–50 each   **GC**

1883 W.M.F. (est. 1880) builds a glassworks in Geislingen, near Stuttgart, Germany.

1922 W.M.F. rebuilds the glassworks destroyed in WWI and modernizes and streamlines production.

1925 W.M.F. develops a prototype for a range of iridescent glass called Myra-Kristall, after an ancient archaeological site in Asia Minor.

1926 W.M.F. develops the prototype for the Ikora-Kristall art-glass range.

1950 Wilhelm Wagenfeld (1900–90) begins designing tableware for W.M.F.

1954 Production of Ikora is discontinued.

1982 The W.M.F. glassworks in Geislingen closes and production of W.M.F. glass moves overseas.

W.M.F.

Probably best known for Art Nouveau metalware and glass, from the 1920s W.M.F. (Württembergische Metallwarenfabrik) developed two highly successful ranges of inexpensive mass-produced colored art glass in distinctive styles.

W.M.F. began experimenting with colored glass in 1925, a move prompted by Karl Wiedmann (1905–92), a talented glass technician who had trained with the company. The first results were the highly successful Myra-Kristall range of lightweight, thinly blown shapes with a thin iridescent gold film (*see p.117*). A year later W.M.F. launched the Ikora-Kristall art-glass range. Ikora included a vast range of shapes, colors, and decoration. The thick cased-glass forms were free-blown, turn mold-blown to produce a smooth surface, or dip-molded. Wiedmann and his colleagues developed some 5,000 color formulas, many discovered in technical trials. Ikora included mass-produced standard ranges and the Ikora Unica series, made mostly for exhibitions. These unique pieces had more complex decoration, including silver or copper leaf, Aventurine, and mica, and some sandblasted and cut patterns. W.M.F. was forced to sell them off after World War II. The Dexel-Ei (egg) vase designed by Walter Dexel is one of the most popular with collectors.

Ikora was predominantly an inexpensive mass-produced line, and most pieces were unmarked, although a few had paper labels.

Above: Ikora-Kristall-range vase of footed, bell-like form, with mottled and streaked green, orange-brown, and red powdered enamel inclusions. *c. 1935. 10¼ in (25.5 cm) high* **$700–900 QU**

Ikora-Kristall-range vase of shouldered and tapering cylindrical form, with air bubbles and streaked milky-yellow, orange, and blue powdered-enamel inclusions. *1930s*
15 in (38 cm) high
$1,000–1,200 QU

"Dexel-Ei" Ikora glass vase in orange and red with fine air bubbles. Designed by Walter Dexel. *c. 1937*
5½ in (14 cm) high
$300–400 QU

Ikora-Kristall-range bowl of shallow, circular form, with crackled and webbed bands of color, ranging from pale green, through to yellow-moss and white, to purple. *1930s*
10¾ in (27.5 cm) wide
$200–250 DN

Ikora-Kristall-range bowl in clear overlaid glass, with an abstract pattern of air bubbles and yellow, black, and red powdered-enamel inclusions. *c. 1935*
12¼ in (31.5 cm) wide
$500–700 QU

Michael Powolny

Michael Powolny is perhaps best known for his figural earthenware ceramics. From 1913, he also began to work in glass and produced a small range of distinctive and highly stylish pieces in association with the Wiener Werkstätte.

Powolny's first loves were ceramics and sculpture. At the Wiener Keramik studio he founded in 1906 with Berthold Loffler, he designed a specialized range of decorative figural ceramics featuring cherubic, distinctly Germanic-looking boys. These small sculptures were made in white earthenware with black detailing and often incorporated stylized flowers and distinctive black chevrons around the base.

The Wiener Keramik studio employed designers from the newly formed Wiener Werkstätte (*see p.65*), with whom, from 1907, Powolny developed close professional contacts. He became one of their leading designers, and they began to sell and distribute his glass designs.

From 1913, Powolny produced designs for such leading Austrian glassworks as J. & L. Lobmeyr (est. 1822) and Loetz (*see p.110*). Many of these designs were in the style associated with the Wiener Werkstätte, and consisted of blown-cased forms with dramatic contrasting black linear detailing that accentuated the shapes. Although first produced about 1914, these stylish linear pieces anticipated the Art Deco style and continued to sell successfully into the 1930s.

Above: Squat, trumpet-shaped vase with a wavy rim, designed for Loetz, in white-cased-in-clear glass with applied strings of black glass. c. 1915. 5¼ in (13.5 cm) high **$2,800–3,500 WKA**

KEY DATES

1871 Michael Powolny is born in Judenburg, Austria, son of a stove-maker.

1885 He begins training as a potter in his father's business.

1894 Powolny becomes a student at the Kunstgewerbeschule in Vienna, where he absorbs the influences of the Vienna Secession.

1906 He and the graphic artist Berthold Loffler (1874-1960) set up the Wiener Keramik Studio.

1912 Powolny becomes professor at the Kunstgewerbeschule in Vienna, where he is responsible for the glass, ceramics, and sculpture workshops. He is a highly influential teacher—one of his students is Lucie Rie—and plays a major role in shaping the decorative arts in his native Austria.

Tall trumpet-shaped vase with tango-orange cased-to-clear glass and vertical black glass stringing and rim. *1914*
8¼ in (21 cm) high
$500–800 **QU**

Footed, oval vase with a broad, flared neck in cased, tango-yellow glass, contrasted with the domed, spreading foot, three oval plaques, horizontal stringing, and rim, all in black glass. *1920s*
4¼ in (10.5 cm) high
$300–500 **DN**

European Blown & Cased

The strong glass-blowing tradition in central Europe gave talented designers free rein, since expert glass-blowers could interpret almost any design. These ranged from art glass designed by members of the Vienna Secession and the Wiener Werkstätte, to pieces by industrial designers such as Peter Behrens (1868–1940) and Wilhelm Wagenfeld (1900–90). Czech glassmakers proved their skills at the 1950 Milan Triennale with designs by Pavel Hlava (b. 1924) and, from the mid-1950s, with the Harrtil art glass made at the Harrachov glassworks.

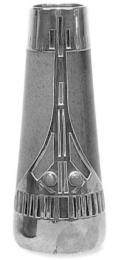

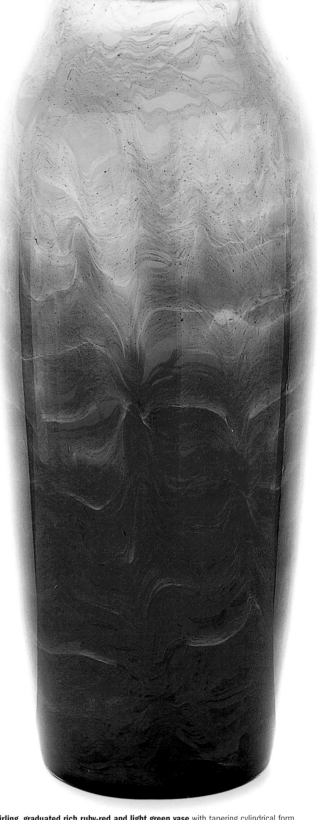

Bohemian Secessionist glass vase (one of a pair). It is set within a geometric-patterned copper mount. *Early 20th century*

7¼ in (18.5 cm) high

$800–1,200 (the pair)　　　　**DN**

Blue conical vase on a heavy clear-glass foot, designed by Heinrich Löffelhardt for Zwiesel. Internally decorated with groups of bubbles. *1970s*

7½ in (19 cm) high

$150–200　　　　**MHT**

Green-blue squat vase with a protruding rim, designed by Heinrich Löffelhardt for Zwiesel. Internally decorated with a large group of bubbles. *1970s*

7½ in (19 cm) high

$150–200　　　　**MHT**

Swirling, graduated rich ruby-red and light green vase with tapering cylindrical form, by Loetz. *1905*

8 in (20 cm) high

$2,500–3,000　　　　**MW**

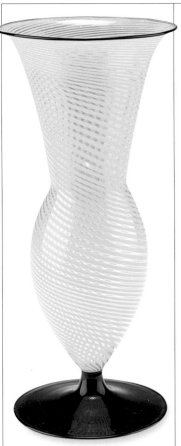

Gray-blue wine cooler with curled integral handles, designed by Bauhaus designer Wilhelm Wagenfeld for the United Lausitz Glass Manufacturers. *c. 1940*

8½ in (22 cm) high

$600–700   **HERR**

Rare purple, mold-blown, shallow dish applied to a heavy, shaped, clear-glass foot, designed by Marie Kirschner for Loetz. Signed "L MK W," with a star above the M. *c. 1905*

6¼ in (16 cm) high

$5,000–9,000   **FIS**

German yellow-and-clear-spiral vase of waisted and trumpet form, with black outlined rim and black foot. Made at Lauscha, which is famous for its glass marble production. *c. 1930*

7¾ in (19 cm) high

$300–500   **QU**

Plain, clear-glass wine glass with slender bowl and stem and simple knop. Designed by Peter Behrens for Poschinger, from a set of 12. *c. 1900*

8¼ in (20.5 cm) high

$600–700 (the set)   **QU**

Light green vase with a lightly textured, polished-glass surface highlighted with a band of stylized gilt rose motifs. Designed by Rudolf Marschall for J. & J. Lobmeyr of Vienna. *c. 1900*

7¼ in (18 cm) high

$7,000–10,000   **WKA**

Spherical brown-glass candle holder by Atelier Schott-Zwiesel, with an internal bubble formation gathered at the top half of the piece. *1970s*

4¼ in (11 cm) high

$100–150   **GC**

Wiener Werkstätte

The Wiener Werkstätte (Viennese Workshops) was a cooperative of leading painters, sculptors, architects, and artists. It was established by Josef Hoffmann (1870–1956) and Koloman Moser (1868–1919) in 1903 to rescue the decorative arts from the poor standards of design and workmanship brought about by mass production. Such ideals did not come cheap, and the Werkstätte designs sold to a small avant garde and rich clientele. Hoffmann, Moser, and Michael Powolny (*see p.63*) all produced designs made by such factories as Moser, Loetz (*see pp.110-11*), and Lobmeyr (est. 1822). The depression of the 1920s and 1930s diminished the market further, and the Wiener Werkstätte was liquidated in 1932.

Scallop-edged bowl of transparent purple glass on a compressed bun foot, designed by architect Josef Hoffmann for the Wiener Werkstätte. *c. 1915*

9¾ in (25 cm) wide

$6,000–9,000   **LN**

Footed purple bowl with scalloped shape and a row of bulbous protrusions under the bowl. The foot is trumpet-shaped. Designed by Josef Hoffmann for Ludwig Moser & Söhne of Karlsbad. *c. 1920*

5½ in (14 cm) high

$1,200–1,500   **QU**

Hand-blown light blue oval glass vase with lip and applied wavy trail decoration to the waist. *1920s*

8 in (20 cm) high

$70–100   **AS&S**

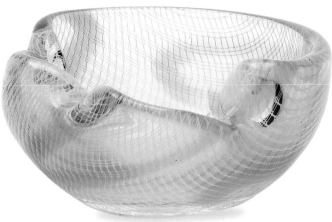

Free-form cased Haartil glass bowl by the Harrachov glassworks of Czechoslovakia, with an internal network of fine white threads and light green stripes, as well as a pulled rim. *1960s*

4¾ in (12 cm) wide

$70–100   **JH**

COPIER

Andries Dirk Copier (1901–91) joined the etching department of the Leerdam glassworks in the Netherlands at the age of 13. He spent several years studying typography, painting, and design, and by 1923 he was a designer at Leerdam, where he became artistic director in 1927. During his long career, he pioneered a range of inventive styles, both organic and geometric, in domestic and art glass. He is probably best known for the enduring Unica series of one-off free-blown art glass as well as the Serica limited-edition series of vases with thick walls and internal bubbled decoration in "seaweed" patterns. These exclusive pieces were launched in the 1920s and continually developed through to the 1980s.

Cased green, red, and clear Czechoslovakian *sommerso*-style vase probably by Pavel Hlava. *1950s*

8¼ in (21 cm) high

$1,200–1,500   **JH**

Cylindrical vase designed by Pavel Hlava, in graduated ruby-red, yellow, and brown colored glass, with eight deep red internal protrusions. *c. 1960*

14 in (36 cm) high

$500–700   **BMN**

Leerdam Unica vase designed by Copier, in clear glass with black crackle surface. Numbered "Unica C 153." *1930s*

4¾ in (12 cm) high   **$4,000–6,000**   **BMN**

Free-blown heavily cased Maastricht vase with random internal wavy brown striations and a thick flared rim. *c. 1955*

8¼ in (21 cm) high

$200–300   **JH**

Leerdam clear glass vase with a graduated, slightly iridescent, pale gray *craquelure* finish. *1930s*

6 in (15 cm) high

$700–1,000   JH

Mold-blown Royal Bohemia glass vase of shouldered form, lined and graduated in red, orange, and yellow. *c. 1970*

6¼ in (16 cm) high

$60–90   GC

Mold-blown Royal Bohemia vase graduated in red, orange, and yellow, and with an elongated neck. *c. 1970*

13½ in (34 cm) high

$80–120   GC

Bimini

In 1923, inspired by lampwork glass he had seen in Berlin, Fritz Lampl (1892–1955) set up the Bimini workshops in Vienna, named after a legendary island in a poem by German poet Heinrich Heine. The factory produced a range of thin-walled glasses, including decorative filigree goblets modeled on Venetian glass, cocktail sticks, lamps, stylized figures, and animals made from blown hollow glass tubes and solid colored rods. In 1938, Lampl emigrated to London, where he set up his Orplid workshop, which specialized in making buttons. Some of the button designs were created by a fellow political refugee from Vienna, the distinguished ceramicist Lucie Rie.

Bimini Werkstätte pair of glasses with filigree inverted conical bowls, flat feet, and stems with spherical bubbles containing lampwork glass roosters. *1930s*

Largest: 8 in (20 cm) high

$300–500 each   LN

Bimini Werkstätte small bud vase with lampwork leaping stag and cylindrical bud vase with a flared rim. *1930s*

4¼ in (11 cm) high

$100–150   JH

Bimini Werkstätte glass cocktail decanter and six glasses (two shown) designed by Fritz Lampl, in pale blue glass, each with a cream-glass lampwork Art Deco prancing lady. *c. 1930*

Jug: 9¾ in (24.5 cm) high

$1,000–1,500 (set)   AL

French Blown & Cased

In the early 1900s, France, already an established name in cameo glass, became known for other blown and cased colored glass in the Art Deco style. The Cristalleries Schneider (est. 1919, also marked Le Verre Français for the cameo range) was a leading proponent of bubbly, marvered cased glass. Daum Frères produced Art Deco designs with frosted, bubbled, and grained effects, but also mastered acid-etching, creating contrasting textures and contemporary designs in one or two colors, as did the glass designer Jean Luce (1895–1959). However, the most original and masterly use of the technique was by Maurice Marinot and his follower Henri Navarre (1885–1970).

Pair of Baccarat Art Nouveau–style crystal vases with gilt-bronze stands whose sinuous stems extend on to the body. Marked "E. Enot Paris" (possible retailer). *Early 20th century*
7¼ in (18.5 cm) high
$2,700–4,500 (the pair)   JDJ

French, violet, thick-walled vase of curving looped form, by the Cristallerie Sèvres. The base has an etched trademark. *1950s*
10 in (25 cm) high
$200–250   HERR

Tapering cylindrical vase by Daum Frères, with a rough frosted body decorated with yellow horizontal threads and dots. Signed "Daum Nancy" with the cross of Lorraine. *1920s*
6¾ in (17 cm) high
$800–1,200   QU

Art Deco–style green tapering vase by Jean Luce, with a geometric sand-blasted or frosted design on the exterior. The vase is signed on the base. *c. 1930*
7¼ in (18.5 cm) high
$1,000–1,500   TDG

Furnace-worked studio-glass vessel by Henri Navarre, with four applied medallions on the rim. c. 1930

6¾ in (17 cm) high

$4,000–6,000   AL

Thick-walled jug by Georges de Feure, made at Daum Frères, with matt finish. Signed. c. 1910

7 in (17.5 cm) high

$200–300   QU

Coupe Bijou footed bowl by Schneider, with internal air bubbles, violet inclusions, and a flared rim. Mounted on a dark purple baluster stem and foot. 1918–22

6 in (15 cm) high

$800–1,000   QU

Tapered glass vase by Daum Frères, which was blown into an armature by Majorelle. 1920–22

14¾ in (37.5 cm) high

$1,000–1,500   HERR

Orange and yellow mottled bowl with a blue rim by Schneider. The brown and yellow striped stem has glass rings. It is mounted on a circular metal base with stylized leaves and three glass "berries." 1920s

14¼ in (36 cm) high

$800–1,200   HERR

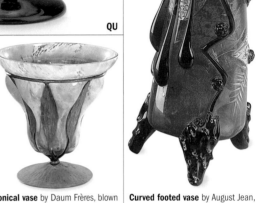

Conical vase by Daum Frères, blown into a brass stand following a design by Louis Majorelle. 1920–25

6¾ in (17 cm) high

$1,200–1,800   FIS

Curved footed vase by August Jean, decorated with abstract blue glass trailed over the body. c. 1900

12½ in (32 cm) high

$800–1,200   HERR

Art Deco-style vase decorated with internal bubbles. Signed "Daum Nancy" on the foot. c. 1930

13½ in (34.5 cm) high

$500–700   DN

Maurice Marinot

A shy and solitary man, Maurice Marinot (1882–1960) originally trained as a painter. His passion for glass developed following a life-changing visit to the Bar-sur-Seine glassworks owned by his friends Eugène and Gabriel Viard. Not content with just designing glass, Marinot also learned how to blow it, and used his talents as a painter to produce colorful textural pieces, some with deep, acid-etched decoration. His glass designs received high acclaim at the Art Deco exhibition in Paris in 1925.

Marinot's technically demanding and imaginative glass was extremely time-consuming to produce and correspondingly expensive. When poor health forced Marinot to abandon glass, the artist-turned-glassmaker reverted to his original loves of painting and drawing.

Maurice Marinot extremely rare flattened oval bottle with stopper. It has a swirling gray and black marblelike decoration, random internal bubbles, and enameled decoration around the rim. 1910–20

6¼ in (16 cm) high

$20,000–25,000   LN

KEY DATES

1922 William John Blenko sets up Blenko glassworks in Milton, West Virginia, specializing in stained glass.

1929 Blenko begins production of colored domestic and ornamental glass to counteract fall in demand for stained glass.

1933 William John Blenko dies and his son William H. Blenko (1897–1969) takes over the factory.

1947 Winslow Anderson becomes the first resident designer.

1952 Wayne Husted becomes resident designer after Anderson's departure.

Blenko

William John Blenko's early and lifelong passion for stained glass allowed him to overcome early difficulties and go on to establish a highly successful glassworks that combined technical expertise with shrewd marketing.

Born and trained in Britain, William John Blenko (1854–1933) had three failed attempts at setting up an American glassworks before succeeding in 1922 with Blenko glassworks. His expertise had initially been applied to stained glass, but when demand fell in the 1920s, Blenko began to develop a range of brightly colored domestic glass.

In 1932, Macy's of New York was carrying the Blenko range, and by 1935 department stores across the United States had followed suit.

In the 1930s and 1940s, Blenko's glassware included vases and bowls in the vibrant range of colors that became the company's trademark and that help to date the glass. Most pieces were in one of Blenko's vivid single colors, although some had applied decoration in a second color. The heat-sensitive Amberina range has graded shades ranging from red to amber.

Three resident designers in particular helped shape Blenko's range. When Winslow Anderson

(b. 1917) joined in 1947, he introduced the softer, more organic forms associated with the Scandinavian style. In 1952, his Bent Decanter was chosen by the Museum of Modern Art in New York, as part of the Good Design exhibition at the Chicago Mart Show. Wayne Husted was designer from 1952 to 1963, and he introduced the range of large, dramatically colored and shaped decanters. While Joel Myers—resident designer from 1963 to 1972—created Blenko's more restrained glass designs: vases and decanters took on the more geometric cylindrical shapes and textured surfaces typical of the 1960s.

Blenko is primarily associated with color, and it is the more vibrant and dramatic colors that tend to be more popular, together with a combination of interesting shapes and sizes.

Above: Orange and yellow Tangerine bottle with elongated, shaped neck and teardrop-shaped stopper. Designed by Wayne Husted. *1958–64. 15¾ in (40 cm) high* **$600–800 EOH**

BLENKO STAINED GLASS

William John Blenko's expertise as a master color-maker was originally dedicated to antique stained glass, which he produced using the traditional method of mouth-blown flat panels of colored "in the pot" stained glass. The company received several commissions for ecclesiastical stained glass, including the magnificent Rose Window in the National Cathedral in Washington, DC. Here Joseph Reynolds used Blenko stained glass for his symbolic depiction of St. John's vision of Heaven, taken from Revelations 4. God is seated on a throne, dressed in a mantle of brilliant gold, surrounded by a rainbow and figures of the Four and Twenty Elders holding golden crowns.

Left: Tall orange and yellow graduated glass vase that was hand shaped, then blown into a mold, with a textured surface and a flared rim. *c. 1960 11½ in (29 cm) high* **$80–120 MHT**

DETAIL OF ROSE WINDOW, NATIONAL CATHEDRAL, WASHINGTON, DC, 1962

Surf Green mold-blown vase designed by Joel Philip Myers in the early 1970s. *1970*

10¼ in (26 cm) high

$1,000–1,500   **EOH**

MAKER'S MARKS

Blenko's pride in its hand-blown colored glass is reflected in the mark used—a label showing a hand carrying the printed words "BLENKO HANDCRAFT." This mark was used from the 1930s to the 1960s. From the 1970s, Blenko used a new mark: a stylized black capital B pierced by a blowing iron. The company also used a number system for patterns, with the first two numbers revealing the year of production. The letters S, M, and L indicate the size of a piece.

Tangerine bottle with teardrop-shaped stopper. Designed by Wayne Husted. *1962–67*

18 in (46 cm) high

$320–380   **EOH**

Emerald-green attenuated bottle designed by Joel Philip Myers. *1969–72*

22 in (56 cm) high

$800–1,200   **EOH**

Charcoal bottle with flat-top stopper, designed by Wayne Husted. *1956–59*

21¼ in (54 cm) high

$600–900   **EOH**

Tall slender yellow bottle with tapered stopper, designed by Wayne Husted. *1958*

20½ in (52 cm) high

$200–300   **EOH**

Tall Persian Blue bottle with crackle effect and tapering, shaped stopper, by Wayne Husted. *1959*

28¾ in (73 cm) high

$400–600   **EOH**

Graduated orange and yellow glass vase with smooth surface, flared rim, and heavy base. *c. 1960*

11½ in (29 cm) high

$80–120   **MHT**

Turquoise squat bottle with shaped stopper, designed by Joel Philip Myers. *1965–67*

14 in (36 cm) high

$300–500   **EOH**

American Blown & Cased

In the 1950s and 60s, American manufacturers produced blown and cased glass in many styles but were united in their use of color. Steuben, well known for cut glass, also produced a range of colored glass. Look for the Cluthra range, known for its internal bubble effect. A postwar group of manufacturers in West Virginia—Bischoff (est. 1942), Pilgrim (est.1949), and Viking (est. 1944)—started producing ranges of colored, often crackled glass, in shapes and colors similar to those of Blenko. Many of their designs also reflected the influence of Scandinavian and Italian glass styles.

Steuben Pomona vase with flared rim designed by Frederick Carder, in an unusual transparent green glass. *c. 1925*
6 in (15 cm) high
$250–350   TDC

Steuben blue jade vase of tapering form with vertical ribbing, fluted and flared rim, and a compressed bun foot. *Early 20th century*
5½ in (14 cm) high
$4,000–6,000   JDJ

Steuben jade green glass vase with a molded diagonal swirl pattern; signed with a Steuben Fleur-de-Lys mark. *c. 1930s*
6¼ in (15.5 cm) high
$300–450   JDJ

Rainbow red bottle of flattened rectangular and shouldered form, with wide rim and original shaped stopper. *1950s*
10 in (25 cm) high
$150–200   EOH

Steuben Cluthra vase, the pink glass urn-shaped body is covered all over with bubbles, giving a mottled appearance. *1920s*
6½ in (16.5 cm) high
$1,500–2,500   JDJ

Pilgrim purple crackle glass tapering bottle with slightly waisted neck and elongated teardrop shaped stopper. *c. 1960*
17¾ in (45 cm) high
$180–250   EOH

Pilgrim yellow crackle glass tapering bottle with slightly waisted neck and replaced spherical stopper. *1950s*
15 in (38 cm) high
$250–350   EOH

Bischoff bottle of circular section with three identical disc-shaped protrusions and inverted cone-shaped clear glass stopper. *c. 1960*

13½ in (34 cm) high

$300–350   EOH

Bischoff bottle with clear glass stem of three spherical knops, and clear glass foot, handle, and teardrop-shaped stopper. *c. 1960*

18½ in (47 cm) high

$200–400   EOH

Two Pairpoint cobalt-blue lidded vases of inverted conical form and a matching footed bowl with wide rim and bulbous body, all engraved with the Vintage pattern. *Early 20th century*

Vases: 12 in (30.5 cm) high

$2,500–4,000 (the set)   JDJ

Three decorative Viking amber mushrooms of typical form, with wide domes atop tapering conical bases. *c. 1960*

Largest: 5½ in (14 cm) wide

Large: $120–180; medium: $30–50; small: $25–40   EOH

Pilgrim orange bottle of squat form decorated with molded dot design, with a cylindrical neck and tall tapering stopper. *1960s*

13½ in (34 cm) high

$200–300   EOH

Large Viking purple shouldered bottle with flared base, cylindrical neck with molded knop, and conical clear glass stopper. *c. 1960*

26 in (66 cm) high

$400–600   EOH

Pilgrim bottle of square section with rounded corners, short cylindrical neck, flared rim, and rounded cylindrical stopper. *1960s*

9½ in (24 cm) high

$150–200   EOH

73

KEY FACTORIES

Cristalleries d'Emile Gallé, Nancy, Lorraine, France (1867–1936).

Daum Frères, Nancy, Lorraine, France (est. 1878); still active.

Legras et Cie, Paris, France (est. 1864); still active.

Loetz, Klostermühle, Bohemia (1836–1948).

Müller Frères, Luneville, France (1895–1933).

Thomas Webb & Sons, Stourbridge, West Midlands, England (1859–1990).

CAMEO GLASS

The cameo technique was originally developed by gemstone engravers. Glassmakers adapted it by blowing and fusing together layers of different-colored glass and then hand-cutting, acid-etching, or sand-blasting away the background layer(s) to create a design that stood proud of the surface.

The Portland Vase (1st century BC–1st century AD), a well-known example of the early two-color hand-carved cameo technique, caused a stir when it was shown at the British Museum in 1810. Later, British glassmakers experimented with hand-carved cameo, introduced the use of hydrofluoric acid to etch away some of the background color, and produced a world-leading range of cameo, usually white on a colored background, in neoclassical shapes and with formal designs.

FRENCH ART NOUVEAU CAMEO

The cameo technique reached new heights in the hands of Emile Gallé, a pioneer of Art Nouveau. He transformed the formal two-color vases into multilayered compositions that expressed his spiritual vision of the natural world. Using combinations of cutting and carving by hand, and wheel- and acid-etching, he created organic designs from as many as five layers of colored

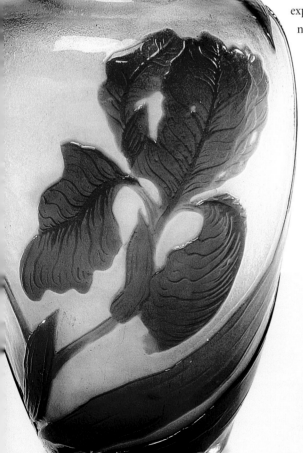

Emile Gallé cameo glass vase with iris blooms carved and etched in shades of purple over a milky yellow ground. *c. 1905 5 in (12.5 cm) high* **$1,200–1,800 VS**

glass. The flora and fauna of his native Lorraine provided inspiration for Gallé's motifs, often highlighted by gold or silver foil, with further detail added by hand-painted enamels or carved or etched designs. Gallé experimented with frosted grounds and mold-blowing to provide further relief for decoration, especially fruit and flower motifs. The piece was then hand-carved to add detail such as veining. Gallé cameo was imitated worldwide.

As commercial imperatives dictated faster production methods, French cameo-makers increasingly replaced hand- or wheel-carving

Emile Gallé drew much inspiration for his cameo work from the natural beauty of his surroundings.

KEY STYLES

Neoclassical symmetrical shapes *with two-color cameo and with formal cut and engraved decoration.*
Organic Art Nouveau forms *with multiple layers of color and flora and fauna decoration; hand- and wheel-cutting, acid-etching, engraving, enameling, and gilding.*
Two-color faux cameo *with acid-etched simplified decoration of either Art Nouveau or Art Deco motifs.*

Small Daum Frères cameo glass vase of footed and flattened tapering form with a rectangular neck. It has carved and etched indigenous French flowers in mauve over a green-gray ground. *c. 1905 3¾ in (9.5 cm) high* **$600–900 DN**

with acid-etching for production ranges of what was known as faux cameo (*see p.81*), reducing the number of colors and simplifying designs.

CAMEO VARIATIONS

In Great Britain, Thomas Webb (*see p.167*) made its own ranges of cameo that combined clear glass and a color. Another, more rarely used, technique was pad cameo: pads of colored glass were applied to a clear flint glass body, which was then cut and etched away to leave the colored pads in

even higher relief. The pads were then hand-carved to add detail.

The Swedish glassworks of Orrefors and Kosta developed their own range of one-color cameo, often clear glass, although blue and green were also used. The top layer was etched away to leave the design in relief on the same-colored background.

Daum Frères vase of tumblerlike shape in cameo glass, with dragonflies, bog flowers, and other pond life etched and enameled in subtle shades of purple, green, and yellow on a sky-blue ground. *c. 1905*
9½ in (24 cm) high
$30,000–50,000 QU

Emile Gallé cameo glass vase
of small ovoid form, with blossoms and leaves indigenous to the Lorraine area carved in shades of purple-through-red glass over a mottled ground. *c. 1905. 3¾ in (9.5 cm) high* **$700–1,000 GORL**

KEY DATES

1873 Emile Gallé sets up a decorating workshop in Nancy.

1874 Gallé takes over a glass workshop from his father.

1878 Gallé wins gold medals at the International Exhibition in Paris.

1894 Gallé builds the Cristallerie d'Emile Gallé in Nancy.

1900 Gallé art glass wins a Grand Prix at the Paris International Exhibition.

1904 Gallé dies, leaving his widow to run the factory with Victor Prouvé as art director.

1936 Factory closes.

Emile Gallé

Initially inspired by historical cameo glass, Emile Gallé went on to develop the technique with a unique blend of artistry and technical expertise that made him the supreme master of Art Nouveau cameo and the inspiration for many French factories.

Gallé's rare early cameo vases are masterpieces of precision and manual dexterity. They were produced using the same techniques that had been used in antiquity: different colored layers of glass were fused, and the top layer of glass was then hand-carved to make the design stand proud.

Gallé took this basic process several steps further. He increased the number of colors, sometimes using as many as five. He eliminated the sharp color contrasts, preferring to cut away the colors at various levels to create shading, subtle color gradations, atmosphere, and perspective. Foil inclusions, fire polishing, and the *martelé* (hammered-metal effect) technique added extra texture, as did further hand-carving of the design, such as leaf veins.

From about 1899, Gallé began commercial production of Art Nouveau cameo, making increasing use of acid-etching. This was employed on Gallé's "standard," or middle-range, cameo pieces, which were of consistently high quality but lacked the creative spirit of the *pièces uniques* that were made either by Gallé or by one of his master craftsmen.

After Gallé's death in 1904, production was streamlined. The "industrial" cameo production included large quantities of lamps and vases in simplified shapes and colors. The majority had two, at most three, layers of color, and the decoration was stenciled on before the piece was acid-etched. Very few had any hand-finishing.

Above: Cameo glass vase of baluster form, with floral imagery acid-etched in tones of pink and amethyst against a yellow-green ground. *c. 1900. 8¼ in (21 cm) high* **$3,500–5,000 MW**

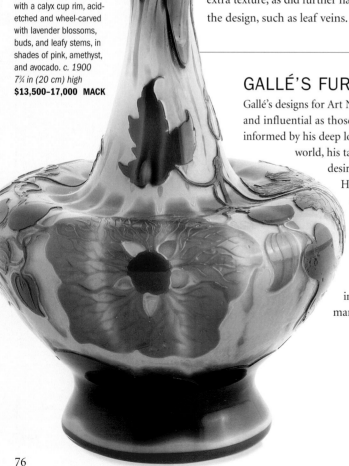

Four-layer cameo glass vase of bulbous form, with a calyx cup rim, acid-etched and wheel-carved with lavender blossoms, buds, and leafy stems, in shades of pink, amethyst, and avocado. *c. 1900 7¾ in (20 cm) high* **$13,500–17,000 MACK**

GALLÉ'S FURNITURE DESIGNS

Gallé's designs for Art Nouveau furniture were as inspiring and influential as those he created for glass. Both were informed by his deep love and knowledge of the natural world, his talent for botanical drawing, and his desire to promote naturalism in design. He challenged traditional furniture conventions and construction by treating wood as a truly plastic medium, employing curving, organic shapes, such as dragonfly wings, for the basic forms and supports. Plants, animals, and insects also featured on the decorative marquetry, handles, and mounts.

Rear of a cabinet with carved floral cresting, branch stretchers, and marquetry panels of birds, trailing branches, and leaf sprays. This piece displays Gallé's characteristic use of motifs and imagery from nature. *Late 1800s 60¾ in (156 cm) high* **$54,000–63,000 MACK**

Crête de Coq cameo glass bowl. The overlaid clear glass has amber and platinum inclusions, under carved grass and floral decoration. *c. 1900*

5 in (12.5 cm) wide

$13,000–17,000   QU

MAKER'S MARKS

All Gallé glass is signed, but the signatures vary considerably. The starred signature below was used as a mark of respect from 1904, after Gallé's death, until 1914. All Gallé marks should be carefully checked in a specialist reference book because fakes have proliferated. On original pieces, the glass surrounding the signature will be of uniform texture.

MARK USED AFTER GALLÉ'S DEATH

Extremely rare cameo marquetry vase with an inlaid daffodil motif, in graduated tones of green, yellow, and blue. Signed; dated. *1900*

7 in (18.25 cm) high

$20,000–24,000   FIS

Rare fire-polished cameo glass vase with etched leaves and blossoming flower-heads. Signed "Gallé" on the side. *c. 1900*

11 in (28 cm) high

$9,000–10,000   JDJ

Cameo glass vase of footed, tapering form, with acid-etched berries, leaves, and branches in greens on a pale amber ground. *c. 1910*

14¼ in (36 cm) high

$2,700–4,500   JDJ

Cameo glass vase with wheel-carved iris blossoms, leaves, and ferns in amethyst and green on pale blues and yellows. *c. 1900*

14¾ in (37.5 cm) high

$5,500–7,500   JDJ

Footed cameo glass vase with autumn crocuses in a misty meadow, acid-etched in dusty pink and purple on pink. *c. 1900*

10¼ in (26 cm) high

$3,500–5,500   QU

Cameo glass floor vase with a pattern of flower-heads, leaves, and trailing stems carved in greens and amethyst. *c. 1900*

17¼ in (44 cm) high

$5,000–7,000   MW

Daum Frères

Inspired by the Gallé pieces shown at the 1889 Paris Exhibition, Daum Frères began to produce art glass. Its cameo work soon gained a reputation that some believed rivalled that of Gallé.

The rich multicolored Art Nouveau cameo designs of the brothers Daum were inspired by the landscape, flora, and fauna of their native Nancy. Many of their trademark innovative techniques—the cloudy, mottled rich background, colored enamel detail, the martelé (hammered metal effect) background, the complex intercalaire pieces with patterns at varying depths, and applied foil-backed decoration—were developed to enhance the naturalistic decoration.

Jean Daum took over the company in 1909, and by the 1920s he began to pioneer the new Art Deco style in which the factory became preeminent.

Shapes became simpler and often featured stylized geometric, rather than naturalistic, floral acid-etched patterns. Vases often had a single layer of opaque colored glass that was acid-etched to reveal a clear colorless body. In the 1920s and 30s, lamps became an increasingly important area of production, some featuring metal mounts by such major designers as Louis Majorelle and Edgar Brandt.

The landscape cameo vases were predominantly made after World War I. The most expensive examples had multiple layers of color that were etched, engraved, carved, and enameled. The most skillful Daum glassworkers could use up to five layers of color—a technically demanding process, since different colors cool at different rates.

Above: Egyptian cameo glass vase in colorless glass with milky powder insertions. The vitrified blue outer layer is acid-etched with stylized papyrus flowers and olive branches. *1926 11½ in (29.25 cm) high* **$8,000–9,000 QU**

Twin-handled cameo glass vase of shouldered baluster form, with an outer layer of trailing-vine decoration acid-etched in green, over a frosted and "hammered" pink ground. *1905–10. 8¼ in (21 cm) high* **$9,000–12,000 MACK**

THE BROTHERS DAUM

Jean-Louis Auguste Daum (1853–1909) had trained as a lawyer and his brother Jean-Antonin (1864–1931) as an engineer before they took over their father's glassworks in Nancy. Jean-Antonin, who headed the Daum decorating studio, was the more artistic of the two. He described himself as preoccupied with the visual, rather than symbolic, beauty of nature, the magic of color, and the "language of flowers." The brothers constantly experimented with new techniques, which they often combined in one piece without losing the overall unity of style, color, and decoration.

JEAN-LOUIS AUGUSTE DAUM

Champignons-pattern vase by Henri Bergé or Emile Wirtz, with mushrooms and insects against a mottled yellow-green ground. *c. 1905*

9¼ in (23.5 cm) high

$12,000–15,000   **HERR**

Footed, baluster-shaped vase by Henri Bergé, with poppies and mountains under a setting sun. *1905*

10½ in (27 cm) high

$35,000–50,000   **QU**

Mushroom-shaped table lamp in clear overlay glass with powdered-enamel inclusions, and etched enamel highlights. *c. 1905*

16¼ in (41.5 cm) high

$4,000–5,000   **QU**

Feuilles de Rosier à l'Automne vase etched in shades of red, green, and yellow enamel against a mottled green ground. *c. 1905*

7 in (18 cm) high

$3,500–5,000   **QU**

Art Deco floor lamp possibly by Louis Majorelle, with a cameo glass shade on a decorated metal stand. *1920s–30s*

64 in (162.5 cm) high

$12,000–15,000   **JDJ**

Art Deco glass vase with textured, stylized blossoms, leaves, and branches acid-etched in orange and green. *1920s*

7 in (17.75 cm) high

$2,000–3,000   **QU**

Cup-shaped, footed vase by Henri Bergé, with an asymmetrical jagged rim and "Narcisse" decoration over a mottled ground. *c. 1910*

7 in (18 cm) high

$9,000–12,000   **QU**

Cameo glass goblet-shaped vase with "bleeding heart" plant-form decoration in powdered and applied enamels. *c. 1905*

8 in (20.5 cm) high

$12,000–18,000   **MACK**

French Cameo

By the late 19th century, French glassworks had displaced British manufacturers at the forefront of cameo production. Gallé and Daum led the field and, from the early 1900s, gradually introduced a range of semi production-line cameo glass that made increasing use of acid-etching to speed up production and reduce costs. Many other French companies followed suit and launched some equally high-quality cameo that was (and still is) more modestly priced. These included Baccarat (est. 1764), which produced both hand-carved and faux cameo, the Saint-Louis Glassworks (using the d'Argental mark, est. 1767), and new glassworks eager to build a reputation.

D'Argental cameo glass vase with stylized flowers, leaves, and trailing stems carved in eggplant over spotted red and caramel-yellow grounds. *c.* 1910

8 in (20 cm) high

$2,800–3,500   **CR**

Verrerie Schneider cameo glass vase from the Le Verre Français line, with acid-etched, stylized *champignons* decoration in red over mottled yellow and turquoise. *c.* 1925

17½ in (44.75 cm) high

$3,600–4,500   **DOR**

Verrerie Schneider cameo glass vase with stylized nasturtium decoration, acid-etched in orange and dark brown glass over a thick, mottled, yellow-gray ground. *1920s*

7¾ in (20 cm) high

$2,800–3,500   **HERR**

Verrerie Schneider cameo glass vase in amethyst-colored glass over clear glass. The former features an acid-etched, frosted-finish, Egyptian-style decoration. *1920s*

7½ in (19 cm) high

$600–800   **JDJ**

André Delatte cameo glass vase of tapering, cylindrical form, with Art Nouveau–style orchid decoration acid-etched in maroon red over an opaque pink ground. *c.* 1925

7 in (18 cm) high

$1,800–2,700   **VZ**

André Delatte cameo glass vase with Art Nouveau–style orchid decoration wheel-carved in shades of maroon and eggplant over an opaque pink ground. *c.* 1925

8 in (20 cm) high

$1,800–2,700   **CR**

Burgun, Schverer & Cie vase with hand-painted intercalaire orchid decoration, etched and wheel-carved in whites and greens, with gilt highlights over a purple-pink ground. *c.* 1900

8½ in (22 cm) high

$21,500–25,100   **LN**

French cameo glass vase with acid-etched floral, leaf, and vine decoration. *1920s*

13 in (33 cm) high

$700–800 JDJ

Müller Frères vase with acid-etched cameo glass fish (in turquoise) and pebbles (in purple). *1925–27*

9 in (23 cm) high

$4,500–5,400 VS

Verrerie Schneider cameo glass vase, from the Le Verre Français line, with acid-etched berries. *1920s*

4 in (10 cm) high

$500–700 JDJ

Acid-etched cameo glass vase in the French style of Gallé by Edward Rigot for Villeroy & Boch. *c. 1930*

12 in (31 cm) high

$3,600–4,500 TO

FAUX CAMEO

In faux cameo, the layer or layers of glass are cut away by acid rather than by hand to create the design. The design area is covered in an acid-resistant substance, such as bitumen of Judea, and the vessel is then plunged into hydrofluoric acid, which eats away the unprotected areas. The process can be repeated several times, producing varying thicknesses of layers and variations in color. The technique, which was introduced to speed up production and reduce costs, almost became an art form in its own right, due to the skill with which many late 19th-century French manufacturers used it. In general, however, faux cameo features less complex designs and fewer and thinner layers of glass.

Baccarat faux-cameo crystal vase of footed baluster form, with leafy plant-form decoration in shades of green and yellow over a pale green ground. *c. 1900*

14 in (36 cm) high

$1,000–1,200 L&T

Burgun, Schverer & Cie vase with hand-painted intercalaire orchid and leaf decoration, etched and wheel-carved in white, yellow, and green over a graduated pink ground. *c. 1900*

7¾ in (20 cm) high

$15,000–20,000 LN

Müller Frères cameo glass vase with acid-etched leaf and stag-beetle decoration. *c. 1900*

6 in (15.5 cm) high

$1,200–1,800 QU

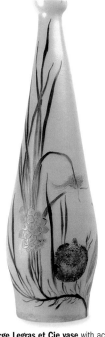

Large Legras et Cie vase with acid-etched shell and marine vegetation on a white ground. *c. 1910*

22 in (56 cm) high

$1,200–1,800 JDJ

Legras et Cie cameo vase with acid-etched and enameled poppies, stems, and leaves. *c. 1910*

14 in (35.5 cm) high

$2,500–4,500 JDJ

European & American Cameo

In spite of the supremacy of the French school, other European and American manufacturers managed to establish their own ranges of cameo glass. Some made cameo glass that emulated the style of late production-line Gallé; others developed a more distinctive style of two-color cameo, or put a twist on Art Nouveau motifs, such as the distinctive blue-gray glass with a single dark-red overlay often used by the Vallerysthal glassworks (est. 1836).

Glassworkers at Haida and Steinschönau produced stylish Art Deco cameo with Bohemian cut detail, and in Great Britain, Thomas Webb developed a range of clear and colored cameo for the 1930s.

French cameo glass vase signed Arsall, its slender ovoid body with hawthorn branches, leaves, and berries acid-etched against a graduated, milky-pink ground. *1918–29*

16 in (41 cm) high

$800–1,200   QU

German cameo glass vase by Vallerysthal, its elongated baluster-shape with Japanese-style chestnut branches and butterflies cut and etched over a blue-gray ground. *c. 1900*

12 in (30 cm) high

$700–1,000   HERR

Bohemian cameo glass vase designed by Hans Bolek for Loetz, of slightly tapering tubular form with a band of cut and enameled leaf decoration above vertical stripes. *c. 1915*

9 in (23 cm) high

$7,000–10,000   TO

English Cameo Fleur vase by Webb & Co., of trumpet form with a conical foot. Decorated with stylized lilies acid-etched in red and pink on a clear glass ground. *c. 1930*

9¾ in (25 cm) high

$500–600   DN

Czechoslovakian cameo glass vase by Prof. A. Dorn, made by Fachschule Steinschönau, with stylized blossoms and leaves carved and etched in purple over clear glass. *c. 1930*

6½ in (16.5 cm) high

$4,000–6,000   FIS

Czechoslovakian cameo vase from the Haida glassworks, probably designed by Adolf Rasche, the trumpet-form body rising from a waisted collar, cut and etched with flowers. *c. 1930*

4¾ in (12 cm) high

$300–400   FIS

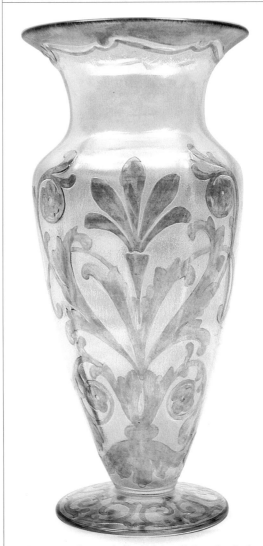

Czechoslovakian pendant ceiling light by Loetz in the style of Gallé, in cameo glass, acid-etched with blossoms and leaves in orange, red, and green over a milky opalescent ground. *c. 1925*

16 in (40.5 cm) wide

$4,000–5,000 QU

Bohemian cameo glass vase from the Harrach glassworks, decorated with acid-etched blossoms and leaves in shades of red and purple on a mottled green ground. *c. 1900*

14 in (36 cm) high

$3,000–4,000 FIS

American cameo glass vase by Handel & Co., of baluster form in clear glass encased in translucent golden amber glass, acid-etched with stylized flowers and scrolling leaves. *c. 1910*

10 in (25.5 cm) high

$1,000–1,500 JDJ

Lalique Suzanne statuette of a woman
with a robe falling from her arms, cast in
opalescent amber glass and with a molded
"R. Lalique" mark. *c. 1925*
9 in (23 cm) **$20,000–30,000 RDL**

Pressed & Molded Glass

Developed in the United States in the 1820s, pressed glass reached its artistic apogee in France some one hundred years later. In the masterly hands of the multitalented René Lalique, some of the most enduring images of the Art Deco style were made in pressed and mold-blown glass. Lalique understood the strengths of the technique: it was ideally suited to the machine aesthetic and the democratic principles of making good design affordable and available to all. Rather than being relegated to mass- producing pale imitations of cut-glass designs, pressed and molded glass offered glassmakers and designers the opportunity to reproduce well-designed tableware or beautiful complex sculptural images time and again, quickly and with no loss of quality or definition.

THE EARLY YEARS

Most modern glass techniques have their roots in ancient glassmaking traditions. Pressed glass is the exception: a mechanical process, it was the child of the age of the machine, mass production, and mass consumption. The first machine for pressing glass was developed in the United States in the 1820s. By the 1830s, American manufacturers were using the technique to mass produce a type of inexpensive "fancy" and functional glass with intricate, high-definition patterns that imitated those found on the more expensive ranges of cut glass. By the 1830s, the technique had crossed the Atlantic to Europe. Manufacturers in Belgium, France, Bohemia, and England—the northeast in particular—were using it to produce domestic wares, trinkets, novelties, and souvenirs in colored and clear glass.

THE TECHNIQUE

Mold-makers, often highly skilled, produced full-sized one-, two-, or three-piece metal molds in which the pattern or design was cut in intaglio. Molten glass was poured into the mold, and

Close-up view of an emerald green Lalique Formose vase clearly showing the low-relief line left by the mold parts when the glass was pressed or blown into them and formed. **RDL**

a plunger was then pushed down into the mold, "pressing" the glass against the mold walls to create the pattern in relief on the outside of the piece and a smooth hollow interior. The end result is unlike mold-blown glass, where the decoration can be felt on the inside of the piece.

The glass used for pressing was usually of slightly inferior quality, and the elaborate patterns and color helped disguise the imperfections. More expensive pressed glass sometimes had an element of hand-finishing, such as rubbing down the mold seams, or

Lalique Esterel vase of oval form with a short neck, in opalescent glass with blue patina, engraved with an "R. Lalique France" mark. c. 1925
6 in (15 cm) high **$1,000–1,500 RDL**

COLLECTORS' TIPS

Perfect condition is essential with any mass-produced, readily found glass.
Look for early pieces with crisp molding; mold definition softens with use.
Pressed glass is mostly unmarked; Lalique is always marked.
There is a wide range of styles to choose from; pieces that capture a particular decade or trend are the most popular.
Many molds were reused at a later date; beware of later reproductions.

Tearoom pattern green Depression glass vase with all-over geometric design and flared and frilled rim. It was made by the Indiana Glass Company for restaurants and soda fountains. *1930s*
6¾ in (17.5 cm) high **$90–120 CA**

Lalique Bacchantes vase with a high-relief frieze of elegant naked women, in opalescent glass with blue patina and original bronze base. It has a wheel-cut "R. Lalique France" mark. c. 1930
9¾ in (25 cm) high **$30,000–50,000 RDL**

it might have further surface effects added, such as frosting or iridescence.

In the United States, the pressed-glass process was refined and further automated. By the late 1850s, most American glass was pressed, and by the 1920s, what became known as Depression glass (*see p.90*) was produced by a completely automatic process in which the molten glass was fed into the molds via pipes and pressed automatically, speeding up production and dramatically reducing costs.

ART DECO LUXURY

René Lalique (*see p.88*) transformed the image of pressed glass with a range of luxury Art Deco pieces that attracted international acclaim. He geared up for mechanical production at his Wingen-sur-Moder glassworks, where, by the 1930s, over 600 workers were mass-producing his pressed and mold-blown glass designs. His pieces ranged from prestigious vases to smaller items such as ashtrays, hood ornaments, statuettes, and tableware in a clear, colored, frosted, and opalescent glass. Lalique adapted the shape of his vases to allow for the wider necks required for pressed glass, and maintained superb quality by regularly replacing molds to ensure high definition. Necks narrower than the body and lighter, thinner glass are features indicative of mold-blown pieces.

Where Lalique led, others followed, and many French manufacturers such as Etling produced high-quality pressed glass. Sabino (*see p.103*) used two-piece molds for his standard range of trinkets and small glass animal sculptures. In Great Britain, Jobling (*see p.97*), George

Davidson and Co. (*see p.96*), and Bagley Crystal Co. (est. Knottingley, Yorkshire, 1871) all used the technique to produce now-collectible Art Deco designs, often with very complex patterns that the technique allowed.

STYLISH AND AFFORDABLE

By the 1950s and 60s, the machine aesthetic was well established and increasingly stylish designs were being mass-produced by press-molding. In Czechoslovakia, the pressed-molded clear glass with abstract geometric patterns (*see* Ashtrays, *p.94*) once again offered a less expensive alternative to similar styles in cut glass. In Great Britain, pressed glass encapsulated the 1950s style for a mass market, while in Scandinavia, pressed glass was used to implement the democratic principle of making good design affordable for all. The latter was characterized by stylish tableware and ornamental ware, such as the classic designs by Kaj Franck for the Finnish Nuutajärvi glassworks (*see p.49*), which acquired automatic pressed-glass equipment in the 1960s.

Cherry Blossom pattern Depression glass flat soup bowl with scrolling, floral, and foliate pattern. It was made by the Jeannette Glass Company, primarily in pink and green glass. *1930–39. 8 in (20 cm) wide* **$90–120 PR**

Art Deco pressed amethyst glass vase (one of a pair) of geometric form with short neck and heavy frieze of scrolling patterns and stylized animals, with bases stamped "Made In France 153." *1930s. 6 in (15.5 cm) high* **$350–500 (the pair) PAC**

Lalique Ronces glass vase of oval form with a short neck and an all-over heavy stylized scrolling pattern. It has a molded "R. Lalique" mark and an engraved "Lalique France" mark. *c. 1920. 9½ in (24 cm) high* **$5,000–7,000 RDL**

René Lalique

The extraordinary talents of René Lalique enabled him to acquire a worldwide reputation both as a designer of Art Nouveau jewellery and of Art Deco glass, with a prolific range from scent bottles to tableware and vases.

René Lalique (1860–1945) began using glass in his jewellery designs in the 1880s, and was soon inspired to create his own glassware. By 1918, he had moved from his glassworks to larger premises. Here he developed his press-molding technique, which he used to create a huge range of glass using mass-production techniques. Lalique's decision to move from exclusive one-off pieces to large-scale manufacture allowed him to reach a wider market without losing his inimitable style. The crisply molded details, the quality of the molding, and, above all, the virtuosity of the designs gave these mass-produced pieces a "one-off" feel.

Between 1920 and 1930, Lalique created designs for more than 200 vases and 150 bowls—the two most popular Lalique forms. He is usually associated with pressed glass, although many of his lighter, thinner vases were formed by blowing glass into a mold.

Pieces were produced in clear, opalescent, frosted, and—more rarely and, therefore, now more sought after—colored glass. The production runs were long—the Formose vase shown at the 1925 Art Deco exhibition in Paris was still in production ten years later—but the molds were replaced at regular intervals to maintain definition and quality. In Lalique's masterly hands, motifs such as Art Deco maidens, naked figures, stylized plants, animals, fish, birds, insects, and abstract designs were transformed into stunning, original vases.

Virtually all Lalique glass is marked with variations of "R. Lalique." After his death in 1945, only the surname was used. Fake signatures on later pieces commonly include an initial "R."

Above: Formose cased glass vase in red and of near-spherical form with a slight creamy white patina and a short neck. The molded decoration shows a swimming fan-tailed goldfish. Signed "R. Lalique." *c. 1925. 7 in (18 cm) high* **$9,000–12,000 RDL**

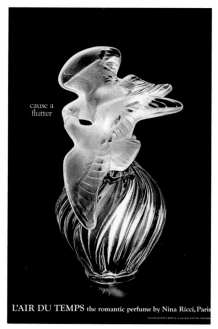

PERFUME BOTTLES

The glamour and indulgence of Lalique's stylish perfume bottles complemented their luxurious contents. The success of the designs for François Coty in 1907 soon developed into commissions from most of the leading French *parfumeurs* of the time. Using demi-crystal glass, Lalique was able to produce quantities of press-molded bottles that needed the minimum amount of finishing. One of the Lalique trademarks was the distinctive *bouchon* or stopper (often numbered to match the bottle). These range from dramatic crescent-shaped designs to the famous L'Air du Temps bottle (*right*).

cause a flutter

L'AIR DU TEMPS the romantic perfume by Nina Ricci, Paris

Douze Figurines avec Bouchon frosted and clear glass vase with a central molded frieze of classical female nudes and a stopper in the form of a kneeling nude. Engraved "R. Lalique". *c. 1920 11½ in (29.5 cm) high* **$7,000–10,000 RDL**

This perfume bottle, designed by René Lalique for Nina Ricci's *L'Air du Temps*, features a dove-shaped stopper symbolizing both peace and romance.

Vichy frosted and clear glass vase with U- and V-shaped garlands and highlighted with a sepia patina. Marked "Lalique France." *c. 1935*

6¾ in (17 cm) high

$800–1,200   **RDL**

Thais statuette in clear and frosted glass, of a nude with a robe draped from outstretched arms. Engraved "R. Lalique." *c. 1925*

8 in (20.5 cm) high

$15,000–25,000   **RDL**

Chardons clear and frosted glass vase of fruit-like form embellished with molded and stylized leaves. Engraved "R. Lalique France No. 929." *c. 1920*

7½ in (19 cm) high

$800–1,200   **RDL**

Domremy grey glass vase with a pattern of thistle leaves and flowers and a sepia patina. It has molded and engraved marks. *c. 1925*

8½ in (22 cm) high

$1,200–2,000   **RDL**

Saint-Tropez clear and frosted glass vase decorated with molded stylized fruiting sprigs. Stenciled "R. Lalique France." *c. 1935*

7½ in (19 cm) high

$2,000–3,500   **RDL**

Pierrefonds bucket-shaped vase with clear glass Art Deco-style handles. Marked "R. Lalique France." *c. 1925*

6 in (15 cm) high

$5,000–8,000   **RDL**

Good, Better, Best

Strongly colored glass is not commonly associated with Lalique, and pieces can vary in price, even if identical, depending on the color. Blue is scarcer than amber and a more vibrant color. Red is even rarer, partly because it is harder to work with, "burning" easily in the heat and, therefore, becoming dull in tone.

$4,000–5,000

Ronces vase in cased amber glass, with molded and engraved marks on the base. *c. 1920. 9½ in (24 cm) high* **RDL**

$5,000–8,000

Ronces vase in electric blue glass, with molded and engraved marks on the base. *c. 1920. 9½ in (24 cm) high* **RDL**

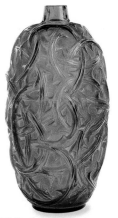

$7,000–10,000

Ronces vase in red glass, with molded and engraved marks on the base. *c. 1920 9½ in (24 cm) high* **RDL**

Rare Inséparables vase with a molded frieze of budgerigars seated on twigs, with a sepia patina. Engraved "Lalique." *c. 1920*

13½ in (34 cm) high

$25,000–30,000   **RDL**

KEY FACTORIES

Federal Glass Co., Columbus, Ohio (1900–79).

Fenton Art Glass Co., Martins Ferry, Ohio (est. 1905); still active.

Hazel Atlas Glass Co., Clarksville, West Virginia (est. 1885); still active.

Hocking Glass Co., Lancaster, Ohio (est. 1905); Anchor Hocking Glass Corp. from 1969; still active.

Indiana Glass Co., Indiana, Pennsylvania (est. 1902); still active.

Jeannette Glass Co., Jeannette, Pennsylvania (est. 1889-1983).

Depression Glass

Ironically, from about 1930 to 1935, mass-produced machine-made glass enjoyed a golden age at the height of the Depression, from which it took its name. This glass is now seen as an important part of American history.

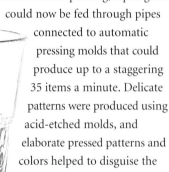

Encouraged by the boom in glass-buying in the 1920s and the Pittsburgh Glass Exhibit of 1925, many glass factories committed themselves to machine-made glass and invested in equipment, molds, and the new technology for automated production. Instead of hand-pressing, liquid glass could now be fed through pipes connected to automatic pressing molds that could produce up to a staggering 35 items a minute. Delicate patterns were produced using acid-etched molds, and elaborate pressed patterns and colors helped to disguise the imperfections of the cheap-quality glass.

This was the glass that was produced in vast quantities, countless patterns, and a variety of colors during the dark years of the Depression. It was used as premiums to promote products and services, collected with coupons, and sold at rock-bottom prices in department stores, some of which were selling a 20-piece set for under $2. All types of tableware and kitchenware were produced: dinner services, luncheon sets, bridge sets, sherbet plates, iced-tea tumblers, banana-split boats, candle holders, candy dishes. The colors brought relief from the gloom, and included varieties of yellow, blue, amber, pink, green, cobalt, burgundy, and amethyst.

Condition is critical—the thin, brittle glass was very vulnerable—and some of the quintessentially geometric Art Deco designs that were less popular at the time are now particularly sought-after.

Above: Moderntone-pattern cobalt blue plate made by the Hazel Atlas Glass Co. Cobalt blue was a desirable color produced in comparatively small quantities. *1934–42 8¾ in (22.5 cm) wide* **$20–30 TAB**

1930s AMERICA

The Wall Street crash of 1929 precipitated a world economic crisis. Conditions grew even worse in the 1930s. In a panic-induced run on the banks, many withdrew their hard-earned savings, forcing most American banks to close by 1932.

Agriculture, factories, and industries could not borrow and were forced to close, retail outlets went bankrupt, and millions of people were thrown out of work, with the unemployment figure reaching some 14 million in the United States. With the election of Franklin D. Roosevelt in 1932, and emergency legislation put in place to ease the bank crisis, confidence and morale were gradually restored and the public used "cheap and cheerful" products, such as Depression glass, for what would today be called "retail therapy."

Sharon Cabbage Rose–pattern iced-tea tumbler made by the Federal Glass Co. of Columbus, Ohio. *1935–39 6 in (15 cm) high* **$60–90 PR**

Spiral-pattern milk jug with pressed swirling band design made by the Hocking Glass Co. *1928–30*

3½ in (9 cm) high

$3–5 TAB

Shell Fire-King Jadeite dinner plate by Anchor Hocking. This size is more valuable than the 9-in (23-cm) size. *1960–70s*

10 in (25.5 cm) wide

$30–50 VGA

Early American Prescut–pattern bowl with a scalloped rim made by the Anchor Hocking Glass Corp. Produced in clear, amber, blue, green, red, black, and painted variations. *1960–99*

11½ in (29.5 cm) wide

$30–40 TAB

Mayfair Petalware covered bowl made by the Hocking Glass Co., with fluted pattern and two handles on the bowl and one on the lid. *1931–37*

11½ in (29 cm) wide

$100–150 CA

Set of four Pillar Optic–pattern mixing bowls with faceted bodies and square feet made by the Hocking Glass Co. *1937–42*

Largest: 9½ in (24 cm) wide

$100–150 VGA

Miss America iced-tea glass by the Hocking Glass Co. The pattern resembles English Hobnail but is far more valuable. *1933–37*

6 in (15 cm)

$100–150 CA

Colonial Block green goblet by the Hazel Atlas Glass Co., with a faceted pattern imitating more expensive cut glass. *1930s*

5¾ in (14.5 cm) high

$12–18 CA

Florentine-pattern yellow gravy boat and platter made by the Hazel Atlas Glass Co., with low-relief molded scrolling and floral design. *1932–36*

Platter: 8 in (20 cm) wide

$80–120 PR

Tearoom-pattern banana-split dish made by the Indiana Glass Co. Found in green, pink, clear, and amber, this form is popular with collectors for nostalgic reasons. *1926–31*

7¾ in (19 cm) wide

$80–120 CA

Sandwich Daisy-pattern red wine or water goblet made by the Indiana Glass Co. with molded dot and floral design. *1920s*

5½ in (14 cm) high

$40–60 CA

Jeannette Glass Co.

The Jeannette Glass Co. in the tiny Pennsylvania community of Jeannette was a major, and now avidly collected, manufacturer of Depression glass. It was one of the first factories to install fully automatic production—by 1927, all hand-production had ceased. The first complete tableware lines in classic colors such as amber, green, rose (pink), and topaz were launched in 1928, and two years later Jeannette was the first factory to produce a complete line of molded tableware in a choice of three colors: the popular pink, apple green, and, less sought-after now, crystal.

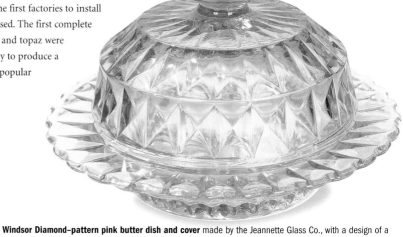

Windsor Diamond–pattern pink butter dish and cover made by the Jeannette Glass Co., with a design of a series of facets emanating from a circle of radial ribs. *1935–46*

6 in (15.5 cm) wide

$50–80 CA

Jadeite egg-cup made by the Jeannette Glass Co. Jeannette's Jadeite tends to have a lighter color than Anchor Hocking's Fire-King range. *1950s*

3 in (7.5 cm) high

$20–30 VGA

Jenny-pattern blue mixing bowl made by the Jeannette Glass Co., with external scalloped rim and facet-cut design to imitate cut glass. *Late 1930s*

6 in (15.5 cm) high

$70–100 CA

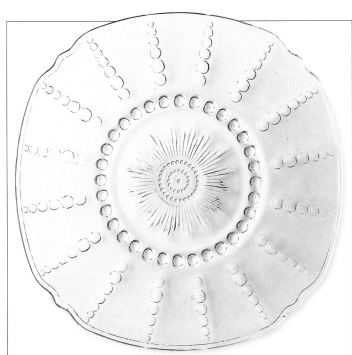

Columbia-pattern crystal glass platter made by the Federal Glass Co., with a ring and lines of dots emanating from a sunburst at the center. *1938–42*

11 in (28 cm) wide

$20–30   **TAB**

Sharon Cabbage Rose–pattern yellow soup cup made by the Federal Glass Co., with panels containing sprigs of cabbage roses and two handles. *1933–37*

6½ in (16 cm) wide

$20–30   **CA**

NEW MARTINSVILLE

Founded in 1901 in New Martinsville, West Virginia, this company had color as an overriding theme, and produced typically styled Depression glassware in a rainbow of colors. The success of New Martinsville was based on vanity sets as well as tableware, with one of its most commonly found patterns being Moondrops. The factory went bankrupt in 1937 and was reopened as Viking in 1944. As before, color played an important part in the very modern designs, from tableware to decorative vases, many with fluid, pulled rims. The factory closed in 1998.

Moondrops-pattern red tumbler by New Martinsville. Although made in a variety of colors, red and blue are the most desirable. *1932–40s. 4¾ in (12 cm) high*

$20–30 CA

American Pioneer–pattern lamp by Liberty Glass Works, with a band of molded bosses on the tapering body. *1931–34*

8 in (20.5 cm) high

$120–180   **CA**

Hermitage-pattern yellow tumbler designed by George Sakier for the Fostoria Glass Co. *1932–45*

4 in (10 cm) high

$10–20   **CA**

Chintz-pattern crystal glass candlesticks by the Fostoria Glass Co., renowned for the brilliant appearance of its glass. *1928–44*

5¼ in (13.5 cm) high

$60–90 (the pair)   **CA**

Rock Crystal–pattern crystal glass double candlestick by the McKee Glass Co., with a scrolling floral and foliate design. *1920s*

5½ in (14 cm) high

$40–60   **CA**

Ashtrays

Before the demonization of smoking and cigarettes, ashtrays were an essential accessory in most homes. Now they offer even non-smoking collectors a chance to acquire attractive and affordable examples of most major 20th-century glass styles.

In the 1920s and 30s, ashtrays were produced in attractive styles and colors, designed to appeal to a fashion-conscious clientele. Pressed-glass ashtrays were made in the fashionable Art Deco pastel colors and geometric and novelty shapes. The Lalique glassworks (*see p.88*) produced press-molded ashtrays with distinctive designs—from feminine shell shapes to masculine boat designs.

The Italian passion for cigarettes and color led to stylish blown-glass ashtrays in a range of exuberant Murano styles. The Venetian decorative techniques included thick-walled cased and colored *sommerso* ashtrays, and fluid, heavy-based organic shapes that combined pretty colors with luxurious gold-leaf inclusions.

Scandinavian ashtrays reflect the Nordic predilection for elegant clean lines, restrained colors, and frosted textures, often combined with the quirky personality of individual designers, as seen in the 1960s piece by Erik Höglund (1932–2001) in which a voluptuous female figure encourages smokers to dispose of their ash safely. Czech glassworks offered a choice of Murano-style *sommerso* ashtrays or more distinctively Czech press-molded abstract geometric patterns. The Belgian Val Saint-Lambert glassworks (*see p.162*) produced ashtrays in a trademark style.

Good condition is essential with such readily found items. Scratches detract from appeal, as does damage from staining or burning. Pieces by a famous designer or factory, or an ashtray that captures the style of a certain decade, can be particularly appealing.

Lalique frosted lion's-head ashtray with stylized mane spreading around the rim. Part of a set including a cigarette holder and a lighter. Signed "Lalique France." *1990s 6 in (15 cm) wide* **$150–200 CW**

Lalique frosted-glass dishlike ashtray with molded ribs leading up to and forming multiple cigarette rests. *Late 20th century 8½ in (21.5 cm) wide* **$250–400 GORL**

American pink and heavily cased art-glass ashtray of flowerlike form. *1960s. 8 in (20.5 cm) wide* **$30–50 TAB**

Murano leaf-shaped *sommerso* ashtray with a pinkish-red body heavily cased in blue glass. *1950s. 5½ in (14 cm) long* **$30–60 PC**

Val Saint-Lambert blue glass triform ashtray heavily cased in clear glass, with cigarette rests at each point. *1950s 3 in (7.5 cm) high* **$50–80 CW**

Swedish amber-colored ashtray designed by Erik Höglund for Boda, with the bust of a woman. *1960s. 2¾ in (7 cm) wide* **$70–100 CW**

Lalique ashtray decorated with a galleon. It has an everted rim with two cigarette rests. *Late 20th century. 7 in (18 cm) wide* **$120–180 GORL**

Textured ashtray with asymmetric rim, probably designed by Asta Strömberg for Strömbergshyttan. *1960s. 7 in (17.5 cm) wide* **$80–120 MHT**

Murano pink glass ashtray cased in clear glass, trapping a layer of air bubbles and gold foil inclusions. The rim is folded inward to create cigarette rests. *1950s. 4½ in (11.5 cm) wide* **$30–50 AG**

Murano triform glass ashtray with mottled blue coloring, internal bubbles, and a layer of internal gold foil inclusions. *1950s 4 in (10 cm) wide* **$50–70 AG**

Novelty clear-glass ashtray in the form of a top hat with an applied gilt rim; from the Ritz Hotel in Paris. *1950s. 3½ in (9 cm) wide* **$70–100 CVS**

Royal Bohemia molded-glass ashtray with deep geometric pattern. Probably designed by Jiri Repasek. *1970–80s. 8 in (20 cm) long* **$30–50 GC**

Murano blue *sommerso* ashtray cased in a layer of yellow glass and then heavily cased in clear glass with textured sides. *Late 1960s. 5¾ in (14.5 cm) wide* **$70–100 P&I**

Scottie dog pressed-glass ashtray in green, with a matchbox holder and model of a seated Scottie dog. *1930s 4¾ in (12 cm) wide* **$30–50 DCC**

George Davidson

The George Davidson glassworks made its name primarily with a range of pressed colored glass that satisfied the growing demand for decorative domestic ware, trinkets, and novelties from the late 19th century until the 1930s.

KEY DATES

1867 George Davidson & Co. is founded at the Teams Flint Glassworks in Gateshead, Northumberland, northeast England, and begins production of pressed-glass tableware in the 1880s.

1891 George Davidson's son Thomas takes charge of the factory, increasing production of existing ranges and introducing new ones.

1922 The factory's pressed glass ranges are redesigned to reflect the new Art Deco style, and Cloud glass is introduced a year later.

1987 George Davidson & Co. ceases production.

Davidson's had notable success with its opalescent Pearline pressed glass in blue or primrose yellow. Matching sets of tableware, vases, and souvenir pieces, such as photo-transfer plates, were mass- produced for an avid and aspirational market from the late 1880s until World War I.

When opalescent glass went out of fashion, Davidson's introduced its Cloud range, with a swirling streaked and mottled colored effect that imitated more expensive materials such as marble or *pâte-de-verre*. The Cloud range was a huge hit and remained in production until World War II, with new colors being added at regular intervals, which can help date the glass. Colors include purple (1923) and a highly sought-after red (1929), with a finish that resembles Chinese lacquer. Early pieces made when the mold still had crisp definition are the most attractive. Davidson's patented a dome-shaped flower block, now commonly known as a "frog," for its vases, and a matching, undamaged frog adds to the value.

After World War II, the company never quite enjoyed the same success. It did not initiate any startling new styles, and its manually produced glass became increasingly uncompetitive.

Above: Amber Cloudy glass powder bowl with cover and faceted sides and lid. Amber is one of the most commonly found colors. *1928–30s. 5 in (13 cm) high* **$30–50 BAD**

Seaweed Cloudy glass vase of plain cylindrical form with flared rim and random, organic green trailed striations. *1930s*
9¾ in (24.5 cm) high
$200–400 BAD

Blue Cloudy glass footed vase in the form of an inverted cone with slightly flared rim. Blue was introduced in 1925. *1925–30s*
8½ in (21.5 cm) high
$100–150 BAD

Amethyst Cloudy glass flower bowl with removable frog for holding the stems of the flowers. If the frog is missing, the value is reduced. *1930s*
9 in (22.5 cm) wide
$80–120 BAD

Pair of Amber Cloudy glass candlesticks often found as part of a dressing table set, including powder bowls and a tray. *1928–30s*
7¼ in (18.5 cm) high
$200–400 BAD

Jobling

The decision to acquire the rights to British production of the heat-resistant Pyrex glassware financed Jobling's range of press-molded Art Deco art glass that is now gaining the recognition it deserves.

KEY DATES

1886 James Augustus Jobling acquires the nearly bankrupt Greener & Co. glassworks in Sunderland, northeast England.

1902 Ernest Jobling Purser (1875–1959) is appointed factory manager and begins to modernize the plant and equipment.

1921 The glassworks is renamed James A. Jobling & Co. and acquires the right to produce Pyrex in Britain.

1933 Jobling introduces Lalique-inspired range of pressed art glass.

1975 Jobling becomes part of the American Corning corporation.

Under Ernest Purser's management from 1902, a failing glassworks was transformed into a thriving, profitable enterprise. Purser acquired the British and British Empire rights to produce the American Corning Corporation's new range of Pyrex. The functional heat-resistant kitchen and tableware range was the financial mainstay of the company from when it was first introduced in 1922.

In 1933, Purser was again eager to expand and diversify and introduced a range of pressed art glass in the Art Deco style. The standard repertoire of decorative vases, ashtrays, cigarette boxes, statuettes, and other trinkets was produced in a range of pressed patterns and in clear flint, pastel, or pale colors, and a matt or satin finish. The story goes that Jobling actually approached Lalique in an attempt to come to a business arrangement, but on refusal developed his own less ambitious Opalique opalescence for his art glass. In spite of the high quality of the mold-making and the fine pressed detail, the range was only moderately successful.

Jobling discontinued its art-glass range in the late 1930s and concentrated on production of tableware and kitchenware.

Above: Bird-pattern bowl in pressed Opalique glass. Design registered February 17, 1933
3¼ in (8.5 cm) high **$400–600 BHM**

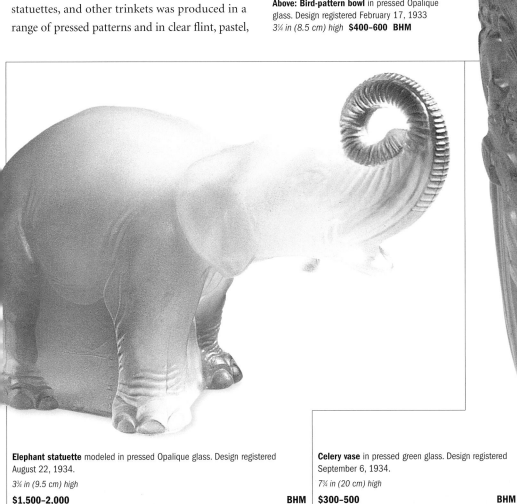

Elephant statuette modeled in pressed Opalique glass. Design registered August 22, 1934.
3¾ in (9.5 cm) high
$1,500–2,000 BHM

Celery vase in pressed green glass. Design registered September 6, 1934.
7¾ in (20 cm) high
$300–500 BHM

97

OPALESCENT GLASS

Opalescent glass is a clear and semi-opaque pressed and mold-blown glass. Its milky, opal-like appearance is created using cloudy or marbled glass, colored accents, or a combination of these. It generally has a milky-blue color that appears in subtle graduations depending on the thickness of the glass—the thicker the glass, the more opaque the color; the thinner, the more translucent it appears.

It was first made by Venetian glassmakers in the 16th century, but its best-known proponents are the art-glass makers of the late 19th and 20th centuries. The opalescent effect is created by adding chemicals to the glass and by alternately heating and cooling it. Sometimes the whole of a piece of glass is made to be opalescent; other times it is restricted to the edge and coupled with wavy effects to give an elegant yet subtle look. The degree and location of the opalescence is controlled by the glassmaking process, as well as by the thickness of the glass itself.

At times the effect is created using one layer of glass, but it may also be obtained using many layers. Any coloration in the glass is illuminated when light shines on it.

Lalique Montmorency vase of bucket form molded in high relief with four bands of cherries and stems. Highlighted with blue staining, and with a metal mount. *1920s. 8 in (20 cm) high* **$9,000–10,000 DN**

EUROPEAN MASTER

French designer René Lalique (*see p.100*) is the best-known manufacturer of opalescent glass, which he used to create a plethora of items including vases, statues, platters, and jewelry, much of it with his unmistakable frosted finish. Lalique was a prolific designer, and his use of metal molds for pressing, casting, or mold-blowing glass allowed him to mass-produce his designs. Consequently, there is a wide variety of items available to collectors. Larger molded pieces may have ripples on the surface, and many pieces, large and small, have visible seams where sections of a mold joined and were left or only partially polished away.

The inspiration for opalescent glass, opals occur in various colors, including white, yellow, red, blue, green, and black, but also display iridescent-like flashes of another color if the light source is changed.

KEY STYLES

Plant imagery is a recurring decoration in opalescent glass. It tends to be presented in the geometric, formalized Art Deco style, as is much of the human imagery employed.

Female subjects were typical models of the 1920s and 30s, with slim, almost-androgynous shapes and boyish haircuts.

Lalique's figures owed more to the Neo-classicism of the late 18th and early 19th century.

Sabino frosted opalescent glass figure of a young woman. This is a copy of Lalique's hugely popular Suzanne au Bain sculpture. Neo-classical in style, it could be ordered with a bronze mount with a concealed light fixture. *1923–39. 9 in (23 cm) high* **$700–1,000 WW**

However, Lalique also made pieces using the lost wax, or *cire perdue*, method of casting. Each of these is unique and rare and will command a high price.

Lalique's work influenced many European glass manufacturers in the Art Deco period. Marius-Ernest Sabino (1878–1961) made a wide range of pieces inspired by Lalique, particularly vases, statuary, and lighting from around 1923 until the closure of his factory in 1939. Few Sabino pieces are as well made or as imaginative as Lalique's, but his figures of stylized women are probably the most successful. He also produced hood ornaments, often directly copying Lalique's work.

Another designer who was heavily influenced by Lalique was Edmond Etling, whose factory was active throughout the 1920s and 30s. The quality of his molded opalescent glass is comparable to that of Sabino, and Etling figures of draped female nudes, which were mass-produced in the 1920s, are most popular with collectors today.

AMERICAN EXPERIMENTATION

Although Lalique is recognized by most as the master of opalescent glassmaking, American glassmakers were among the first to evolve the technique in the late 19th century, taking the stained glass used for church windows and transforming it into milky opalescent glass. The aim was to challenge the traditional approach of painting on glass to create multicolored effects.

Louis Comfort Tiffany was one of the first glassmasters to try this. Before 1885, when he founded his own firm, Tiffany had registered for a patent on a new glassmaking technique that combined different colors in opalescent glass to create vibrant, multidimensional hues never before seen in glass.

MASS PRODUCTION

Opalescent glass was mass produced in both Great Britain and the United States. The most notable American manufacturers include Fenton, Northwood, Hobbs, and American Glass, while the British firm George Davidson & Co. of Gateshead, County Durham, was the major European manufacturer and it gave its opalescent glass the name of Pearline. Introduced in 1889, Davidson's opalescent range included tableware, and was produced in various colors including blue and yellow. The latter was known as primrose glass, and the color was made by adding uranium to the batch.

Today, few glassmakers make opalescent glass, mainly because the chemicals needed to execute the complex glassmaking process are poisonous and have to be handled extremely carefully.

Lalique Formose vase
molded in deep relief with a school of fish in blue-tinted opalescent glass. *c. 1925*
7 in (18 cm) high
$2,500-4,000 RDL

G. Vallon milky opalescent shallow glass bowl
molded with leaves and three groups of cherries forming a tripod support on the underside of the base. *1930s.*
9¼ in (23.5 cm) wide
$250-400 CHEF

Lalique Opalescent

Lalique's opalescent glass, which has a soft sheen that resembles the moonstones he used in his jewellery, is the best known and most popular of the Art Deco period. Most of his pressed-glass shapes, including tableware and car mascots, were produced in opalescent versions, but it is the luxurious vases and statuettes that are particularly popular. Additional color was often added in the form of a patina—an enamel wash that was applied after the molding and then fired at a low temperature. One or several colors could be applied, often to highlight certain features or areas of the design, creating subtle, form-enhancing hues.

Perruches circular fruit bowl in opalescent glass, featuring budgerigars with a blue-green tint set among dense flowers and foliage. *c. 1930*

9¾ in (24.5 cm) wide

$4,500–5,000   **RDL**

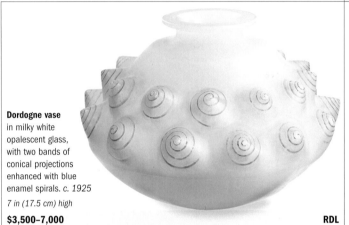

Dordogne vase in milky white opalescent glass, with two bands of conical projections enhanced with blue enamel spirals. *c. 1925*

7 in (17.5 cm) high

$3,500–7,000   **RDL**

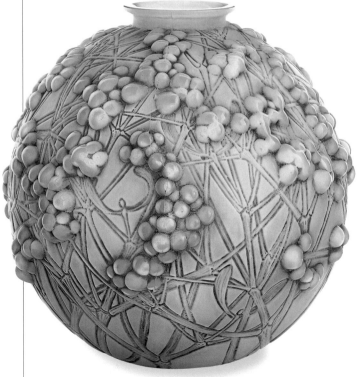

Druides vase molded in deep relief with vines and grapes, in opalescent glass with green staining. *c. 1925*

7 in (17.5 cm) high

$2,000–3,500   **RDL**

Ceylan demi-crystal vase depicting pairs of budgerigars under scrolling foliage; in brown-tinted opalescent and frosted glass. *c. 1925*

9¾ in (25 cm) high

$5,000–8,000   **L&T**

Ceylan vase (as left), but this time the glass is tinted blue—both colors are Lalique specialities. *c. 1925*

9¾ in (25 cm) high

$6,000–9,000   **RDL**

Perruches vase with pairs of wooing budgerigars, molded in green tinted and stained opalescent glass. *c. 1920*

10 in (25 cm) high

$3,500–5,000   **RDL**

Tulipes vase molded with large, stylized tulip blooms and stems in opalescent glass with green-blue patina. *c. 1925*

8 in (20.5 cm) high

$4,000–5,000　　　　**RDL**

MARKS AND FAKES

Virtually all Lalique glass is marked with a variation on his signature, "R. Lalique." From the late 1920s, the words "France" or "Made in France" were often included. The marks may be engraved, stencilled through sandblasting, etched, or molded in intaglio or relief. A molded mark with good definition suggests that the piece was made using the power press; poorer definition suggests a mold-blown piece. After Lalique's death in 1945, only the surname was used. The perfume bottles (*see p.186*) carry a pattern number on both the bottom of the bottle and on the stopper. Any discrepancy suggests that the stopper is a replacement.

Because of the value and popularity of Lalique's work, fakes abound. Even genuine post-1945 Lalique pieces are sometimes "rejuvenated" by the addition of an "R" in front of the surname to suggest an earlier, more valuable piece.

Marks may be deceptive and the ultimate tests of a piece of genuine Lalique glass are the quality of the molding, clear and crisp definition, subtle color and enameling, and originality of design.

Béliers footed cup- or chalice-like vase in opalescent glass, with twin ram's-horn handles. Wheel-cut "R. Lalique." *c. 1925*

7½ in (18.75 cm) high

$2,500–4,000　　　　**RDL**

Languedoc vase with a short, cylindrical neck and an alternating concave and convex trellis-like pattern on the body, molded in opalescent glass. *c. 1930*

6 in (15 cm) high

$7,000–8,000　　　　**RDL**

Chamonix vase molded with vertical fluting to the body in selectively blue-tinted opalescent glass. *c. 1935*

6 in (15 cm) high

$1,000–1,500　　　　**RDL**

Espalion gourd-like vase with an all-over fern pattern molded in opalescent glass with an olive-green patina. *c. 1925*

7 in (17.5 cm) high

$1,200–1,800　　　　**RDL**

Malesherbes gourd-like vase in opalescent and frosted glass with selective green patination. *c. 1925*

8¾ in (22.5 cm) high

$2,500–3,500　　　　**RDL**

Rampillon tumbler vase molded in high relief with lozenges against a floral motif ground, in blue-grey opalescent glass. *c. 1925*

5 in (12.5 cm) high

$1,200–1,500　　　　**RDL**

Moyenne Nue statuette in tinted opalescent glass. The nude female is in a flowing robe in Neo-Classical style. *c. 1910*

6 in (15 cm) high

$6,000–8,000　　　　**RDL**

French Opalescent

In the 1920s and 1930s, French glassmakers shared the 16th-century Venetian fascination with opalescent glass and used it to produce molded luxury glass in the Art Deco style. René Lalique and Marius-Ernest Sabino led the field, producing pieces with molded patterns of flowers, plants, fish, animals, and, particularly popular, female forms. Other French glass factories sought a share of the market, among them the Verrerie d'Andelys, set up in the 1920s by the American Holophane Co. to produce Verlys art glass, and Edmond Etling et Cie, which was better known for bronzes and statuettes in the Art Deco style before moving into opalescent vases and bowls.

One of a pair of Art Deco *plaffoniers* by Sabino, with a mold-blown floral and basketweave pattern in frosted, milky-white opalescent glass. Needle-etched "Sabino 4330 Paris." *c. 1930*
17 in (43 cm) wide
$3,500–4,500 (the pair)　　　　　　　　　　　　　　**FRE**

French press-molded glass bowl with a wispy floral pattern in yellow-tinged, milky-white opalescent glass. Made by and signed Etling. *c. 1930*
12 in (30.5 cm) wide
$600–800　　　　　　　　　　　　　　　　　**SWT**

French press-molded glass bowl by Verlys, with repeat dragonfly and plant-form decoration around the perimeter. In frosted and yellow-tinged, milky-white opalescent glass. *c. 1930*
9½ in (24.5 cm) wide
$2,800–3,500　　　　　　　　　　　　　　　**QU**

Shallow glass bowl press-molded with a ring of rosettes set among a bed of stems and leaves. In milky-white opalescent glass. Marked "Made in France." *c. 1950*
12¼ in (31.5 cm) wide
$300–500　　　　　　　　　　　　　　　　　**CHEF**

Molded glass bowl by Etling et Cie, with eucalyptus leaves and gum nuts in opalescent glass with distinct milky-white, blue, and yellow sheens. *1920–30*
9 in (23 cm) wide
$600–900　　　　　　　　　　　　　　　　　**OACC**

Molded glass vase by Sabino with a *raies* (stingray or skate) pattern in pale blue and frosted opalescent glass. Needle-etched "Sabino. France" on the base. *1920s*

8½ in (22 cm) high

$1,500–2,000   QU

Press-molded glass vase of footed-tumbler form, with stylized berries and vine-leaf decoration in frosted and blue-tinted opalescent glass. *c. 1940*

6½ in (16.5 cm) high

$100–300   SL

Sabino

Italian-born Marius-Ernest Sabino (1878–1961) set up his glassworks in Paris in the 1920s. He originally manufactured light fixtures but soon produced a range of molded opalescent glass, from large-scale architectural panels, chandeliers, and lampshades, to vases, bowls, car mascots, and small figures and animals. In 1925, Sabino glass won a gold medal at the Art Deco exhibition in Paris. After closing in 1939, Sabino reopened in the 1960s and reused many of the original molds for small animals and birds, marked "Sabino Made in France," which can make dating difficult. Less problematic are the larger molded interwar pieces with an engraved Sabino signature.

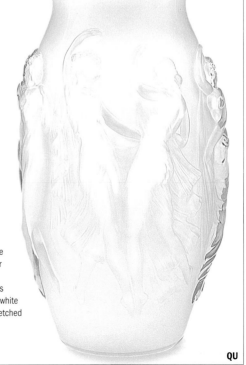

Sabino press-molded glass vase with etched stylized skates or stingrays in blue-tinged, milky-white opalescent glass. *c. 1925*

10 in (25.5 cm) high

$1,500–2,000   QU

Sabino press-molded glass cabinet vase with a leaf pattern in milky-white opalescent glass. Needle-etched "Sabino. Paris." *c. 1930*

5 in (12.5 cm) high

$300–400   QU

Sabino La Danse Gaité vase, with highly collectible decoration comprising four pairs of dancing girls in diaphanous classical robes engraved in frosted, milky-white opalescent glass. Needle-etched "Sabino. Paris." *c. 1930*

14¾ in (37.5 cm) high

$1,200–1,800   QU

Pâte-de-Verre

In the late 19th century, a group of French glassmakers revived and redeveloped the complex ancient Egyptian technique of *pâte-de-verre* and reintroduced it into the 20th-century studio glassmaking repertoire.

Pâte-de-verre (literally "glass paste") is a sophisticated technique used to make exclusive unique or limited-edition pieces. A mold of the design is filled with crushed glass colored with metallic oxides and heated until the glass fuses. When the glass has cooled, it is removed from the mold and hand-finished. For unique pieces, the mold was made using the *cire perdue*, or lost-wax, process and used only once. With limited-edition or semi-production-line *pâte-de-verre*, a reusable mold was employed.

French glassmakers excelled in the technique. Almaric Walter (1870–1959) was probably the most prolific proponent of *pâte-de-verre*. In the Daum workshop in Nancy, between 1906 and 1914, both he and Henri Bergé (1868–1936) produced small animals, insects, and reptiles either as small sculptures or decoration. Walter set up his own *pâte-de-verre* workshop in 1919, using the "A Walter Nancy" mark. He continued with designs similar to those he created for Daum, as well commissioning designs from other artists, who often signed their work.

François-Emile Décorchemont (1880–1971) and Joseph-Gabriel Argy-Rousseau (1885–1953) were both former ceramicists turned glassmakers who specialized in *pâte-de-verre* after World War I. Décorchemont is best known for his thick-walled vases with veined and streaky decoration. Argy-Rousseau produced a prolific range of small, richly colored Art Nouveau and Art Deco–style pieces at his workshop Les Pâtes de Verres d'Argy-Rousseau (1921–31) in Paris.

Almaric Walter scarab pendant on which the glass bead and string may not be original. *1920s. 1½ in (4 cm) long* **$3,000–5,000 LN**

Almaric Walter bowl with bumblebee detail. Signed "AWalter Nancy Bergé sc." *1920s. 4¼ in (11 cm) wide* **$1,200–1,800 QU**

Almaric Walter box with a grasshopper on the lid. Signed "AWalter Nancy, HBergé." *1920s 3¼ in (8 cm) high* **$3,000–4,000 QU**

Almaric Walter bowl with stag beetle and pine branches. Signed. *1920s 5¾ in (14.5 cm) wide* **$5,000–6,000 QU**

Almaric Walter bowl with bees and honeycombs. Signed "HBergé Sc. AWalter Nancy," restored lid. *1920s. 7 in (18 cm) wide* **$10,000–15,000 QU**

Argy-Rousseau Scarabées vase with dark brown and red band and applied scarabs on a pale green ground. Signed. *1920s. 6 in (15 cm) high* **$15,000–20,000 MACK**

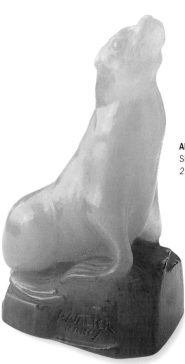

Almaric Walter lidded bowl with roses.
Signed "AWalter Nancy." *1920s*
2½ in (6.5 cm) wide **$3,500–4,500 QU**

Almaric Walter sculpture of a woman with
flowing hair, by A. Finot. *1910–20*
9 in (23 cm) wide **$8,000–10,000 LN**

Almaric Walter model of a seal on
a stand. Signed. *Early 20th century*
6¾ in (17 cm) high **$30,000–40,000 LN**

Almaric Walter *vide poche* with fish
decoration. Signed "A Walter, Nancy."
1920s. 5½ in (14 cm) wide
$15,000–20,000 MACK

Daum sculpture of an owl by Maurice
Legendre. Molded "M. Legendre DAUM
61/100." *c. 1965. 9½ in (24 cm) high*
$500–800 FRE

Argy-Rousseau vase decorated with eight
figures. Signed on the side "G. Argy
Rousseau." *Early 20th century* *6¼ in
(16 cm) high* **$15,000–18,000 JDJ**

Joe Descomps for Daum *vide poche* with
snail decoration. Signed "J Descomps,
Daum Nancy." *1920s. 9¾ in (24.5 cm) wide*
$12,000–18,000 MACK

Almaric Walter dish with decoration of a
lizard on leaves. Signed "A. Walter Nancy."
1920s. 6¾ in (17 cm) wide
$6,000–8,000 JDJ

Almaric Walter vase *au lézard* shaped as a cup on a
trumpet-shaped foot. Signed "AWalter Nancy HBergé Sc."
c. 1920. 8½ in (21.5 cm) high **$12,000–18,000 QU**

Almaric Walter *vide poche* with salamander
design, possibly by Henri Bergé. Signed
"A Walter." *1920s. 6½ in (16.5 cm) wide*
$15,000–20,000 MACK

Quezal Jack-in-the-Pulpit iridescent vase
in the form of the flower of the poisonous
Arisaema triphyllum. Stevens & Williams and
Tiffany are among the earliest known makers
of this complex form. *c.1915*
13 in (33 cm) high **$10,000–12,000 LN**

Iridescent Glass

Iridescent glass has a lustrous, rainbowlike surface that changes color depending on how the light hits it. It was first made in the 19th century in imitation of Roman glass that was being excavated at sites across Europe. The Roman glass had a natural iridescence, the result of being buried for centuries in the damp earth. Glassmakers discovered they could imitate this by exposing glass to metal-oxide fumes or by spraying or painting it with metal oxides.

The popularity of iridescent glass was helped by the introduction of domestic electric lighting, which showed the colors and the sparkling iridescence of the glass to the best effect. Most iridescent glass is in the Art Nouveau style. Its best-known proponents are Louis Comfort Tiffany, the Steuben glassworks, and Quezal in the United States, and Loetz and Pallme-König & Habel in Austria. Iridescent glass was mass produced in the United States as Carnival glass.

INSPIRED BY THE PAST

In the 19th century, archaeologists across Europe unearthed numerous pieces of Roman glass that had become iridescent as a result of exposure to chemicals in the soil or sand during their years underground. The chemicals had corroded the surface of the glass, giving it an otherworldly, lustrous sheen. Inspired by these archaeological finds, glassmakers tried to recreate the finish using the latest chemical processes. The result was an increasingly sophisticated and attractive look.

We may never know who made the first piece of iridescent glass, but the manufacturers most likely to have done so are Tiffany in the United States and Loetz in Austria. What we do know is that Louis Comfort Tiffany patented his iridescent glass in 1894, giving it the name Favrile and using it to make a range of glassware, most notably decorative vases in organic shapes. Max Ritter von Spaun of Loetz exhibited a similar range at the Chicago World Fair of 1893.

Loetz iridescent glass vase
in a characteristically innovative waisted and bulbous cylindrical shape. In clear over dark blue over ruby-red glass, with iridescent yellow-tinted silver, configured in wavelike and "pulled-feather" patterns. *c. 1900*
5 in (12.5 cm) high **$9,000–10,000 VZ**

Loetz glass is typically bluish-green in color and is sometimes streaked with red or golden yellow or silvery threading. Vivid colors such as red, yellow, and purple were also made and are highly sought-after today. The surface may be splashed with patches of silvery iridescence that looks like a butterfly's wing but is known as "oil spots." Loetz made vases in many shapes and sizes, and pinched forms are typical of the factory's designs.

From around 1900, the company started to collaborate with outside designers. Among those who designed pieces for Loetz are Josef Hoffmann, Koloman Moser, and Maria Kirschner.

INCREASING VARIETY

Another European manufacturer of iridescent glass was Pallme-König & Habel in Kosten near Teplitz. It made purplish or pea-green ware with trailed decoration in the style of Loetz from around 1887, including small, squat glasses with ruffled rims, brass-bound inkwells, and vases with applied floral motifs. The glass tends to be thicker and of a lesser quality than pieces made by Loetz.

Louis Comfort Tiffany experimented widely and produced more than 5,000 new types of glass. However, he is probably best known for his Favrile range of iridescent glassware. As well as stunning finishes, Tiffany created amazing shapes—his floriform vases can encapsulate the spirit of an entire plant in one fluid shape. Decoration was usually integral to the object and could be on the interior or the exterior of the glass.

COLLECTORS' TIPS

Many pieces display organic motifs in their form or decoration, or both. Of these, plant forms – flowers, leaves, and fruits – are prevalent, but animal, fish, bird, and insect imagery is also a recurring theme.
Imagery can be stylized almost to the point of abstraction in some cases.
Ancient Roman glass was the main source of inspiration for late 19th- and 20th-century iridescent glass, so many shapes and forms are inspired by Classical antiquity.

Left: Tiffany Favrile glass bowl in amber glass with pink and gold iridescence. The rippled surface of its flared rim is typical of the plantlike forms or motifs evident in many Tiffany pieces. *1900–28*
7¼ in (18.5 cm) wide **$400–500 S&K**

Right: Carnival glass vase in iridescent orange and marigold glass, possibly by Fenton. It is patterned with elongated spearhead motifs and vertical ribbing. Plant-form ruffled rims, as here, are found on many Carnival glass vases. *1907–22*
10¾ in (27.5 cm) high **$60–90 BB**

collected today include Wilhelm Kralik & Sohn, Harrach, and F. van Poschinger in Bohemia; Amédée de Caranza in France; and Quezal, Kew Blas, and Durand in the United States.

MASS PRODUCTION

The majority of designer-made iridescent glass is typical of the Art Nouveau style. However, the finish on mass-produced Carnival glass was made in a similar way, with an iridized surface treatment. The glass was exposed to sprays and fumes of hot metal oxides before it cooled. When light hit the glass, the result was a rainbow effect on the surface similar to that seen when gasoline floats on water.

Carnival glass was press-molded by companies in the United States and Great Britain in the early 20th century. It was made in a variety of colors, including green, amethyst, marigold, amber, and red. Created as an inexpensive alternative to highly priced glass by Tiffany and his competitors, Carnival glass has since become highly collectible.

Archaeological discoveries of ancient Roman glass with naturally occurring iridescence—as at the excavation of this wine bar in Pompeii (c. 1912)—were the inspiration for manufactured iridescent glass.

Tiffany's greatest rival was probably the Steuben glassworks in Corning, New York. From 1904 to around 1930, the factory produced an Aurene range inspired by—but not a copy of— Tiffany's Favrile. The iridescence on Aurene glass is usually brighter than that on Tiffany glass. The Aurene range is a rich gold in color, while Blue Aurene is a bright blue. It was Steuben's most popular range from its introduction until the mid-1920s.

Other manufacturers in the United States and Europe followed suit. Some names are lost forever because their work was never signed. Those we know about and whose work is

Loetz small Cytisus-design vase, with a globular body tapering to a flared and pinched triangular neck. The pealike blooms of this sought-after floral pattern are rendered in iridescent polychrome tones. *c. 1900. 4½ in (11 cm) high* **$7,000–9,000 TEL**

Conical-shaped glass vase with a candle-cup neck, by Amédée de Caranza. Decorated with leaves and red cherries—fruit motifs were a de Caranza favorite—on a mustard ground. The iridescent finish was created using an adaptation of a technique originally employed to produce metallic lusters on ceramics. *1900–03 6¼ in (16 cm) high* **$3,000–4,000 MACK**

Durand art-glass footed bowl with a flared rim. The interior has an iridescent gold finish, while the exterior is decorated with an iridescent blue-on-gold King Tut pattern. The pulled coils and swirls of the latter resemble similar designs by Tiffany and Quezal but are crisper and more regimented. *1924–31 10½ in (26.5 cm) wide* **$900–1,100 JDJ**

KEY DATES

1852 Susanna Gerstner, widow of Johann Lötz, acquires a glassworks in Klostermuhle, subsequently known as Johann Lötz Witwe, then shortened to Lötz, before being anglicized as Loetz.

1879 Max Ritter von Spaun, Susanna's grandson, acquires the Loetz glassworks and develops the company's international reputation.

1893 Loetz iridescent glass is exhibited at the Chicago World Fair.

1906 Loetz begins a fruitful collaboration with Josef Hoffmann, employed as a freelance designer.

1913 Johann Lötz Witwe GmbH established following insolvency in 1911.

1948 Loetz glassworks closes.

Loetz

From the 1890s, Loetz's iridescent art glass married inventive Art Nouveau organic forms with controlled surface decoration. Sometimes known as the "Austrian Tiffany," Loetz's iridescent glass is avidly collected.

Max Ritter von Spaun (1856–1909) presided over the Loetz glassworks during the company's golden years of 1895–1905. During this time, the company produced an extensive range of Art Nouveau pieces (mainly vases), some Tiffany-inspired, with applied and multiple handles, wavy rims, forms based on rose-water sprinklers, and other organic shapes.

The solid, somewhat thick, glass pieces produced by Loetz were complemented by a wide spectrum of strong, rich iridescent colors, often used in startling contrast. Many pieces had a characteristic rich blue iridescence, often with a gleaming oil-on-water effect. Unusual ground colors include red, purple, and yellow. The controlled but startling patterns were often based on traditional Art Nouveau motifs, such as

peacock feathers and stylized plants. Others were decorated with random designs—spotted, splashed, and feathered patterns, with gold and silver iridescence. Among the most popular patterns were Papillon, usually in red, gold, or blue, which resembled butterfly wings, and Phänomen glass, with wavy internal decoration. Some pieces had specially designed silver mounts.

As the vogue for Art Nouveau faded, the Loetz style changed. From 1905, forms became less organic and more regular, and the decoration became freer and less obviously controlled.

Identifying Loetz glass can pose problems. It was widely copied, and not all Loetz glass is signed. Pieces with a Loetz or Loetz/Austria mark were usually produced for export.

Above: Iridescent green-yellow vase decorated with waves of darker strings and iridescent silvery blotches. The shape is known as number 2485. *c. 1900. 8¾ in (22 cm) high* **$20,000–30,000 WKA**

Floriform vase with iridescent blue flower, a crimped rim, applied iridescent light green-amber curling leaves, and a textured foot. *Early 20th century. 12 in (30.5 cm) high* **$3,500–5,000 JDJ**

DESIGNERS AT LOETZ

Max Ritter von Spaun was a cultured and artistic man. His circle of friends included artists and architects, and he was eager to build links and commission designs for modern glass from leading Austrian designers of the time. Many of these designers were associated with the Vienna Secession, formed by Koloman Moser (1868–1919) in 1897, and the Wiener Werkstätte (*see p.65*), established by Koloman Moser and Josef Hoffmann (1870–1956) in 1903. Hoffmann produced designs for Loetz from 1906 until 1914, and other members of the Wiener Werkstätte followed suit, including Jutta Sika (1877–1964), Otto Prutscher (1880–1949), Dagobert Peche (1889–1923), and Michael Powolny (1871–1954; *see p.63*).

Phänomen vase with iridescent green "reeds," an iridescent swirling lake effect, moon, and linear trailed "clouds." The shape and decoration were designed by Franz Hofstätter. *c. 1900. 9½ in (24 cm) high* **$30,000–40,000 WKA**

Bulbous footed iridescent Feather bowl with a deep-red "pulled-feather" design over an opaque yellow ground. It has a clear glass foot. *1898–1904*

6½ in (16.5 cm) high

$1,500–2,000 AL

Bulbous Delphi bowl with iridescent body etched with sinuous foliate and floral design; with a crimped rim. *c. 1900*

4½ in (11.5 cm) high

$2,000–3,000 VS

Octagonal matt iridescent Phänomen vase in dark green, with four silver-yellow leaf applications. *c. 1905*

6 in (15 cm) high

$2,000–3,000 FIS

Light green vase with the appearance of blades of grass bound together with applied iridescent glass trails. *c. 1905*

4½ in (11.5 cm) high

$4,000–7,000 TEL

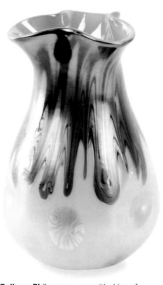

Bulbous Phänomen vase with drips of iridescent finish on the exterior and interior. The neck tapers to a flared triform rim. *1902*

6½ in (16.5 cm) high

$15,000–18,000 TEL

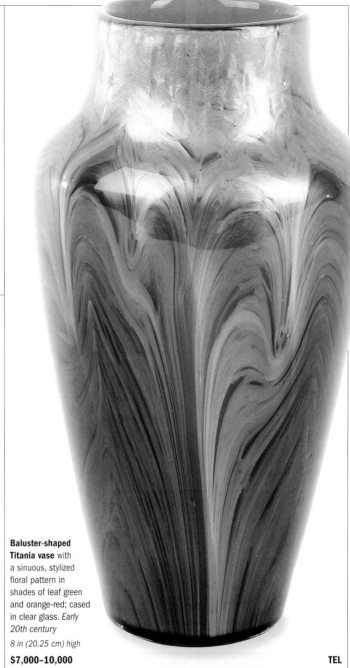

Baluster-shaped Titania vase with a sinuous, stylized floral pattern in shades of leaf green and orange-red; cased in clear glass. *Early 20th century*

8 in (20.25 cm) high

$7,000–10,000 TEL

Large Crater vase with a splayed and undulating rim, made from clear glass decorated with a random bubble pattern in vibrant orange-red. *c. 1900*

10½ in (27 cm) high

$4,000–6,000 MW

Bohemian Iridescent

The Loetz glassworks (*see p.110*) was working in parallel with Tiffany (*see p.120*) to produce fashionable iridescent glass from the late 19th century onward. Other Bohemian glassworks soon followed suit with their own similar, but inferior-quality, iridescent glass, which tended to be heavier, with less controlled iridescence. Among them were the Harrach glassworks (est. 1712), whose work frequently employed Art Nouveau–style metal mounts, and Wilhelm Kralik Sohn (est. 1831), whose work was mostly unsigned. The Glasfabrik Elisabeth, which merged with Pallme-König in 1889, produced vases with applied iridescent trailed decoration.

Unsigned footed bowl with knopped stem, in amethyst-colored glass with gold iridescence on the lower half. *1900–10*

6 in (15 cm) high

$1,200–1,800   JDJ

Small Harrach vase of waisted, flasklike form in blue iridescent glass within an Art Nouveau copper mount. *c. 1900*

4¾ in (12.25 cm) high

$500–700   QU

Wilhelm Kralik Sohn bowl with a combed pattern in iridescent blue, green, and gold glass. It is raised on a four-footed base with two looped handles of gold-plated tin. *c. 1900*

14 in (36 cm) high

$1,500–2,000   HERR

Unsigned Secessionist-style bowl of bulging rectangular form, with an amethyst-colored glass body and faint iridescent sheen. The applied copper mount features two foil-backed, ruby-red glass cabochons. *c. 1900*

5½ in (13.5 cm) wide

$800–1,200   DN

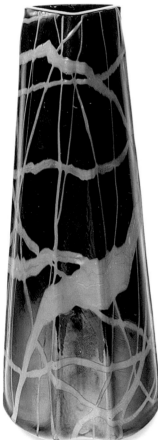

Wilhelm Kralik Sohn vase with an indented round base and square rim, in iridescent deep purple with bands of silver foil. *1902*

10½ in (26.5 cm) high

$150–200   FIS

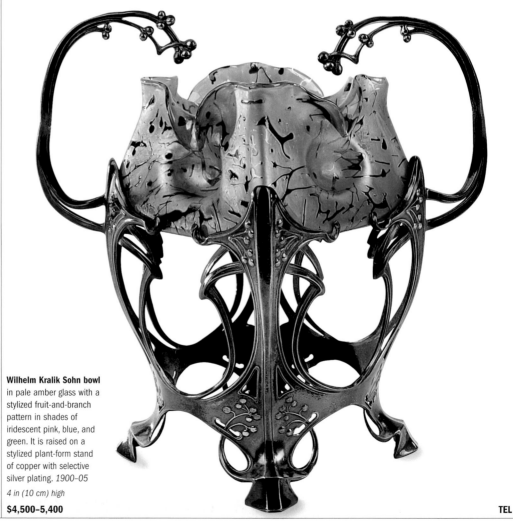

Wilhelm Kralik Sohn bowl in pale amber glass with a stylized fruit-and-branch pattern in shades of iridescent pink, blue, and green. It is raised on a stylized plant-form stand of copper with selective silver plating. *1900–05*

4 in (10 cm) high

$4,500–5,400   TEL

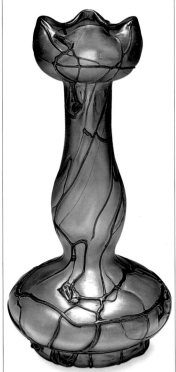

Glasfabrik Elisabeth double gourd-shaped vase made in iridescent green glass and covered while cooling with asymmetrical applied threading decoration. *1900–05*

9½ in (24 cm) high

$1,500–2,000   **QU**

Harrach oval vase in iridescent red and purple glass, with acid-etched cameo decoration of cloud formations on the rim, tulips on the body, and vegetation around the base. *c. 1905*

12 in (30.5 cm) high

$1,200–1,800   **QU**

Unsigned Bohemian vase of baluster form made in iridescent glass with random and mottled orange, green, blue, and purple streaks. *c. 1900*

11 in (28 cm) high

$200–250   **FIS**

Glasfabrik Elisabeth vase in pink iridescent glass, with darker pink and silver inclusions and four-leaf-clover motifs and trailing stems in green. *c. 1900*

10½ in (26.5 cm) high

$1,200–1,800   **QU**

Pallme-König

By 1900, the family-owned Gebrüder Pallme-König & Habel glassworks (est. 1786, Steinschönau, Bohemia) had a workforce of some 300 craftsmen who were producing iridescent art glass and table glass, some with metal mounts, in the Art Nouveau style. The forms and iridescence were similar to those used by Loetz (*see p.110*) but lacked the quality, delicacy, and controlled iridescence of the superior Loetz pieces. However, because Pallme-König glass is usually unmarked, it can be incorrectly attributed. One of the company's trademarks was the use of trailed "spiderweb" decoration in contrasting colors, as shown on the vase far right—again, rather similar to the Loetz Phänomen range.

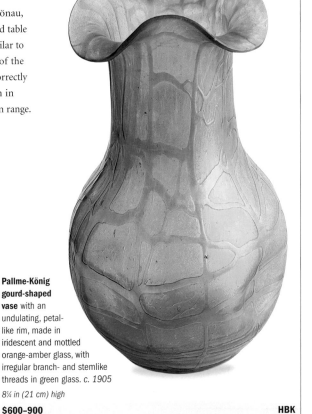

Pallme-König centerpiece glass bowl in iridescent golden, green, and mauve glass above a pewter stand with foliate supports and base. *c. 1905*

9¼ in (23.5 cm) high

$1,000–1,500   **DN**

Pallme-König electric table lamp suspended from a branchlike bronze base. The iridescent pink glass shade has irregular applied trailings. *c. 1905*

11¾ in (30 cm) high

$500–700   **HERR**

Pallme-König gourd-shaped vase with an undulating, petal-like rim, made in iridescent and mottled orange-amber glass, with irregular branch- and stemlike threads in green glass. *c. 1905*

8¼ in (21 cm) high

$600–900   **HBK**

Animals

Small sculptural animal figures have an innate appeal for collectors and offer glassmakers a chance to show off their technical skills. In the 20th century, the trend moved away from molded animals and toward free-blown stylized pieces that sought to capture the essence of the creature.

Throughout the 20th century, highly skilled Murano glassmakers explored the plastic nature of glass to produce ranges of animal figures, from elegant, stylized animals to more naturalistic models. Czech and British glassworks were also renowned for their animal ranges: the Czech Exbor Studio glassworks produced high-quality cut-glass animals, including limited-edition fish sculptures, and both Whitefriars and Wedgwood made delightful, collectible blown-glass animals.

The most attractive pieces are a combination of a good factory, good workmanship, good condition, and a charming or humorous design. Such pieces will be correspondingly expensive. Far more affordable, but sometimes just as appealing, are the quirky designs, such as the molded Scottie dog inkwell, opposite.

Murano glass wild-boar figure by V. Nason & Co. in gray and clear glass, with sticker. *1950s* *5½ in (13.5 cm) wide* **$50–80 P&I**

Glass chicken designed and made by Vittorio Ferro in three separate sections. *2004* *8¾ in (22.5 cm) high* **$2,500–3,500 VET**

Green glass dragon paperweight, unmarked but probably early 20th century. *4½ in (11.5 cm) high* **$30–50 AG**

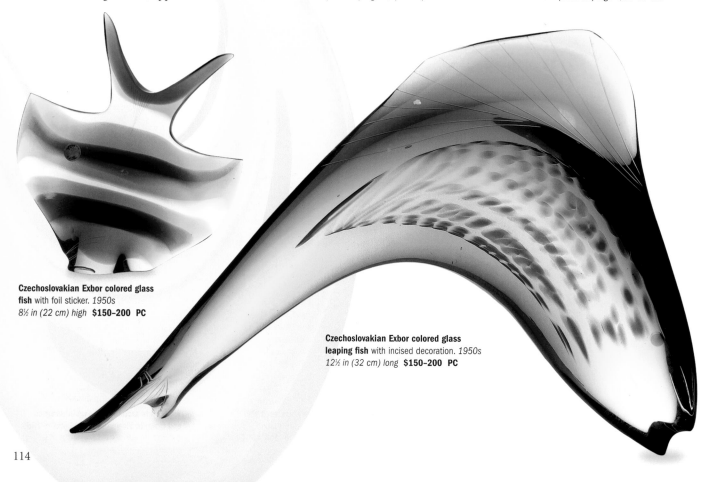

Czechoslovakian Exbor colored glass fish with foil sticker. *1950s* *8½ in (22 cm) high* **$150–200 PC**

Czechoslovakian Exbor colored glass leaping fish with incised decoration. *1950s* *12½ in (32 cm) long* **$150–200 PC**

Pressed glass Scottie dog inkwell with silver-plated mounts. It turns black when full. *c. 1900. 3½ in (9 cm) high* **$200–300 DCC**

Venetian glass Scottie dog with black glass and gold inclusions and original foil label. *1950s. 9 in (23 cm) long* **$150–200 ROX**

Lalique letter seal rabbit, in topaz glass, engraved "R. Lalique France." *1930s 2½ in (5.5 cm) high* **$700–1,000 DRA**

Squirrel model in red and clear glass, probably Venetian. *Late 20th century 7 in (18 cm) high* **$20–30 JH**

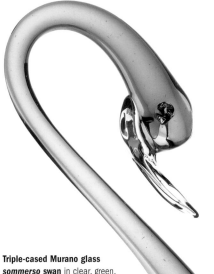

Triple-cased Murano glass *sommerso* **swan** in clear, green, and amber glass. *1950s. 14½ in (37 cm) high* **$200–300 PC**

Murano glass figure of a dove with gold foil inclusions encased in clear glass. *Late 20th century. 3¾ in (9.5 cm) high* **$20–30 GAZE**

Contemporary glass model of a bird by R. Sperl, from an edition of 99, signed "R. E. S." *c. 2000 13½ in (34 cm) high* **$2,000–3,500 FM**

Large Whitefriars clear glass duck with repeated rings of bubbles decoration. *1950s. 6½ in (16.5 cm) high* **$60–90 GC**

Whitefriars arctic-blue penguin designed and blown by Vicente or Ettore Boffo. *c. 1960 6½ in (16.5 cm) high* **$500–700 TCS**

German & Austrian Iridescent

Just as Loetz was inspired by Tiffany, so Loetz in turn inspired numerous German and Austrian manufacturers to produce their own ranges of iridescent Jugendstil art glass from the 1890s. Much of this glass is unmarked and difficult to attribute, since so many factories used similar styles, typically adopting wavy or ruffled rims and dented or dimpled forms with metallic iridescent finishes.

Among the more original ranges are the Ikora series by W.M.F. (*see p.62*), pieces by known designers such as Josef Schneckendorf (1865–1949), or the iridescent glass created by freelance designers for Ferdinand von Poschinger's Buchenau glassworks.

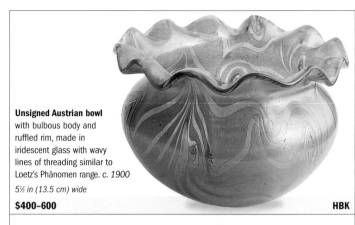

Unsigned Austrian bowl with bulbous body and ruffled rim, made in iridescent glass with wavy lines of threading similar to Loetz's Phänomen range. *c. 1900*

5½ in (13.5 cm) wide

$400–600   HBK

W.M.F. Ikora-range vase by Karl Wiedmann, in clear-cased, mottled yellow and green iridescent glass. *c. 1930*

9 in (23 cm) high

$900–1,200   QU

Baluster-shaped vase designed by Karl Schmoll von Eisenwerth for the Ferdinand von Poschinger glassworks, Bavaria. *c. 1900*

12 in (30.5 cm) high

$3,000–4,000   QU

Squat vase designed by Josef Emil Schneckendorf, painted and etched with stylized floral motifs in metallic iridescence over clear glass. *1908*

3 in (7.5 cm) high

$2,000–3,000   QU

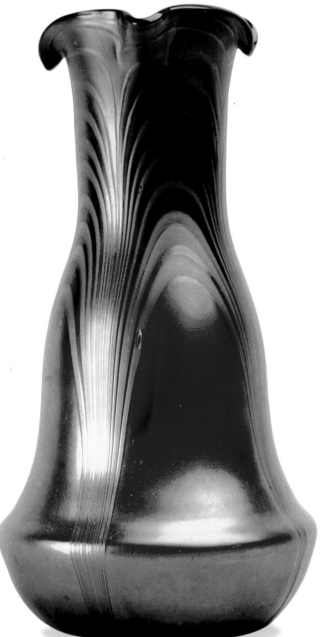

Unsigned Austrian vase with a pinched, splayed rim and stepped, tapering body. In iridescent red glass with pink and blue "pulled-feather" decoration. *c. 1905*

12 in (30.5 cm) high

$600–800   JDJ

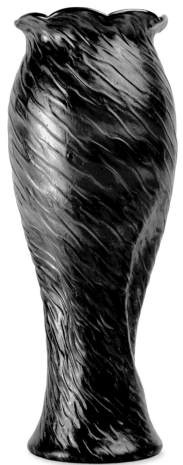

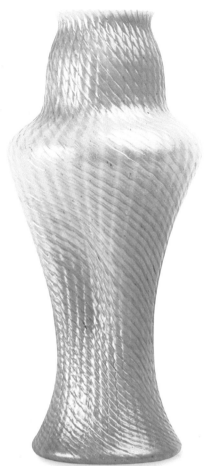

Unsigned Austrian vase of slender baluster form with pinched sides, a ruffled rim, and a rippled finish. In iridescent green glass with purple and blue highlights. *1920s*

13 in (33 cm) high

$350–450   **JDJ**

Unsigned Austrian vase of unusual baluster form in iridescent pink glass, with a ground rim, three dimples on the tapering body, and a textured and swirling "woven" finish. *1920s*

12 in (30.5 cm) high

$200–300   **JDJ**

Unsigned Austrian vase with a pinched rim, tapering round body, and spreading bulbous base, in shades of dark red and purple iridescent glass with an all-over crackle finish. *c. 1905*

11 in (28 cm) high

$400–600   **JDJ**

W.M.F. Myra-Kristall range

The Myra-Kristall range produced by W.M.F. (*see p.62*) took its name from a site in Asia Minor, where archaeologists discovered ancient glass with a natural iridescence. Karl Wiedmann developed the prototype in 1925, and the successful range was launched in 1926. The forms were not innovative; the attraction lay in the silky matt surface with a shimmering golden iridescence that reflected through green, blue, and purple. Later, Myra Red Kristall and Mother-of-Pearl iridescence were added to the color range. W.M.F. had to run double shifts to meet the huge demand for the range. Production ceased in 1939, resumed in 1948, and was finally discontinued in 1954.

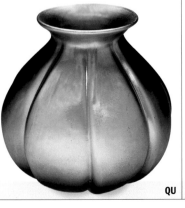

W.M.F. Myra-Kristall vase of bulbous and ribbed budlike form, with a metallic iridescent cast. Examples made in the 1930s were often mold-blown and had thicker walls than 1920s versions. *c. 1935*

6¼ in (15.5 cm) high

$300–500   **QU**

W.M.F. Myra-Kristall vase of bulbous and ribbed budlike form, but more thinly blown than the later example (*left*). It displays the iridescent golden-amber luster developed by Karl Wiedmann and commonly associated with the Myra range. *c. 1925*

6 in (15 cm) high

$600–900   **QU**

KEY FACTORIES

The Quezal Art Glass & Decorating Co., Queens, New York (1902–1924).

Steuben Glass Co., Corning, New York (est. 1903); still active.

Tiffany Glass & Decorating Co., Corona, New York (1892–1932).

Union Glass Works, Somerville, Massachusetts: produced Kew Blas art glass (1890s–1924).

Vineland Flint Glassworks, Vineland, New Jersey: produced Durand art glass (1924–31).

AMERICAN IRIDESCENT

The introduction and development of iridescent glass in the United States can be attributed to one influential and inspirational man—Louis Comfort Tiffany (1848–1933). Tiffany had decided at a young age to dedicate himself "to the pursuit of beauty." Although he trained as an artist in the 1860s, his first business venture was as an interior designer. His commissions included designs for the White House and Mark Twain's house in Hartford, Connecticut. Tiffany had become fascinated by the qualities of glass, especially the way it refracted light, while painting. He then studied under Andrea Baldini, a Venetian glass-blower.

Tiffany traveled extensively abroad and, after seeing the work of Emile Gallé at the Paris Exhibition of 1889, he was inspired to create art glass. Furthermore, he wanted to replicate the aged appearance of excavated Roman glass, with its luminous iridescence caused by the effects of mineral deposits in the sand. Europe was resonating with the embryonic Art Nouveau movement, with its rejection

Louis Comfort Tiffany (1848–1933), photographed in the late 1880s, just a few years before he founded the Tiffany Glass & Decorating Co.

of Victorian clutter and stifling historicism. Art Nouveau offered an aesthetic of the natural world. Tiffany's glass designs were not only inspired by nature, but also by the art of Japan, China, and the Middle East.

Back in New York, Tiffany was determined to produce the world's most acclaimed art glass. In 1893, he persuaded Arthur J. Nash (1849–1934)

Metallic gold luster vase by Tiffany, of budlike form with vertical ribbing to the upper body and the rim configured as five splayed back petals. *1900–05*
4¼ in (11 cm) high **$1,500–2,000 JDJ**

KEY STYLES

Flora and fauna are the major recurring themes in American iridescent glass.
The most distinctive themes are the iridescent, orchid-like blooms of Jack-in-the-Pulpit vases and the "pulled feather" (notably peacock), elongated stem, and acanthus scroll patterns.
Plain iridescent finishes are much sought after.
Roman, Islamic, Venetian, and old German forms are much in evidence.

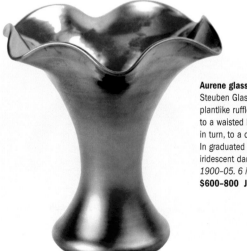

Aurene glass vase by the Steuben Glassworks, its plantlike ruffled rim tapering to a waisted body flaring, in turn, to a conical foot. In graduated shades of iridescent dark blue glass. *1900–05. 6 in (15 cm) high* **$600–800 JDJ**

from the White House Glass Works in Stourbridge, England, to found him to found the Stourbridge Glass Co. at Corona, New York. The glass they produced was of the best quality, its colors achieved by the addition of metallic oxides.

THE SECRET SPARKLE

Tiffany patented his famous iridescent glass Favrile (from the Old English "fabrile," meaning "belonging to a craftsman or his craft") in 1894. This luster technique, with its iridescent effect, became Tiffany's hallmark. The technique involved dissolving salts of metallic oxides in the molten glass, thereby creating the luminous colors: the golds and vibrant shades of autumn, the soft yellows and sea greens, the mysterious blues. The glass was then held in a reducing flame and sprayed with chloride. This caused the surface to form a series of tiny lines that refracted light. This was a highly complex and skilled technique, and speed and accuracy was of the essence.

THE IRIDESCENT INSPIRATION

Several American companies, including Steuben, Durand, and Quezal, also produced iridescent glass. Steuben, under the direction of Frederick Carder (1863–1963), was particularly successful. In 1904, Carder patented a velvety, iridescent glass called Aurene (from the Latin "aurum" meaning gold), which was an immediate commercial success. Tiffany threatened a lawsuit, believing it to be a copy of his Favrile glass, but Carder proved he had developed it independently.

This was a particularly productive time for the Steuben works; over the next three decades Carder is credited with producing over 6,000 shapes in 100 finishes, including Verre de Soie (1903), Aquamarine (1915), Cyprian (1915), Calcite (1915), Tyrian (1916), Cintra (1917), Cluthra (1920s), and Ivrene (1920s).

Although producing some interesting pieces, most of the other factories were content to create pieces very much in the Tiffany style. They all helped to satisfy the increasing demand for the iridescent glassware popularized by Tiffany.

Louis Comfort Tiffany's studio, completed in 1885, at his 72nd Street and Madison Avenue apartment in New York City.

Pale green overlay glass vase by Quezal, of shouldered oval form with irregular bands of pulled leaf and scroll motifs in yellow and silver, and with blue iridescence to the lower body. *1901–23* *6¼ in (16 cm) high* **$2,700–3,500 DOR**

Favrile glass vase by Tiffany, of waisted and bulbous double-gourd shape with an elongated neck, in the plain, iridescent gold finish Tiffany also used on tableware and drinking glasses. *c.1900* *11¾ in (30 cm) high* **$3,500–4,500 JDJ**

KEY DATES

1879 Louis Comfort Tiffany establishes Louis Comfort Tiffany & Associated Artists.

1885 Tiffany sets up the Tiffany Glass Co. in New York to produce modern stained-glass work.

1892 Tiffany Glass & Decorating Co. is established. It is renamed Tiffany Studios in 1902.

1894 Favrile, the first iridescent art-glass range, is launched.

1924 Tiffany dissolves Tiffany Furnaces.

Tiffany

The name of Tiffany is virtually synonymous with American Art Nouveau art glass. Tiffany refined and developed the technique for iridizing contemporary glass to produce an exclusive and now extremely valuable range of trail-blazing shapes and finishes.

Louis Comfort Tiffany (1848–1933) was essentially a designer rather than a glassmaker, and it was the technical expertise of English glassmaker Arthur J. Nash (1849–1934), with whom he collaborated at the Tiffany Furnaces in New York, that transformed Tiffany's designs into the stunning glass that made Tiffany a household name.

Tiffany's Favrile range of iridescent art glass, launched in 1894, was an immediate success. The glowing colors—blue and gold are most common—were produced by spraying the surface of the molten glass with metallic lusters, and were applied to truly innovative plant-inspired Art Nouveau forms. These included the distinctive Jack-in-the-Pulpit vase, based on the native wildflower; the gooseneck vase that resembled a Persian rose-water sprinkler; and the magnificent but highly vulnerable and valuable tall Floriform vases with gently flaring ruffled rims. On less complex forms, the decoration included the trademark but technically complex peacock pattern, feathering, tooled threading, and patterns created by marvering hot glass into the surface of the vase to create the trailing leaf and flower shapes favored in Art Nouveau. On other pieces, the naturalistic floral decoration was created by painting the design onto the surface in metal oxides.

Other iridescent ranges had experimental textured surfaces. The Lava range was inspired by the molten lava from a volcano and decorated with iridescent molten trails that ran down the irregular cracked iridescent surface. Tiffany's Cypriote range sought to recreate the pitted iridescent surface found on ancient Roman glass.

Above: Rare Cypriote vase with confetti-style cypriote technique on a golden ground. Signed "L.C. Tiffany," and with a paper label. *c. 1900. 3¾ in (9.5 cm) high* **$20,000–30,000 MACK**

ROMAN GLASS

The popular iridescent glass of the late 19th and early 20th centuries was inspired by the glass of ancient Rome. Archaeologists excavating ancient sites around the Mediterranean had uncovered Roman glass of which the textured pitted surface and iridescent finish was the result of the reaction of metal oxides during years of burial. Inspired by the finds, in the late 19th century, European and American glass manufacturers experimented widely to find a way of recreating, with the help of new technology, what nature had managed to create simply by the passage of time.

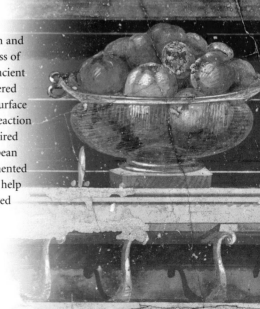

Iridescent vase of waisted baluster form with a deep-honey ground with trailed gilt decoration. It is signed on the base "L.C. Tiffany E1940." *c. 1900. 9 in (23 cm) high* **$10,000–15,000 MACK**

DETAIL OF A ROMAN FRESCO DEPICTING A GLASS VESSEL, POMPEII

Floriform vase with transparent green stem and iridescent pulled-feather bowl. *Early 20th century*

14 in (35.5 cm) high

$3,600–4,500   JDJ

Favrile double gourd-shaped vase with cream opaque neck trailing into the deep-green iridescent finish of the body. It is marked "W5812" and has a Tiffany paper label. *c. 1905*

7½ in (19 cm) high

$10,000–15,000   MACK

Oval-bodied and footed vase with vine-leaf motifs in shades of green. The underside is signed "L.C. Tiffany Favrile. 244G." *Early 20th century*

7 in (17.5 cm) high

$4,000–6,000   JDJ

Favrile pitcher with green leaf-and-vine decoration and an applied iridescent gold handle. Signed "L.C. Tiffany Favrile." *Early 20th century*

6½ in (16.5 cm) high

$4,000–6,000   JDJ

Blue iridescent vase with leaves and vines and flashes of green, gold, and blue. Signed "Louis C. Tiffany LCT D1420." *Early 20th century*

4½ in (11.5 cm) high

$6,000–9,000   JDJ

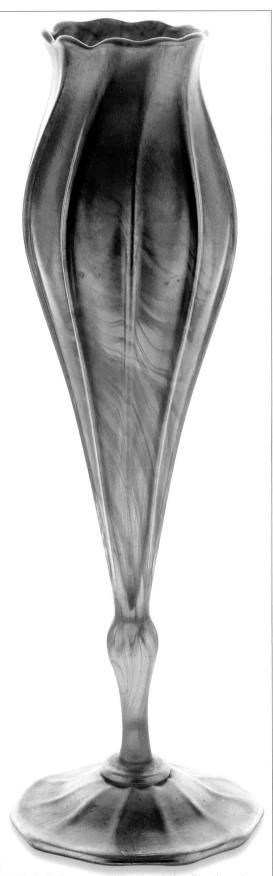

Tall Favrile floriform vase with ribs and a pulled motif in yellow and green. The base is etched "L.C. Tiffany/Favrile/9042J." *Early 20th century*

12 in (30 cm) high

$3,600–4,500   CR

121

Steuben Glassworks

Steuben's early range of iridescent art glass played a major role in establishing the company's fortunes and prestigious reputation. It also made a major contribution to the development of modern American art glass.

Frederick Carder, co-founder of the Steuben Glassworks, was an innovative and talented designer and glass technologist. His early experiments with colored art glass resulted in his now famous Gold Aurene (from the Latin *aurum*, meaning gold) iridescent range, which he patented in 1904. The gleaming, lustrous surfaces of Steuben's iridescent pieces proved highly popular with the American public—so popular that they challenged Tiffany's Favrile ware, which they closely resembled.

Carder went on to develop new iridescent color ranges. Blue Aurene was launched in 1905, and Red Aurene—a difficult and often unstable color—followed, together with opaline, brown, and shades of green. Verre de Soie—clear glass with a silky, silvery iridescence—was produced from 1905, and

Ivrene was launched in the 1920s. Steuben's iridescent colors were somewhat brighter than those of Tiffany. They were often combined in one piece and, although Carder believed that the colors spoke for themselves, pieces were frequently decorated with flat surface effects such as pulled feathering.

The Aurene range was Steuben's major output between about 1904 and 1933. Vases, dishes, and bowls were staples. The forms were mostly standard and were designed to appeal to a broad public, but they were transformed by the soft, even-colored sheen, and it is the color, decoration, and quality of the finish that determine value today. Decorated Aurene glass—in particular, pieces with interesting surface decoration and color combinations—is the most valuable.

Above: Large Blue Aurene vase of shouldered oval form. Its iridescent light blue finish shades into pale green iridescence at the neck. Signed "Steuben Aurene" on the base. *c. 1905–30* *10¼ in (26.5 cm) high* **$1,800–3,500 JDJ**

FREDERICK CARDER

British-born Frederick Carder (1863–1963) played a seminal role in American art glass as the "guiding genius" at the Steuben Glassworks. His expertise as a designer and glass technologist, combined with his passion for experimentation, helped establish the reputation of what Carder always regarded as *his* factory. During his long career at Steuben, he designed for many different types of glass, creating some 6,000 shapes and numerous colors. A man of action to the end, he was still exploring techniques such as *cire perdue* and *pâte-de-verre* when he retired at the age of 96.

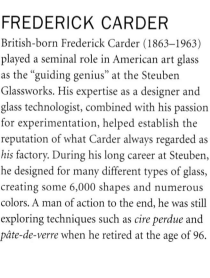

Very rare Aurene vase by Frederick Carder, of baluster shape. It has a flared and ruffled rim and pulled feather decoration in iridescent green and gold. *c. 1915. 9 in (23 cm) high* **$9,000–11,000 TDC**

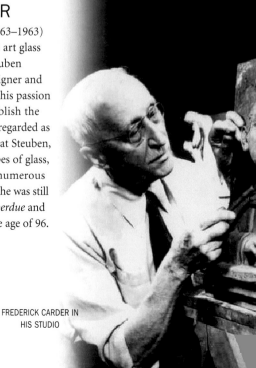

FREDERICK CARDER IN HIS STUDIO

Rare footed bowl by Frederick Carder, of floral-like form in Gold Aurene over translucent ivory calcite glass. *c. 1915–25*

11¼ in (28.5 cm) wide

$1,500–2,000   TDC

Large center bowl of circular form. It has an iridescent blue-green finish on the interior and upper rim, above a white calcite exterior. *c. 1920s*

14¾ in (37.5 cm) wide

$600–900   DRA

Pair of trumpet-shaped footed vases, with a swirling, iridescent Gold Aurene finish and iridescent blue and purple highlights. *c. 1920s*

12 in (30.5 cm) high

$4,500–5,500 (the pair)   JDJ

Blue Aurene glass with a concave body flaring down to a round foot and up to a wider, ruffled rim—all in graduated shades of iridescent blue. *c. 1905–30*

6 in (15 cm) high

$1,000–1,500   JDJ

Blue Aurene candlestick with a flared rim to the candle cup, above a twisted stem rising from a domed, circular foot—all with a blue iridescent finish. *c. 1910–30*

8 in (20 cm) high

$1,000–1,500   JDJ

Blue Aurene glass bowl by Frederick Carder. The squat form is relatively rare. *c. 1925*

4¾ in (12.5 cm) high

$1,500–2,000   TDC

Trumpet-shaped footed vase with a broad rim and finished in iridescent Gold Aurene over ivory-white calcite. Designed by Frederick Carder. *c. 1925*

8 in (20 cm) high

$1,800–2,800   TDC

Quezal

The Quezal company, named after a South American bird noted for its gorgeous iridescent plumage, was established to produce iridescent glass in the Tiffany style, and its finest pieces are of comparable quality and price.

As former Tiffany employees, Thomas Johnson and Martin Bach were familiar with the company's decorating techniques and glass recipes. They made no attempt at technical or design innovations, and Quezal's range of vases, bowls, and lampshades were unashamed imitations of Tiffany's Favrile art glass. Forms included the famous Jack-in-the-Pulpit shape and other flower-inspired designs. Quezal pieces had slightly thicker walls and a high-quality iridescent finish. The decoration was more regular than that on Tiffany pieces, with an emphasis on pulled-feather decoration that created distinctive patterns. Undecorated blue or purple pieces are rare.

The superb technical quality of Quezal's glass more than compensated for the lack of originality found in the Tiffany pieces, and Quezal became a serious rival. However, Quezal's fortunes were dependent on the fashion for iridescent glass, and when it fell out of favor, in the 1930s, the firm struggled, and production switched to lampshades.

The high quality of Quezal glass made it popular. From 1902, most pieces were marked with an engraved name. Quezal glass made in 1901 was unmarked, and some of these pieces have been given spurious Tiffany signatures.

Above: Pulled-feather-decoration vase of oval form, with iridescent green and gold threading set against a creamy-white ground. *1902–20. 6 in (15 cm) high* **$2,000–3,000 JDJ**

Lustre Art lampshade of oval form with a ruffled rim and a wavy, white, sponged pattern on a gold-luster ground. Marked "Lustre Art." *1902–20*
4¾ in (12 cm) high
$300–400   **CR**

Iridescent glass vase of shouldered and waisted baluster form, with pulled-feather decoration in iridescent blue, green, and gold against an opaque white ground. *1902–20*
13 in (33 cm) high
$6,500–7,000   **LN**

Footed glass compote with a flat rim in iridescent green shading to iridescent blue. *1902–20*
9½ in (24 cm) wide
$1,000–1,500   **JDJ**

Squat vase with a hexagonal rim, in pale green glass with fumed iridescence from light blue to purple. *1902–20*
6 in (15 cm) high
$700–1,000   **JDJ**

Durand

The iridescent glass produced at the Vineland Glass Co. in New Jersey is better known as Durand, the name of the enterprising French-born glassmaker whose commercial success allowed him to fund his range of art glass.

Staffed by former employees of Quezal (*see opposite*), the art-glass workshop at Vineland initially produced glass whose forms and decorations closely resembled those of Tiffany's rival. However, the team soon produced its own distinctive range of colors and patterns.

Forms were regular and simple. The basic golden amber iridescence was called Ambergris, but it was the patterns that distinguished the Durand Vineland pieces. Some vases were decorated with fine random trails of glass threads, a technique known as "spiderwebbing." Other decoration included peacock feathers and King Tut swirls, following the fashion for all things Egyptian after the 1923 discovery of Tutankhamun's tomb.

On some pieces the iridescent pattern was allowed to drip down the sides to create a random pattern. Other iridescent ware had cameo or intaglio designs in the surface. In the late 1920s, a range of crackled glass vases was introduced under the exotic names of Moorish Crackle and Egyptian Crackle.

Durand's early cut glass is mostly unmarked. Later pieces are usually signed "Durand," with the lettering sometimes across the letter V.

Above: Art-glass, footed, baluster-form vase in shades of iridescent blue, with applied and woven threading in complementary shades. *1924–31*
9¼ in (23.5 cm) high **$700–1,000 JDJ**

KEY DATES

1870 Victor Durand Jr. is born in Baccarat, France. He joins Baccarat glassworks at the age of 12.

1884 Durand emigrates to the United States to join his father, Victor Durand Sr.

1897 Father and son take on the lease of the Vineland Glass Manufacturing Co. in Vineland, New Jersey, where they build a new kiln and diversify production.

1925 An art-glass workshop is set up at the Vineland Flint Glassworks under Martin Bach Jr. and other former Quezal employees.

1931 Durand Jr. dies in a car crash. Vineland merges with Kimble Glass Co. and art-glass production ceases.

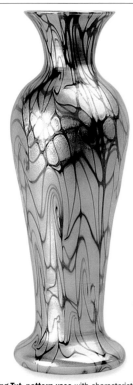

King Tut–pattern vase with characteristic coils and swirls in blue-black set against an iridescent, pink-tinged gold. *1924–31*
10 in (25.5 cm) high
$1,800–3,600 JDJ

Iridescent blue vase with a squat, bulbous base and trumpet-shaped neck. Decorated with hearts and trailing vine motifs. *1924–31*
6½ in (17 cm) high
$1,500–1,800 JDJ

Shouldered oval vase with a flared rim. Its pulled-feather decoration is in iridescent green and gold and is wrapped in applied-gold threading. *1924–31*
7¼ in (18.5 cm) high
$800–1,200 JDJ

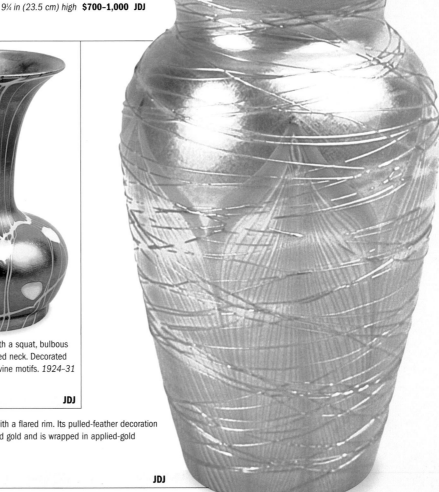

American Iridescent

The superb art glass produced by Tiffany and Quezal started the fashion for iridescent glass in the United States in the late 19th century, spawning numerous similar ranges in the early 20th century. Some were exclusive and expensive, such as those by A. Douglas Nash, a former manager at Tiffany. Other companies, such as Imperial Glass Co., developed iridescent art glass in a range of quality and price. Many other manufacturers made unmarked pieces resembling those by the leading makers. These are sometimes attributed on the basis of style, but the price should reflect this, as it should for pieces "in the Tiffany style," where there is uncertainty over the "LCT" mark.

Pair of lampshades attributed to Luster Art, with iridescent gold and green pulled-feather and creamy-white trailed decoration. The interior is iridescent gold. *Early 20th century*

6 in (15.5 cm) high

$900–1,200 (the pair)   JDJ

Pair of unsigned iridescent lampshades of lily-like form with vertical ribbing and flared, ruffled rims. The interiors are decorated with brown-gold coloring. *Early 20th century*

10 in (25 cm) high

$150–200 (the pair)   JDJ

Rare gold iridescent lamp by Douglas Nash. The shade has a shaped matching finial; the stem has multiple spherical knops. *c. 1930*

16 in (40.5 cm) high

$4,000–6,000   JDJ

Iridescent vase by Imperial with three looped handles. The body has a pulled, trailed design with an iridescent finish. *Early 20th century*

9½ in (24 cm) high

$1,200–1,500   JDJ

Jack-in-the-Pulpit vase with a pulled-feather design to the exterior and a plain gold iridescent interior. The base is signed "LCT," but it is not thought to be by Tiffany. *Early 20th century*

13½ in (35.5 cm) high

$800–1,100   JDJ

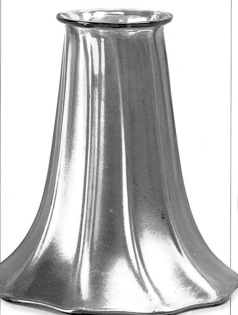

Tiffany-style gold iridescent oval vase featuring a cylindrical neck and ribbed design on the body. *Early 20th century*

8¼ in (21 cm) high

$350–500   **S&K**

Unsigned gold iridescent lampshade of lily-like form, with vertical ribbing and a flared rim with a scalloped edge. *Early 20th century*

5¼ in (13.5 cm) high

$120–180   **JDJ**

Small gold iridescent oval vase with vertical ribbing and a flared and scallop-edged top. Although unsigned, it is attributed to Kew Blas. *Early 20th century*

3 in (7.5 cm) high

$350–500   **JDJ**

Kew Blas Art Glass

The Union Glass Co. was established in 1851 in Somerville, Massachusetts. Company president Julian de Cordova modernized and re-equipped the glassworks and employed William S. Blake as factory manager. From about 1893, the glassworks began to produce two ranges of art glass. The iridescent range was called Kew Blas, an anagram of W.S. Blake, and the name is used as an engraved mark on the base. Kew Blas glass was influenced by Quezal's art-glass range (*see p.124*) and is dramatic rather than subtle, with symmetrical shapes and clearly defined feathered decoration executed in strong, brilliant colors.

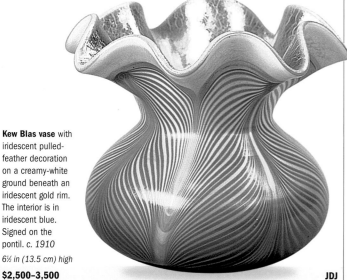

Kew Blas vase with iridescent pulled-feather decoration on a creamy-white ground beneath an iridescent gold rim. The interior is in iridescent blue. Signed on the pontil. *c. 1910*

6½ in (13.5 cm) high

$2,500–3,500   **JDJ**

Kew Blas vase with pulled-feather decoration on a creamy-white ground. The interior is iridescent gold. *c. 1910*

8¼ in (21 cm) high

$1,200–1,800   **JDJ**

Kew Blas vase with green and gold pulled-feather decoration. The inside is iridescent gold. Signed "Kew Blas" on the base. *c. 1910*

9 in (23 cm) high

$1,000–1,500   **JDJ**

KEY FACTORIES

Dugan Glass Co., Indiana, Pennsylvania (est. 1892); known as Dugan from 1895 and Diamond Glass from 1913; destroyed by fire in 1931.

Fenton Art Glass Co., Martins Ferry, Ohio (est. 1905); still active.

Imperial Glass Co., Bellaire, Ohio (1904–1985).

Millersburg glassworks, Holmes County, Ohio (est. 1909); from 1911 known as Radium Glass Co.; closed 1913.

Northwood Glass Co., Martins Ferry, Ohio (1908–1985).

CARNIVAL GLASS

The fashion for iridescent glass was not confined to the exclusive art glass produced by Louis Comfort Tiffany. From about 1908 to the late 1920s, other American manufacturers produced a range of less expensive pressed iridescent glass, sometimes called "the poor man's Tiffany," which far outsold its more exclusive namesake. Originally given names with spurious classical overtones—Etruscan, Pompeiian, Venetian Art glass—it became known as Carnival glass in the 1950s, when it had fallen out of fashion and was often given away as at fairs.

PRIME CARNIVAL GLASS

The golden age of Carnival glass was between about 1911 and 1925. At this time, the major Carnival glass manufacturers were producing a huge range that sold both in the United States and abroad. Most of the glass was hand-pressed in cast-iron molds, whose crisp, deep molding with intricate detail was a tribute to the advanced skills of the mold-makers and hand-pressers. The glass was then hand-finished. A few pieces were mold-blown. Shapes were many and varied. The ubiquitous shallow bowl was quickly pressed and then crimped, pleated, and pulled to form an

almost infinite variety of bonbon dishes, nut bowls, compotes, berry sets, banana bowls, orange bowls, footed tazzas—the list is endless— and the standard range of punch, water, and wine sets with matching tumblers was also produced. Vases ranged in size from 4-in (10-cm) bud vases to impressive 22-in (56-cm) versions; any vase over 16 in (40 cm) tall is known as a funeral vase.

Patterns included oriental motifs inspired by the Aesthetic Movement of the 1880s—dragons, peacocks, lotuses, chrysanthemums—as well as idealized landscapes, animals, plants, and flowers. Fenton had the largest range of patterns—some 150—and many manufacturers produced their own versions of successful patterns such as Grape & Cable—the most prolific Northwood design.

Prime Carnival is also found in the widest range of colors. Most popular at the time, and so readily found today, are the various shades of orange known as marigold, purple—ranging from an inky violet to a delicate amethyst—blue, and green. Pastel shades were less popular and rarer.

SECONDARY CARNIVAL

As the fashion for Carnival glass waned in the United States in the mid-1920s, manufacturers in Europe, Scandinavia, and even Argentina began to produce their own Carnival glass to supply their home markets. This so-called Secondary Carnival was still hand-pressed but with less hand finishing and was made until the late 1930s. In Great

Peacock & Grape-pattern bowl by Fenton in iridescent marigold glass (also made in blue, green, red, white, and lavender). *c. 1910* 8½ in (22 cm) wide **$90–120 BA**

KEY STYLES

Pressed-glass forms *of standard late 19th-century "fancy" tableware.*
Colors refer to base glass *rather than the iridescent overlay, the exception being marigold (orange on a clear glass base).*
Elaborate, *mostly naturalistic, patterns.*
Hand-finished *crimped, pleated, or otherwise decorative rims.*
Prime Carnival glass *is mostly unmarked, except for Northwood and some Dugan/Diamond pieces.*

Grape & Cable-pattern bowl by Fenton, in the form of a large, tazza-like centerpiece in iridescent vaseline glass. Northwood also made a version of this pattern in many colors, including cobalt blue, smo teal, lime green, and laven 1910–20s. 8¼ in (21 cm) high **$50–70 MACK**

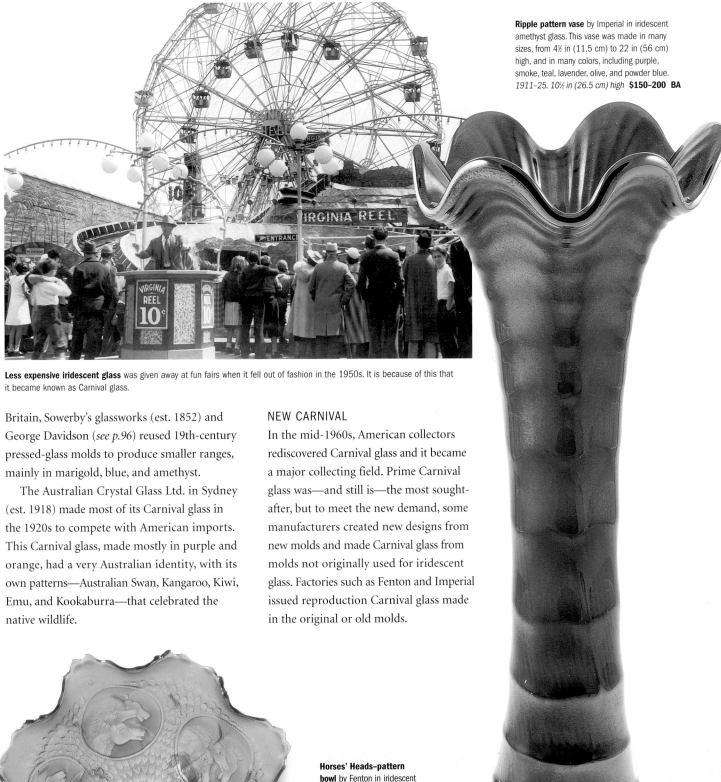

Ripple pattern vase by Imperial in iridescent amethyst glass. This vase was made in many sizes, from 4½ in (11.5 cm) to 22 in (56 cm) high, and in many colors, including purple, smoke, teal, lavender, olive, and powder blue. *1911–25. 10½ in (26.5 cm) high* **$150–200 BA**

Less expensive iridescent glass was given away at fun fairs when it fell out of fashion in the 1950s. It is because of this that it became known as Carnival glass.

Britain, Sowerby's glassworks (est. 1852) and George Davidson (*see p.96*) reused 19th-century pressed-glass molds to produce smaller ranges, mainly in marigold, blue, and amethyst.

The Australian Crystal Glass Ltd. in Sydney (est. 1918) made most of its Carnival glass in the 1920s to compete with American imports. This Carnival glass, made mostly in purple and orange, had a very Australian identity, with its own patterns—Australian Swan, Kangaroo, Kiwi, Emu, and Kookaburra—that celebrated the native wildlife.

NEW CARNIVAL

In the mid-1960s, American collectors rediscovered Carnival glass and it became a major collecting field. Prime Carnival glass was—and still is—the most sought-after, but to meet the new demand, some manufacturers created new designs from new molds and made Carnival glass from molds not originally used for iridescent glass. Factories such as Fenton and Imperial issued reproduction Carnival glass made in the original or old molds.

Horses' Heads–pattern bowl by Fenton in iridescent glass. Also known as the Horse Medallion, this pattern appeared on bowls and plates. Other colors included red rose (rare), amethyst, celeste blue, green, and white. *1912–23. 7½ in (19 cm) wide* **$100–120 BA**

Fenton

The "cheap and cheerful" range of iridized press-molded glass launched by Fenton in 1907 is now known as Carnival glass and has become one of the most popular collecting areas, with prices to match.

Fenton's original relief-molded iridescent range was inspired by Tiffany glass and is sometimes known as the "poor man's Tiffany." Pieces were produced in a range of press-molded relief designs based on animals, plants, and fruit. Fenton's staple patterns included Peacock & Grape and Dragon & Lotus; rarer patterns included Red Panther. The wide range of iridescent colors included royal blue, purple, and green—all readily found. Marigold—various shades of orange on a clear base—was one of the most popular. In the 1920s, Fenton introduced red—a technically demanding color; early red pieces

are now rare and sought-after. Fenton experimented with short runs, unusual colors and shapes, and some hand finishing, all of which have added to the appeal of its glass, as does the crisp quality of the early molds.

Such was the demand for Carnival glass in the late 1960s that from 1970, Fenton began to issue reproductions from original molds sold as a new range of Carnival glass. All New Carnival glass is marked with a script Fenton in an oval cartouche, unlike the early Carnival pieces, which are often unmarked.

Above: Panther-pattern marigold Carnival-glass bowl. This design was also produced in amethyst, blue, aqua, Nile green, red, amberina, clambroth, and lavender. *c. 1907–18. 5 in (12.75 cm) wide*
$180–200 BA

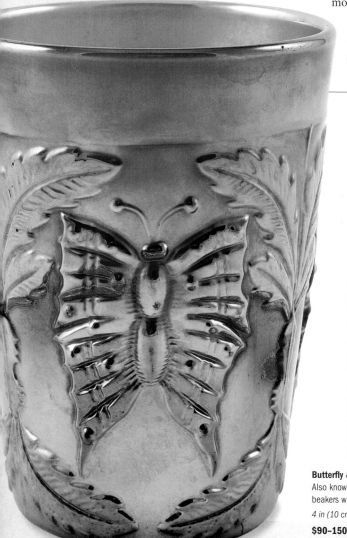

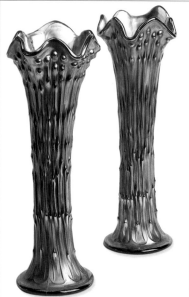

Pair of April Showers–pattern Carnival-glass vases. This design appeared in marigold, amethyst, green, cobalt blue, and white. *c. 1911–18*
14 in (35.5 cm) high
$500–700 (the pair) AOY

Butterfly & Fern–pattern amethyst Carnival-glass beaker. Also known as Butterfly & Plume, this design for jugs and beakers was also made in other colours. *c. 1907–18*
4 in (10 cm) high
$90–150 BA

Dragon & Lotus–pattern Carnival-glass bowl. Produced in many colors, this design was common for bowls, but plates are much rarer. *c. 1907–18*
8½ in (21.5 cm) wide
$200–250 BA

Stag & Holly–pattern Carnival-glass rose bowl. This design was also applied, in many colors, to spatula-footed and ball-footed bowls. *c. 1912–18*
8½ in (21.5 cm) wide
$150–200 BA

Northwood

Like its major rival Fenton, Northwood was one of the earliest and most important manufacturers of the prime, or top-quality, Carnival glass produced in the United States from about 1908 until the 1920s.

KEY DATES

1881 Harry Northwood, son of leading British glassmaker John Northwood, leaves Britain for the United States.

1887 Harry Northwood sets up Northwood Glassworks in Martin's Ferry, Ohio.

1895 Northwood relocates to Indiana, Pennsylvania.

1902 H. Northwood & Co. moves again, this time to Wheeling, West Virginia, and begins production of iridescent glass using techniques developed at British glassworks.

1908 Northwood begins producing Carnival glass, which soon becomes the factory's most popular range.

One of Northwood's most prolific and popular patterns was Grape & Cable, which appeared on more than 40 different pressed-glass items—from bowls, water jugs, and tumblers to candlesticks and hatpin holders. Skilled mold-makers and pressers produced the deeply molded, crisp patterns that were often hand-finished. Bowls with hand-crimped and wavy edges were the mainstay of Carnival glass, and Northwood's Good Luck motto-ware bowl was one of its best sellers.

Among the most popular Northwood items today are the elaborate punch-bowl sets, especially those with a full set of matching cups. Rare and sought-after are the plain flat plates that show off the elaborate pressed patterns without

distortion. The staple Northwood colors are strong cobalt blue, green, and a purple that ranges from a deep, rich hue to a pale amethyst; it is the quality of the iridescence that determines appeal, or rarer colors such as smoke, amber, and gray blue.

Northwood was the only company to mark its early Carnival glass. From about 1909, many, but not all, pieces were generally marked with an underlined capital N. This was usually set in a circle, but it occasionally appeared without a circle or within a double circle.

Above: Singing Birds–pattern green Carnival-glass beaker. Other shapes with this design include berry, water and table sets, sherbets (rare), and mugs. *c. 1908–18*
4 in (10 cm) **$120–180 BA**

Wishbone-pattern marigold Carnival-glass footed bowl. Other colors include purple, horehound, ice blue, lavender, electric blue, and lime green. *c. 1908–18*
7½ in (19 cm) wide
$100–150 BA

Grape & Cable–pattern Carnival-glass milk jug. This bestselling pattern was made in several colors and nearly 40 shapes. *c. 1910–18*
3 in (7.5 cm) high
$100–150 BA

Good Luck–pattern amethyst Carnival-glass bowl. This design is found on both plates and bowls. The latter can have pie-crust or, as here, ruffled rims and basketweave or ribbed exteriors. *c. 1908–18*
8½ in (21.5 cm) wide
$350–450 BA

133

Carnival glass

The elaborate pressed patterns and forms of Carnival glass offered an inexpensive and popular alternative to cut glass for a mass market. The Imperial Glass Company specialized in cut-glass patterns under its Nu-Cut trademark, and fancy vases and plates under its Nu-Art trademark. Other major manufacturers included the Dugan-Diamond Glass Company, known for its peach opalescent ware.

Good condition, crisp molding, elaborate patterns, and rare shapes, such as the tall "funeral" vases, all add to value. The various shades of orange, known as Marigold (or Rubigold by Imperial), were among the most popular colors and are readily found today.

Amethyst Diamond Lace–pattern water pitcher and six beakers by Imperial. This pattern was first shown in the company's 1909 catalog and was primarily used for sets. *1930s*
Pitcher: 8¾ in (22 cm) high

$500–900   **MACK**

Marigold-pattern punch bowl with a band of molded bunches of grapes near the crenellated rim and alternating molded discs and lines imitating cut glass. *1930s*
12¼ in (31 cm) wide

$100–150   **OACC**

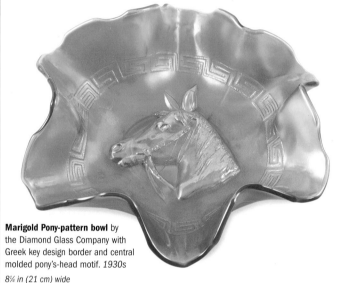

Marigold Pony-pattern bowl by the Diamond Glass Company with Greek key design border and central molded pony's-head motif. *1930s*
8¼ in (21 cm) wide

$80–100   **BA**

Rare marigold Golden Harvest-pattern decanter, possibly by the Diamond Glass Company. These were cheaper than cut-glass examples. *1920s*
12 in (30.5 cm) high

$100–150   **BA**

Green Butterflies-pattern, two-handled compote with wavy rim, by Fenton. This form is commonly found in Carnival glass, either with or without handles. *1930s*
7 in (18 cm) wide

$70–100   **BA**

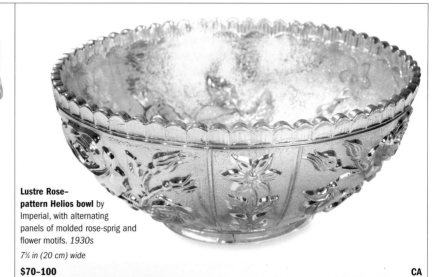

Lustre Rose–pattern Helios bowl by Imperial, with alternating panels of molded rose-sprig and flower motifs. *1930s*

7¾ in (20 cm) wide

$70–100 CA

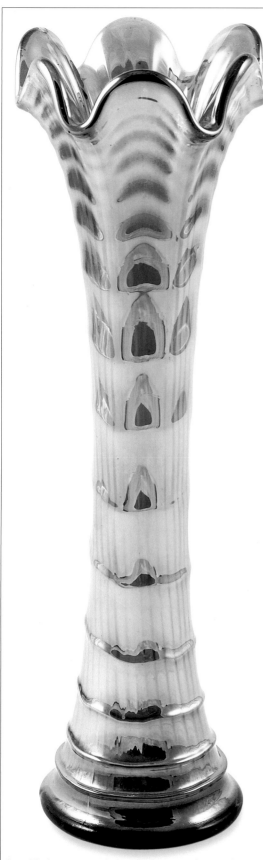

Green Ripple-pattern vase by Imperial. The organic, flowerlike form harks back to Art Nouveau styles and can be found in a range of patterns. *1920s–30s*

9 in (23 cm) high

$50–90 BA

Green Pansy-pattern amethyst nappy by Imperial, with a very good level of iridescence. A nappy is a shallow serving dish or bowl. *1930s*

6½ in (16.5 cm) wide

$100–120 BA

Marigold Kangaroo-pattern bowl with molded kangaroo motif in the center. Produced in Australia. *1920s*

5 in (12.5 cm) wide

$100–150 BA

Marigold Flower Block–pattern rose bowl with a metal liner to hold the flowers. This piece would have been made to compete with more expensive cut-glass examples. *1930s*

6 in (15 cm) wide

$250–350 BA

133

Wisteria blossom Favrile glass chandelier
with a domed drapery shade and a bronze
mount. This piece is exceptionally rare, and
there are only two other known examples in
existence. *c. 1910. 24 in (61 cm) wide*
$350,000–500,000 SL

Enameled, Painted, & Stained Glass

The urge to decorate and celebrate the colors of the
natural world seems to be as old as civilization itself.
The ancient art of enameling on glass, known from
Roman times, was explored and refined by succeeding
generations of decorators in the Islamic world, in 15th-
century Venice, and in Europe from the 16th century.
By the 1920s, enameling flourished both in exclusive
freehand-painted art glass and in a range of "cheap and
cheerful" tableware. The alternative to applying color to
glass was to incorporate it into the material itself and
exploit and enhance its natural translucence. Inspired
by the glorious colors of medieval stained-glass
windows, 20th-century American manufacturers
created miniature masterpieces of colored glass
that could be enjoyed in a domestic setting.

ENAMEL PAINTING

Decorating techniques such as enameling and painting were not exclusive to glass: they were the specialty of skilled decorators who worked in other media such as ceramics. Glass decorators used enamel paint or, more rarely, lacquer or oil paint. The last two could not be fired, so were mainly employed on pieces that were too big to fit into the low-temperature muffle kiln used to fire enamels. Paint was applied to the reverse of the piece, where it was less likely to become worn through handling. The more hard-wearing enamel colors were made from metallic oxides mixed with finely ground glass and suspended in an oily medium. The decorator applied them to the glass with a brush. The painted piece was then fired (often several times to accommodate the different colors) to remove the oiliness and fuse the colors to the glass surface.

PERFECTING THE TECHNIQUE

In the mid-15th century, enameling, a specialty of Islamic glassmakers, reached Venice, where it proved an ideal way of decorating the thin *cristallo* glass, which was too brittle for deep cutting or engraving. As the fashion waned in Venice in the late 16th century, enameling became the forte of German and Bohemian decorators, who used it on drinking vessels in particular. They refined the technique, introducing thin, transparent colored enamels that gave the appearance of watercolor, and transparent black or brown enamels (*Schwarzlot*). At the Great Exhibition in London of 1851, British, Bohemian, and French glass manufacturers showed stunning ranges of luxury art-glass vases with polychrome enameled decoration, often combined with gilding.

ART NOUVEAU DETAILING

Emile Gallé's Art Nouveau glass incorporated enameling to highlight and create detail, as did that of Daum Frères. The Daum factory also used free painterly enameling, both on its own and in combination with acid etching to create naturalistic decoration based on landscapes and more stylized detail on later ranges of Art Deco glass. Jean Luce and Marcel Goupy (*see p.138*), who were first and foremost designers rather than glassmakers, used increasingly abstract enameled decoration influenced by contemporary painting styles.

German and Bohemian 20th-century designers built on their strong traditions of decorative enameling, with members of the Wiener Werkstätte (*see p.65*) and students at the specialist State glass schools using polychrome enameling in Secessionist designs on a range of clear art glass.

ART DECO ENAMELING

By the 1920s and 30s, most glass factories were producing enameled ware. Fashionable decorative cut glass such as perfume

Daum Frères etched and enameled Winter Landscape glass vase depicting a forest of winter trees on a snowy ground against an early morning or evening sky. It is signed "Daum Nancy" with the Lorraine cross. *Early 20th century* *7¼ in (18.5 cm) high* **$15,000–20,000 MACK**

COLLECTORS' TIPS

Enameling cannot be restored, so any wear or damage will reduce its appeal.
Look for pieces that combine enameling with another interesting technique.
Designer pieces will be expensive; tableware is better priced and readily found.
Mass-produced Czech enameled Art Deco glass is reasonably priced, but lighter and less brilliant than better-quality lead glass.
Transfers usually leave an outline; these patterns tend to be less expensive than freehand designs.

Enameled clear-glass Jean Luce vase with bulbous form, hand painted with a linear and geometric pattern with panels, each containing a stylized flower. It is mounted on a cylindrical base with bands of trailed glass highlighted with blue enamel. *c. 1930* *5 in (13 cm) high* **$200–300 VZ**

Wine glass made by Theresienthaler Krystallglasfabrik (Theresienthal Crystal Glassworks). The bowl is hand-painted with stylized leaves and thorns in colored enamels, and has a slender, shaped, dark-green stem, and a foot with a gilded rim. *c. 1920. 8½ in (21.5 cm) high* **$250–350 VZ**

Below: Tiffany & Co. Crocus table lamp with mushroom-shaped leaded glass shade decorated with Art Nouveau-style crocus blossoms. Signed "TIFFANY STUDIOS NEW YORK 25904," it is mounted on a patinated bronze base with a shaped foot. *c. 1910* *23 in (58.5 cm) high* **$30,000–40,000 QU**

A stained-glass craftsman uses a hot iron to melt the metal that seals the sections of colored glass together in the panels.

bottles, vases, decanters, and dressing table sets were often enlivened with enameled transfer patterns. The technique truly came into its own on Art Deco tableware, and was ideally suited to the new "jazzy" motifs. The enameling was applied either freehand, or to transfer-printed outlines, on the newly fashionable cocktail sets and matching tumblers, decanters, the whole gamut of drinking glasses—from hand-painted elegant stemware to chunky cut-glass tumblers with geometric enameled decoration—and bowls by leading designers such as Goupy and Ludwig Kny at Stuart (*see p.166*).

Transfer-printed enameled decoration reached its peak in the 1930s. After World War II, this type of decoration was gradually replaced by new technologies, such as screen-printing.

STAINED GLASS

True stained glass is clear glass covered with a thin stain of color and then fired to fix the color—an inexpensive way of coloring glass developed and used by Bohemian glassmakers. The "stained" glass used by Louis Comfort Tiffany and other manufacturers for their lampshades and glass panels was usually small pieces of colored sheet glass with, in Tiffany's case, an almost infinite range of tones. The glass was selected and cut to shape from a design, following precise instructions, and then assembled in a metal framework. Tiffany enclosed the pieces of glass in thin strips of copper rather than lead, which were joined together to accommodate the curving shapes of his shades.

Enameled vase by Haida, the Bohemian state training school for glassmakers. The baluster form with flared rim is hand painted with an Art Nouveau stylized foliate and scrolling pattern. *c. 1910. 6½ in (16.5 cm) high* **$300–400 VZ**

Daum Frères Champignon vase of dishlike form with two handles and a heavy foot. It is etched and enameled with colored mushroom motifs on a yellow, amber, and brown graduated ground and is signed "Daum Nancy" with the Lorraine cross. *Early 20th century* *8¾ in (22.5 cm) wide* **$15,000–25,000 MACK**

KEY DATES

1919 Georges Rouard acquires the A La Paix retail outlet in Paris, which he renames Geo. Rouard, and employs Marcel Goupy to run the decorating shop.

1923 Goupy shows his designs at the first exhibition of contemporary decorative arts in Paris.

1925 Goupy is vice-president of the jury in glass at the *Exposition Internationale des Arts Décoratifs et Industriels Modernes* in Paris.

1929 Rouard dies. Goupy becomes artistic director at Geo. Rouard, a post he holds until 1954.

Marcel Goupy

A multitalented designer in a variety of media, Marcel Goupy created a distinctive series of elaborate enameled designs for a wide range of decorative tableware and art glass in the Art Deco style.

Marcel Goupy (1886–1954) was primarily a designer rather than a glassworker. He studied architecture, sculpture, and interior decoration and was also a talented painter, silversmith, and jeweler. From 1918, Goupy began to design a range of clear glass tableware that included carafes, jugs, and liqueur and lemonade sets. His attractive clean designs had simple, enameled decoration, much of which has survived in good condition as it was evenly applied and fused well with the glass.

Goupy's range expanded to include hand-blown vases and bowls, which were often decorated both inside and out. The inner enameling provided color or shading that set off the increasingly stylized motifs on the outside. The motifs included such Art Deco standards as leaping deer, repeating patterns, and figural and floral subjects. The vases offered the best surface for decoration and provided scope for complex designs in colors that were typically bright, but harmonious rather than garish.

Many of Goupy's designs were executed by August Heiligenstein (1891–1976). A talented designer in his own right, Heiligenstein was not allowed to sign his work for Goupy. Most Goupy pieces carry an enameled "M. Goupy" signature.

Above: Clear glass bowl painted around the rim with garlands of berries in red enamels with gilt highlights, over a black enamel grid. *1920s. 2½ in (6.25 cm) high* **$800–1,000 QU**

Clear glass vase painted with a landscape in shades of blue, green, and gray enamel. The rim and base have thin bands of black enameling. *1920s–30s*
7 in (18 cm) high

$6,000–8,000   **LN**

Clear glass vase of gourdlike form, with thin bands of brown and black enameling on the rim, neck, foot, and body—the latter is also painted with deer in a forest. The neck features (worn) gilding. *1920s–30s*
9¾ in (25 cm) high

$8,000–9,000   **LN**

Clear glass decanter with a club-shaped stopper, annular knops on the neck, and a teardrop body painted with sprigs of flowers, fruits, and leaves. *1920s–30s*
11 in (28 cm) high

$400–500   **L&T**

Legras & Cie

The Legras glassworks was a great commercial success. Its early cameo range in the Art Nouveau style catered for the huge market created by the popularity of the glass of Emile Gallé and Daum Frères and followed their style of enameled decoration.

At the turn of the century, the Legras glassworks employed some 150 decorators and well over 1,000 glassworkers. This workforce for the most part concentrated on following prevailing styles rather than initiating them. One of Legras's more original contributions was a range of acid-etched cameo vases and bowls with an opaque pinky-beige glass body that resembled cornelian. The other was the Indiana range, which also successfully incorporated acid-etching, cutting, and enameling. The red enameled interior surface was used to create the dramatic poppy design. The outer color casing was removed to allow the red enamel to shine through the transparent glass and create the illusion of depth.

In the 1920s and 30s, when the factory had reopened after World War I with Charles Legras as director, production concentrated on acid-etched Art Deco intaglio designs. Legras also produced a range of vases and lamps with a mottled surface that was then hand-painted with enamels. Many of the floral and landscape patterns were in the style of pieces by Daum Frères, with similar designs, as well as the technique of taking the effect of the design over the lip or rim. Most pieces are signed "Legras."

Above: Slim club-shaped vase in clear glass, polychrome-enameled with a snowy forest landscape at sunset. *c. 1910. 13½ in (34 cm) high* **$400–500 QU**

KEY DATES

1864 Auguste-Jean-François Legras acquires the Verreries et Cristalleries de Saint-Denis et des Quatre Chemins in Paris, where production centers on table and fancy glass.

1897 Legras takes over a glassworks in Pantin, Paris.

1900 Legras introduces Art Nouveau cameo glass and wins the Grand Prix at the Paris Universal Exposition.

1914 The glassworks closes for the duration of World War I.

1919 The Legras glassworks reopens as Verreries et Cristalleries de St-Denis de Pantin Réunis and continues today.

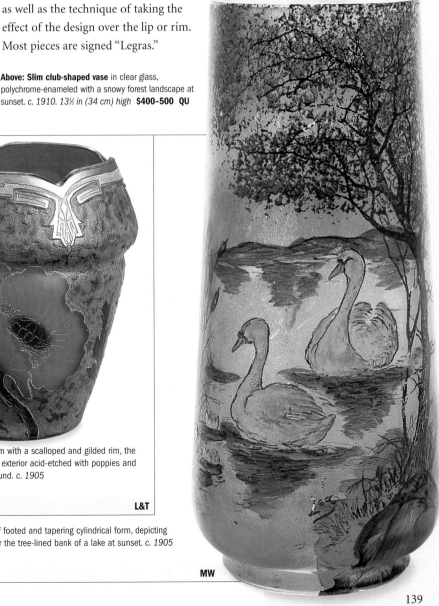

Indiana glass vase of oval form with a scalloped and gilded rim, the interior enameled red, and the exterior acid-etched with poppies and foliage on a mottled green ground. *c. 1905*

6 in (15.5 cm) high

$1,000–1,200   **L&T**

Slender clear glass vase of square and tapering form, polychrome-enameled with trees and snowy ground against a winter sunset. *c. 1900*

13¾ in (35 cm) high

$400–500   **MW**

Polychrome-enameled vase of footed and tapering cylindrical form, depicting a pair of swans swimming near the tree-lined bank of a lake at sunset. *c. 1905*

10½ in (27 cm) high

$200–300   **MW**

Daum Frères

The decorators employed by Daum Frères specialized in delicate hand-painted patterns in colored enamels and grisaille, often highlighted with gilding. Their themes were inspired by the surrounding countryside—its weather, landscape, and seasons—and the many species of plants in the company's greenhouse. This love of nature and botanical knowledge was combined with techniques such as intercalaire decoration, which trapped painted landscapes between two layers of glass, and etched, mottled, and frosted backgrounds, which enhanced the enamel details, creating atmosphere and perspective for autumnal and wintry scenes.

Tapering, opalescent, enameled bottle decorated with a seascape showing two ships in full sail. It retains its original matching spherical stopper. *1900*

8 in (20 cm) high

$1,800–2,800　　　　MW

Translucent cameo enameled vase decorated with green leaves and applied red berries. It is signed "Daum Nancy." *Early 20th century*

13¾ in (35 cm) high

$10,000–15,000　　　　JDJ

Heavily cased and textured, matt clear glass octagonal footed dish in light green, with enameled floral sprigs on the exterior. It is mounted on four rectangular feet. *c. 1900*

6¼ in (16 cm) high

$700–1,000　　　　MW

Flattened translucent vase with a rectangular rim, decorated with a scene showing trees in an open landscape at dawn in spring. *c. 1900*

6¾ in (17 cm) wide

$3,500–5,000　　　　MW

Solanées translucent and opalescent circular box with slightly domed lid. It is decorated with etched and colored flowering deadly nightshade sprigs and signed "Daum Nancy" with the cross of Lorraine. *c. 1910*

5 in (12.5 cm) wide

$1,800–3,800 QU

Coeurs de Jeanette cameo vase decorated with finely painted bleeding-heart flowers. *c. 1910*

4¾ in (12 cm) high

$2,800–3,500 QU

ADOPTING THE STYLE

The fine, highly detailed, hand-painted decoration characteristic of Daum's glass was similar to that used on ceramics, and many decorators moved easily between the two media. Typically, the enamel colors were cold-painted onto the surface of the glass and then fired. The style was adopted by other French glassworks capitalizing on the nostalgia for floral decoration.

French opalescent and yellow bowl with a wavy rim. Signed "Peynaud." *Early 20th century. 8½ in (21.5 cm) high*

$700–900 JDJ

Small Summer Scenic vase with an etched and enameled landscape scene. Signed. *Early 20th century*

3½ in (9.5 cm) high

$5,500–6,500 MACK

Bulbous vase with tapering rim and enameled scene of rose-pink flowers and leaves on a mottled, golden-yellow and brown ground. *c. 1905*

6 in (15.5 cm) high

$5,000–7,000 MW

Cameo glass vase with a bulbous base tapering into a trumpet-shaped mouth. It has an etched montbretia pattern and is enlivened with enameling. *1910*

13½ in (33.75 cm) high

$6,000–7,000 QU

A CLOSER LOOK

Limited-edition cobalt-blue plate designed by Salvador Dalí, decorated in gold enamel with a head motif in the center, surrounded by abstract designs. This image possibly represents the head of John the Baptist. It would reflect Dalí's religious background; its placement on a circular platter seems appropriate. It is signed "Daum Made in France" and numbered "151/2000." *c. 1980. 10¼ in (26 cm) wide* **$600–800** JDJ

Gold-enamel head motif

Abstract designs around edge

Central European Painted & Enameled

The strong German and Bohemian enameling tradition established in the mid-16th century continued into the 20th century. The transparent colored enamels first used on Biedermeier beakers became a distinctive feature of the Art Nouveau and Art Deco drinking glasses produced by Theresienthal (est. 1836), Moser, J. & L. Lobmeyr (est. 1823), and Meyr's Neffe (est. 1841).

Members of the Wiener Werkstätte (*see p.65*) used enameling as part of their decorative repertoire. At state glass schools, enameled designs were created in new styles featuring both bright colors and black highlighted with gold.

Clear glass footed bowl made in Haida, with a gilded rim, a floral centerpiece, and arabesque borders. *1910-20*

8 in (20 cm) wide

$500–600   QU

Haida covered and footed clear glass bowl, decorated with thin bands of gilding and a silhouette frieze of children engaged in playful pursuits. *c. 1910*

7½ in (19 cm) high

$250–300   DN

Conical vase made in Steinschönau in clear blown glass. It is faceted around the base, painted with a hunting scene in black and gold enamel, and has a gilded rim. *c. 1915*

4¼ in (11 cm) high

$800–1,000   VS

Pair of goblet-shaped vases from the Wiener Werkstätte in clear glass. Painted by Vally Weisenthiel with bands of blue and red enamel, interspersed with stylized polychrome floral motifs. *1910-20*

8¼ in (21 cm) high

$18,000–24,000   LN

Wiener Werkstätte drinking glass with a clear-glass, trumpet-shaped bowl showing a battle scene in polychrome enamels. *1917*

7¼ in (18.5 cm) high

$1,200–1,500 QU

Circular lidded bowl made in Steinschönau, in clear glass with thin bands of black enameling and a risqué silhouette of a lady and dog against a garden landscape. *c. 1915*

3¾ in (9.5 cm) wide

$300–500 FIS

Meyr's Neffe wine glass designed by Otto Prutscher, in clear glass with selective faceting. The rim features enameled olive motifs. *c. 1910*

8¼ in (21.25 cm) high

$7,500–8,500 QU

Glass beaker from the Artel group in Prague. Its clear glass body depicts a church, animal grotesques, and arabesques. *1908–25*

4 in (10.5 cm) high

$1,500–2,000 FIS

Clear glass bowl made in Steinschönau, with a band of stylized flower-heads and scrolling foliage, in black, blue, and green enamels, and with gilding to the base and rim. *c. 1915*

5½ in (13.5 cm) wide

$300–500 FIS

Haida footed cup with domed lid and ball finial. The clear and honey-yellow glass is painted with stylized floral motifs in blue, green, yellow, and black enamels. *c. 1920*

10½ in (26.5 cm) high

$3,000–4,000 FIS

Fritz Heckert iridescent vase designed by Willy Meitzen with enameled butterflies and flowering plants and tendrils heightened with gilding. Signed "F.H. 537/6 M. 66." *c. 1900*

8¾ in (22 cm) high

$500–600   **QU**

Haida vase designed by Karl John. The clear glass is internally decorated in subtle colors and depicts a flying fish and a dragonfly. Signed "Jonolith." *c. 1930*

6 in (15 cm) high

$800–1,000   **FIS**

Silesian small vase by Josephinenhütte. The blue glass is decorated in colorful enamels, and a bird is shown resting on golden stylized flowering stems that are surrounded by butterflies. *1920s*

4¼ in (10.5 cm) high

$400–700   **VS**

Moser of Karlsbad vase of clear glass that is tinted green at the base. Engraved with flowering stems applied with green and blue stained-glass florets. Signed. *c. 1905*

9¼ in (23.5 cm) high

$2,700–3,600   **VZ**

Fritz Heckert enameled twin-handled vase designed by Max Rade. Decorated in naturalistic colors with fruiting branches and a formal border around the base. Signed "5826 MR." *c. 1900*

4¾ in (12 cm) high

$500–600   **FIS**

Meyr's Neffe hock glass with the clear bowl enameled with red and blue floral decoration and gilding, on a green stem. *c. 1910*

5¾ *in (14 cm) high*

$250–350   **BMN**

Meyr's Neffe hock glass with the clear bowl enameled with pastel floral decoration and gilding, on a green stem. *c. 1910*

5¾ *in (14 cm) high*

$250–350   **BMN**

Meyr's Neffe hock glass with the clear bowl enameled with blue floral decoration and gilding, on a green stem. *c. 1910*

5¾ *in (14 cm) high*

$300–400   **BMN**

Meyr's Neffe champagne glass enameled with stylized flowers and leaves. It has a gilded rim and a knopped stem. *c. 1905*

8¾ *in (22.5 cm) high*

$1,000–1,500   **QU**

Meyr's Neffe glass with the bell-shaped bowl engraved and enameled with floral decoration, and with a knopped green stem. *c. 1900*

8 *in (20.5 cm) high*

$250–350   **BMN**

Theresienthal enameled hock glass painted with an open flower-head and supported on a green stem. *Early 20th century*

8½ *in (21.5 cm) high*

$250–350   **DN**

A CLOSER LOOK

Fritz Heckert ovoid iridescent vase designed by Willy Meitzen with enamelled butterflies and flowering plants and tendrils heightened with gilding; signed "F.H. 537/6 M. 66". *c. 1900.* 8¾ *in (22 cm) high*

$540–630   QU

Motifs from the natural world are characteristic of the Art Nouveau style; butterflies were particularly popular

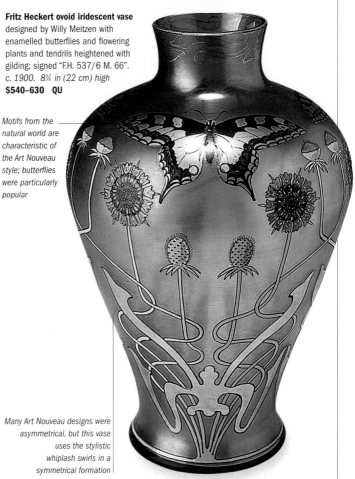

Many Art Nouveau designs were asymmetrical, but this vase uses the stylistic whiplash swirls in a symmetrical formation

Handel Reverse-Painted Lamps

The rapid spread of domestic electricity in the late-19th-century United States created a burgeoning market for lighting, which Handel met with a range of highly decorative reverse-painted lamps in multiple styles.

The Handel Company was primarily a decorating workshop. The casting shop created plaster molds of the shades, which were then made up by glassmaking companies and returned to Handel for the all-important decoration, which still determines appeal and value. The shades were made in various shapes—cone, dome, hemispherical, cylindrical, and loaf-shaped for desk lamps. One of the most popular was the 18-in- (46-cm-) diameter domed shade made for table lamps. The shades had different textured surfaces—the "chipped ice" effect that diffused the light so well was particularly successful.

Handel designers produced a master watercolor for the decoration, with very specific directions on color.

These directions would then be executed on the inside of the shade. Designs ranged from standard and readily found all-over patterns of flowers and autumn leaves, to butterflies and colorful exotic birds such as macaws and flamingos. Two other popular themes were landscapes and seascapes, both local and familiar, as well as the more exotic and collectible featuring Egyptian scenes, Dutch windmills, and tropical islands.

Shades usually have a painted mark on the bottom of the inside of the shade with the four-figure design number. Some also have a designer's mark. From 1910, shades usually included an impressed "Handel Lamps" mark and a patent number on the metal rim at the top of the shade.

Above: Table lamp with a domed shade reverse-painted with a river-and-fields landscape on a pinky-orange sunset ground, above a bulbous base. *1903–30. 23½ in (60 cm) high* **$6,000–8,000 JDJ**

REVERSE-PAINTING

Reverse-painting was the technique used by American lamp manufacturers who hand-painted the insides of their glass lampshades. The original watercolor design was transferred to steel engraving plates. A piece of thin tissue paper was then placed over the plates, and the pattern was traced using tiny holes made with a fine metal point. The tissue was placed on the inside of the shade and the pattern was transferred using a swab dipped in charcoal. The decorator then completed the outline and applied the color following the detailed instructions on the master design.

Table lamp with a domed shade reverse-painted with a tropical landscape under a setting sun. The four-footed, baluster-form base retains a little of its original copper finish. *1903–36 22½ in (57 cm) high* **$9,000–12,000 JDJ**

THE REVERSE-PAINTING TECHNIQUE

Desk lamp with a bronze-tone adjustable base, supporting a shade that is reverse-painted with a tropical coastal scene. *1920s*

14½ in (37 cm) high

$2,000–2,800   **JDJ**

Domed-shade table lamp reverse-painted shade with a rural landscape of architectural ruins among trees. *1910–30*

27 in (69 cm) high

$5,000–8,000   **AAC**

Table lamp with a domed shade reverse-painted with yellow daffodils and green foliage, above a cylindrical base. *1904–30*

23 in (58.5 cm) high

$10,000–13,000   **JDJ**

Hexagonal-shade table lamp with two sides reverse-painted showing a knight jousting on horseback within a floral border. *1904–30*

20½ in (52 cm) high

$2,800–4,500   **JDJ**

Table lamp with a domed shade reverse-painted with a rural landscape of woods, fields, and water under streaking clouds and a full moon. The bronze-painted base is embossed. *1904–30*

24 in (61 cm) high

$8,000–9,000   **JDJ**

Octagonal-shade table lamp reverse-painted with a border of roses, stems, and leaves in pink, green, and brown. *1910–36*

22 in (56 cm) high

$4,500–5,500   **JDJ**

Teroma table lamp with a domed shade, reverse-painted with oak leaves, branches, and acorns in browns and greens on a "chipped ice" ground. The dark patinated bronze base features acorn pulls. *1904–36*

22½ in (57 cm) high

$4,500–5,500   **JDJ**

Reverse-Painted Lamps

In the late 19th century, domestic use of electricity was spreading across the United States, and glassmakers were inspired to design shades that would be enhanced by the new technology. They were produced by several manufacturers, including the Miller and Jefferson companies and the Phoenix Glassworks, in a variety of shapes and designs using the reverse-painting technique associated with leading producers such as Handel (*see p.146*). When the lamp was switched on, the hand-painted design sprang to life, while textured outer surfaces diffused the light. The lamp bases were an integral part of the design, and unusual or figural designs are particularly prized.

Unsigned reverse-painted American lampshade showing a log cabin in a snow-covered rural landscape, in white and shades of gray, brown, and orange. *1920s–40s*

6 in (15 cm) wide

$700–900 JDJ

Phoenix glass table lamp with a reverse-painted nocturnal rural landscape. The base is embossed with flower and leaf motifs. *1930s–40s*

22 in (56 cm) high

$300–500 JDJ

Moe Bridges lamps favor landscape scenes, usually with a water element

This large shade offers a good landscape perspective

Pair of Jefferson mantle lamps with cylindrical shades, reverse-painted with views across land and out to sea at sunset. *1910–30*

15½ in (39.5 cm) high

$1,000–1,800 JDJ

Jefferson "boudoir" lamp with a domed shade reverse-painted with poppies and foliage on a yellow ground. *1910–30*

8 in (20.25 cm) high

$700–1,000 JDJ

Moe Bridges table lamp with a reverse-painted rural-landscape shade, supported on a copper-colored metal base. *1910–30*

22½ in (57 cm) high

$3,500–5,000 JDJ

Table lamp with domed shade reverse-painted by A. Frederick with grazing elk. A moose stands at the base. *1910–30*

12 in (30.5 cm) high

$6,000–8.000 JDJ

Pairpoint

The Pairpoint Corporation (1880–1958) of New Bedford, Massachusetts, was one of the leading manufacturers of reverse-painted glass lampshades. It produced a range of high-quality scenic shades, ribbed designs such as those shown here, and a blown range known as Puffy table lampshades, with floral decoration in high relief. Typically, Pairpoint bases were made in a variety of metals, including copper, bronze, and silver plate. The design of the base usually complemented the shade (*see bottom center*), but customers could choose from a selection of interchangeable models. Pairpoint shades and bases are usually signed, and marks sometimes include those of the designer.

Table lamp with a domed shade depicting a church in a rural landscape by A. Fox. The base has a brass-trimmed foot. *1910–30*
24 in (61 cm) high
$3,500–4,500   JDJ

Domed-shade table lamp reverse-painted by C. Durand with a Roman temple surrounded by water and trees. *1900–20*
22 in (56 cm) high
$4,000–6,500   JDJ

Table lamp with a bronze-patinated base of Neo-Classical form, supporting a shade reverse-painted with men and a horse in a landscape of trees, rivers, and mountains. *1910–30*
22 in (56 cm) high
$5,000–8,000   JDJ

Florence table lamp with a silver-plated base. The shade features chrysanthemums and foliage. *1905–20*
21 in (53.5 cm) high
$8,000–12,000   JDJ

Table lamp with a reverse-painted shade showing clippers at sea. The wooden base has three fish supports. *1920s–30s*
20½ in (52 cm) high
$4,500–5,500   POOK

Reverse-painted Florence table lamp with stylized floral motifs. The base is silver-plated. *1905–20*
19½ in (49.5 cm) high
$4,500–5,500   JDJ

American Stained-Glass Lighting

With the advent of domestic electric lighting, Louis Comfort Tiffany was able to fulfill his desire to bring beauty into the average home with his stained-glass lamps that inspired similar ranges from other American manufacturers.

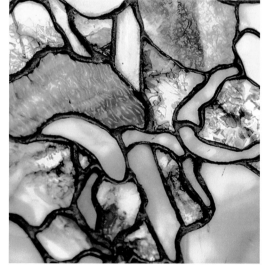

Tiffany's experiments with new formulas for colored glass resulted in a range of some 5,000 different colors that were used from the 1890s, when Tiffany lamps first emerged, until the 1930s, when the company closed. Where Tiffany led, others followed, and companies such as Handel (*see p.146*), Pairpoint (*see p.149*), and Duffner & Kimberly (1905–11) also produced stained-glass light fixtures, although their glass never quite matched the quality of Tiffany's. The table-lamp designs gradually increased in complexity. Early geometric patterns were regular and symmetrical, often in just one or a few colors, and could be

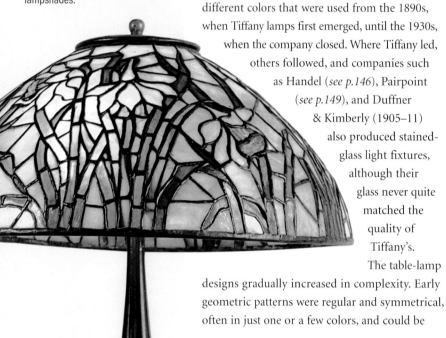

assembled on a wooden mold by most skilled craftsmen following a detailed pattern. These patterns were gradually embellished with flower borders and belts and scattered flowers, often with irregular lower borders. The "natural" designs—with all-over flower, tree, or shrub patterns, or incorporating insects—demanded greater expertise, in both assembly and choice of glass. The finest stained lampshades are inspired and original paintings in glass. They present a dazzling array of color and texture and have eclectic upper and lower borders.

Stained-glass ceiling fixtures were often more utilitarian, with the marked exception, of course, of the large cone-shaped shades. These offered a broad surface for the all-important and elaborate designs.

Above: Tiffany Lily-Pad table lamp on which the lily-pad design is picked out in light blue and light and dark green. The bronze lily-pad base has four feet. *c. 1910*
25¼ in (64 cm) high **$70,000–100,000 QU**

USE OF COLOR

Stained-glass designs were a combination of science and artistry. The aim was to reproduce the subtle play of light, color, shade, tone, and texture found in nature. Skilled colorists recreated these effects using fibrillated and striated glass for the sky, rippled glass for the sheen on a dragonfly wing, and fractured glass for a sunset or a flower. Colors were also dependent on reflected light—from an outside source such as daylight—and transmitted light from the light bulb. A flick of a switch could change purple to red, blue to brown, and green to yellow.

Tiffany Daffodil table lamp with the shade decorated with yellow daffodils on a green and cream background. Signed "TIFFANY STUDIOS NEW YORK 1449-2," mounted on a base marked "Handel." *Early 20th century. 22 in (56 cm) high* **$25,000–40,000 JDJ**

DETAIL OF TIFFANY NASTURTIUM TRELLIS LAMP (OPPOSITE)

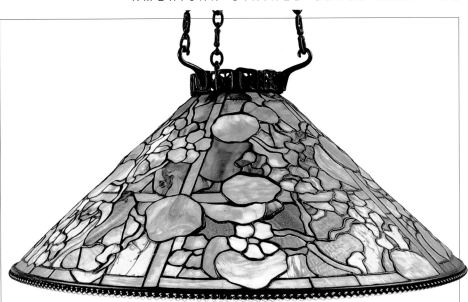

Rare Tiffany Nasturtium Trellis, confetti-glass shade with the popular trellis-and-nasturtium pattern on a blue-gray background. It has a beaded bronze rim, and is marked "TIFFANY STUDIOS NEW YORK." *Early 20th century*

28 in (71 cm) wide

$90,000–120,000 JDJ

Tiffany table lamp with a leaded green-and-white hemispherical shade mounted on a base in the form of an urn supported by three arms. Signed. *c. 1900*

21¾ in (55 cm) high

$10,000–15,000 VZ

Tiffany Studios dome-shaped leaded shade with squares and triangles of mottled green and yellow glass and leading with verdigris. Stamped "TIFFANY STUDIOS." *Early 20th century*

16 in (40.5 cm) wide

$8,000–12,000 DRA

Tiffany Poinsettia table lamp with a shade of variegated red, amber, green, and blue poinsettias on a green ground. Signed "TIFFANY STUDIOS NEW YORK 1558." *Early 20th century*

26 in (66 cm) high

$70,000–100,000 JDJ

Tiffany Zodiac table lamp with an angular leaded shade containing mottled, green geometric glass panels. The base has a molded zodiac pattern. *Early 20th century*

16½ in (42 cm) high

$10,000–13,000 JDJ

Tiffany standard lamp with a geometric green-white and amber-white leaded shade mounted on a tall base with molded spiraling foliate arabesques. Signed "TIFFANY STUDIOS NEW YORK" and "Tiffany/New York/230." *c. 1905*

81¼ in (203 cm) high

$150,000–200,000 VZ

Handel stained and leaded hanging shade of domed form with everted rim and an abstract, brightly colored floral pattern. Signed with factory mark. *Early 20th century*

20½ in (52 cm) wide

$1,200–1,800   **L&T**

Handel stained and leaded hanging shade of hemispherical form with an all-over floral design made up of triangular sections. Signed with factory mark. *Early 20th century*

12 in (30.5 cm) wide

$700–1,000   **L&T**

Leaded glass table lamp with a bamboo-pattern shade. Possibly by Suess. *Early 20th century*

25 in (63.5 cm) high

$1,500–2,000   **JDJ**

Handel table lamp with leaded shade. The skirt border has a floral design. Mounted on a baluster base. Signed. *Early 20th century*

24 in (61 cm) high

$2,500–4,000   **JDJ**

Large leaded table lamp with an all-over daisy-and-leaf-pattern shade. Mounted on a bronze base of tree-trunk appearance. Probably by Suess. *Early 20th century*

31 in (78.5 cm) high

$10,000–15,000   **JDJ**

Good, Better, Best

The colors of the shade and the complexity of its design, as well as the form and design of the base, are what determine the value of American stained-glass table lamps. A well-known maker adds value, with Tiffany being the most sought-after.

$3,600–4,500

With a stepped green floral shade and a basic four-legged base, this **early 20th-century table lamp**, attributed to The Suess Ornamental Glass Co., is a good example of the style. *22 in (56 cm) high* **JDJ**

$7,000–10,000

Attributed to Gorham, this **early 20th-century table lamp** has garlands of oak leaves and acorns encircling the shade, and a flared rim. The base has a tree-trunk appearance. *20 in (51 cm) high* **JDJ**

$10,000–13,000

Made by the desirable company Duffner & Kimberly in the early 20th century, the complex design, variety of colors in the umbrella-shaped shade, and bronze stand with four paw feet make this **leaded glass lamp** a sought-after piece. *21 in (53.5 cm) high* **JDJ**

Spherical leaded ceiling shade comprising six curved and shaped slag-glass panels and with a crown-shaped finial. Attributed to Duffner & Kimberly. *Early 20th century*

22 in (55.5 cm) high

$1,500–2,000   JDJ

American conical leaded shade with skirt and alternating facets of pink flowers on a green foliate background and mottled green, purple, and white abstract designs. *Early 20th century*

24½ in (62 cm) wide

$1,500–2,000   SL

Unusual Prairie School bronze lantern with four frosted, leaded glass panels with amber "Glasgow roses." *Early 20th century*

12 in (30.5 cm) high

$2,800–3,500   CR

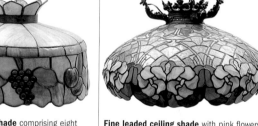

Jeweled and leaded hanging shade of tapering form, with a skirt featuring red jewels in a Greek key design. *Early 20th century*

21¾ in (55 cm) wide

$300–500   JDJ

Leaded hanging shade comprising eight bent-glass panels with a fruit-and-foliate design on a green ground. *Early 20th century*

8 in (20.5 cm) wide

$300–500   JDJ

Fine leaded ceiling shade with pink flowers on a brown-and-tan background. Attributed to Duffner & Kimberly. *Early 20th century*

22 in (55.5 cm) wide

$12,000–18,000   JDJ

Fine leaded table lamp with a complex, oval-and-circular design on the shade. Attributed to Duffner & Kimberly. *Early 20th century*

23½ in (59.5 cm) high

$7,000–10,000   JDJ

Handel Hawaiian Sunset table lamp with a shade featuring palm trees and tropical vegetation. Signed. *Early 20th century*

24½ in (62 cm) high

$18,000–25,000   JDJ

Handel Apple Blossom leaded shade with a skirt of mottled lavender and pink flowers amid green foliage. *Early 20th century*

25½ in (64.5 cm) high

$5,000–8,000   SL

American table lamp with a leaded shade of mint-green tiles and a floral-design skirt. It has an urn-form bronze base. *Early 20th century*

22 in (56 cm) high

$4,500–6,500   SL

Stained-Glass Panels

Stained-glass panels were very popular in the early 20th century, when they were used as part of the design of many homes. The panels were positioned to make the best use of natural light or were set into screens that could be directed toward the sun. Designers such as Louis Comfort Tiffany, Charles Rennie Mackintosh, and Alphonse Mucha all designed glass panels, but many unknown and unnamed factories and designers also made them.

From the mid-20th century, glass panels went out of fashion. However, designers are now using them again, and original early 20th-century examples are becoming more collectible.

CHARLES RENNIE MACKINTOSH

Scottish designer Charles Rennie Mackintosh (1868–1928) incorporated stained-glass panels into his designs. The effect of light on the glass suited the contrast between the "light-feminine" and "dark-masculine" rooms he designed at his own home and for commissions. At the Ingram Street Tea Rooms in Glasgow, for example, Mackintosh used a wooden screen with leaded glass inserts to separate the hallway from the White Dining Room, allowing visitors to glimpse the room before they entered it.

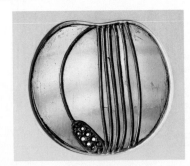

Detail of stained-glass panel designed by Mackintosh, showing a stylized floral design.

American arched window with stained and painted glass panels including one with George Washington bust, with spouting dolphin and spewing dragon side panels. *Early 20th century*

54 in (137 cm) high

$2,000–3,500   NA

Stained and leaded window with frosted crackle glass stained with flowers on both the front and back to give a 3-D effect; the bordered design is set with faceted jewels. *Early 20th century*

37½ in (95.5 cm) high

$8,000–10,000   JDJ

One of a pair of stained glass windows, probably British, with a stylized yellow butterfly between two red Glasgow roses. *Early 20th century*

38 in (96.5 cm) wide

$600–700 (the pair)   FRE

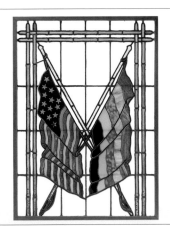

American leaded stained glass window featuring an American flag and the five-color flag of the Republic of China (1912–28); the frame is not original. *Early 20th century*

44 in (112 cm) high

$1,200–1,500   CHAA

La Plume, a stained glass and painted leaded glass panel *after the original design by Art Nouveau graphic designer Alphonse Mucha. c. 1900*

39 in (99 cm) square

$2,000–3,500   L&T

155

Poured-Glass Jewelry

The fragile luminosity of poured-glass jewelry has attracted fashion designers and followers for more than a century. Today, the same techniques are being used to create these handmade works of art for the body.

In the early 20th century, a number of Parisian factories diversified from making poured-glass buttons and beads to create jewelry. The technique—also known as *pâte-de-verre*—involved mixing crushed glass with colored metal oxides before being molded and fired. The glass components were often set in metal wire, which formed part of the setting.

One company that became renowned for its poured-glass jewelry was Maison Gripoix, which started making inexpensive copies of the flamboyant Art Nouveau pieces worn by the actress Sarah Bernhardt. The company was commissioned to make pieces for designers such as Piguet, and by the 1920s, Coco Chanel was among their clients. Gripoix also worked with Yves Saint Laurent, Balmain, Worth, and Christian Dior, for whom it made signature lily-of-the-valley pieces.

Gripoix also made—and continues to make—handmade poured-glass jewelry under its own name. Since the 1990s, these have been marked Histoire de Verre. Pieces often feature crystal rhinestone highlights and pearls.

In the late 1990s, a group of four former Gripoix workers set up L'Atelier de Verre, making poured-glass pieces in a similar style. The company was bought by Chanel in 2003.

Other jewelers who produced poured-glass pieces include New York-based Miriam Haskell, who used French poured-glass beads in her hand-wired jewelry, and costume jewelry designers Cristobal, who incorporated poured glass into their Secret Garden collection in the late 1990s.

Maison Gripoix poured-glass necklace with red berries and green leaves. *1980s* *17¾ in (45 cm) circ* **$700–1,000 RITZ**

Maison Gripoix poured-glass flower pin, petals and leaves set in gilt wire. *c. 2001* *2¾ in (7 cm) wide* **$300–500 RITZ**

Histoire de Verre poured-glass flower necklace and earrings highlighted with rhinestones. *1990s. Earrings: 2¼ in (5.75 cm) wide* **$1,200–1,800 CRIS**

Histoire de Verre poured-glass leaf-motif necklace set in gold-plated brass wire. *1990s* *19 in (48.25 cm) circ* **$300–500 CRIS**

L'Atelier de Verre poured-glass earrings with rhinestones in gold-plated settings. *c. 2000* *2¼ in (5.5 cm) long* **$300–500 SUM**

L'Atelier de Verre poured-glass flower pin in gold-plated metal with rhinestones. *c. 2000* *2½ in (6.5 cm) long* **$500–600 SUM**

L'Atelier de Verre poured-glass flower necklace with faux pearls and rhinestones. *c.2000. 16 in (41 cm) circ* **$500–600 SUM**

Maison Gripoix for Chanel poured-glass flower necklace and earrings with gold-plated links. *c. 1930. Earrings: ¾ in (2 cm) wide* **$2,000–3,000 CRIS**

Chanel couture poured-glass bracelet, the glass set in gilded metal. *1950s* *6¾ in (17 cm) long* **$3,000–4,000 WAIN**

Maison Gripoix for Chanel poured-glass dragon pin with gold-plated wire frame. *1940s* *4¼ in (10.5 cm) wide* **$400–600 RITZ**

Rare Chanel poured-glass peacock pin with pavé-set clear-crystal rhinestones. *1930s* *5½ in (14 cm) long* **$3,000–5,000 BY**

Miriam Haskell poured-glass flower necklace and earrings with glass beads and rhinestones. *c. 1950. Earrings: 1¼ in (3 cm) long* **$1,800–2,400 SUM**

Miriam Haskell poured-glass flower pin with faux pearls and rose montée. *c. 1940* *4 in (10 cm) long* **$1,200–1,500 SUM**

Cristobal poured-glass bouquet-of-flowers pin with rhinestones in a brass wire frame. *Late 1990s. 3½ in (9 cm) high* **$500–700 CRIS**

Deep Water clear and cobalt blue glass cased vase made by Waterford. The body is engraved and cut with a swordfish swimming among rising bubbles and water plants.
c. 1960. 8¾ in (22 cm) high **$350–500 JH**

Engraved & Cut Glass

Engraving and cutting are "cold" techniques, used once the glass has cooled. Both involve using a tool to create a design on the surface of glass; the difference is largely the depth of the cuts. Engraving is shallow and can be done with a flint, diamond, needle, or small copper wheels. The engraver holds the piece under the wheel and presses up against it, using a series of wheels, fed with water and an abrasive, to produce the design.

To create cut glass, the piece is held above the wheel and pressed down onto robust stone or iron wheels, again fed with water and an abrasive, to cut the design. The wheels come in different sizes and with a choice of profiles to create flat facets, V-shaped grooves, and shallow depressions. Skilled glass-cutters combine these three basic cuts into a variety of patterns. The cut glass is then polished to create a prismatic surface that reflects light.

THE WHEEL-ENGRAVING TECHNIQUE

Although Roman glassmakers used shallow wheel-engraving on their glass, the technique fell out of favor in the 15th century, when the fashion for Venetian *cristallo* glass, better suited to diamond-point engraving, was at its height. Wheel-engraving was revived in the 16th century by a gem engraver at the Prague court of Emperor Rudolph II. It flourished in Bohemia thanks to the use of water power instead of foot power to drive the wheel, and the development of a robust, hard, and brilliant glass that was ideally suited to both intaglio (*Tiefschnitt*, or under the surface) and relief (*Hochschnitt*, or proud of the surface) designs. Skilled Bohemian engravers emigrated to other European glassmaking centers, taking their engraving and cutting skills with them.

DIAMOND-POINT AND STIPPLE ENGRAVING

These techniques, both produced using a diamond stylus, were initially developed for use on brittle Venetian *cristallo* glass and the Dutch *façon de Venise* glass it inspired. With diamond-point engraving, a popular amateur pastime, the design is made up of hundreds of minute, shallow scratches.

A glassworker in Prague engraves a glass plaque using a rapidly spinning wheel to cut the design into the surface of the panel. The Czech Republic has a long-standing tradition of engraving and cutting.

With stipple engraving, a more technically demanding 17th-century technique revived and given new impetus in the 20th century by such designers as Laurence Whistler (b. 1912), the design is built up from hundreds of shallow dots or stipples, which can be applied to both the front and back of the glass.

BOHEMIAN CUTTING

The golden age of cut glass followed the development of hard brilliant potash glass in Bohemia and, in 1676, George Ravenscroft's soft, heavy-bodied, and brilliant lead glass in Britain.

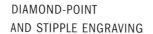

Saint-Louis ruby-red cased glass vase, the ovoid body cut with arcs of spots that reflect in the surfaces, giving an optical effect. It was made for the 250th anniversary of the Saint-Louis Glassworks and has an acid stamp on the base. *1982. 15¼ in (39 cm) high* **$500–800 JH**

COLLECTORS' TIPS

Cased cut glass is rarer than uncased.
Engraved surfaces cannot be restored, so check carefully for flaws; light scratches on cut surfaces can be polished out.
Pieces by well-known British participants in the Harrods exhibition command top prices, as does the work of Keith Murray.
Smaller glassworks offer modestly priced examples of the Scandinavian style.
Good, bold Art Deco design can be as important as attribution.

Webb Corbett decanter attributed to John Webb and cut with an all-over design of squares and loops. It has its original factory label and stopper and was made for the export market. *c. 1940. 13½ in (34 cm) high* **$500–800 JH**

Ariel glass vase by Edvin Öhrström for Orrefors. It has an internal design of a woman examining a flower and swirling patterns in pink-purple glass. It is heavily cased in clear glass. *1938. 6¼ in (16 cm) high* **$20,000–30,000 LN**

Both were ideally suited to deeper, more elaborate cutting. At the Great Exhibition of 1851 at Crystal Palace in London, Bohemian glassworks showed their cased, colored, and cut glass, to great acclaim, and a second generation of Bohemian craftsmen was encouraged to migrate to other glassmaking centers.

ENGRAVED AND CUT STYLES

In the early years of the 20th century, many glassworks were still producing traditional heavily cut 19th-century variations of "prickly monstrosities" alongside Art Nouveau–inspired designs. The major shift in style followed the *Exposition Internationale des Arts Décoratifs et Industriels Modernes* in Paris in 1925, the showcase for the new Art Deco style. Here, the Swedish designers swept the board with their stunning engraved exhibition pieces (*see p.174*); they continued to dominate the field of engraved glass with an increasingly modern range that combined clear glass with matt engraving, using contemporary motifs.

This highly influential Scandinavian style was disseminated through a series of touring exhibitions and influenced a whole generation of British and American designers. It may also have influenced the artists who took part in the Harrods Modern Art for the Table exhibition in 1934 (*see p.164*). Scandinavian designers also pioneered such innovative use of cut and engraved decoration as the Ariel and Graal techniques (*see p.177*) and, in the 1950s, abstract cutting and engraving on clear glass that launched another influential style (*see Karhula-Iittala, p.49*).

BOLD EUROPEAN DESIGNS

Continental glassworks embraced the Art Deco style as they had the Art Nouveau, and moved smoothly between the two. French and Belgian glassworks with a strong tradition of cut glass, such as the Saint-Louis Glassworks (est. 1767), Baccarat (est. 1764), and Val Saint-Lambert (*see p.162*), produced clear and colored cut pieces with strong abstract geometric designs on quintessentially Deco forms, as did the designers of the Wiener Werkstätte (*see p.65*). Daum produced a stunning range of cut and engraved glass in new bold shapes and pastel colors, using acid-etching to produce the fashionable frosted ground.

TRADITIONAL LINES

British glassworks remained for the most part deeply conservative. They clung to the heavy cutting associated with perennially popular traditional designs or produced an uneasy mix of Art Nouveau and Art Deco. Many of the Stourbridge factories, with a strong tradition of cutting, were more adventurous, in particular Stuart (*see p.166*), where Ludwig Kny developed a distinctive cutting style and designs, Webb Corbett (*see p.168*), and the shining star of Keith Murray at Royal Brierley (*see p.169*). However, even these enlightened companies maintained their traditional cut and engraved ranges and, in the absence of determined designers, often abandoned their modern lines in the 1960s and 70s.

Val Saint-Lambert tall cased vase cut with vertical bands and a section of horizontal step cutting. The rim has an applied silver band with a stamped "800" mark for Belgian silver. *1930s 10 in (25.5 cm) high* **$2,500–4,000 MAL**

Rare vase designed by David Hammond for Webb, with alternating panels of miter cut and engraved leaf motifs, marked "Webbs England." This is pattern number 52873/52563 and is a rare design. *1950s. 8½ in (21.5 cm) high* **$800–1,200 JH**

Daum Frères Art Deco-style vase in pale green glass. The near-spherical form is deeply cut with vertical fluting flanked by circular, concave cut panels against a frosted ground. It is signed "Daum Nancy France" near the base. *1930s. 7¾ in (19.5 cm) high* **$700–1,000 DN**

Val Saint-Lambert

In the early 1900s, Val Saint-Lambert was one of the world leaders in luxury cut lead crystal and moved smoothly from the Belgian Art Nouveau style to a distinctive range of Art Deco colored cut glass.

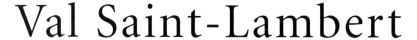

The Val Saint-Lambert glassworks had close associations with principal members of the Belgian Art Nouveau movement and collaborated with leading architects Victor Horta (1861–1947) and Henry van de Velde (1863–1957). The latter designed deeply cut patterns that the company's chief designer, Léon Ledru (1855–1926), used on a number of transparent, cased colored vases, such as the one shown on the left.

The factory specialized in dramatic cut patterns that echoed the forceful line of Horta's whiplash motif rather than the more organic, fluid French Art Nouveau style. As a result, it was well prepared for the move toward the new style inspired by the Art Deco exhibition of 1925 in Paris. Here, Val Saint-Lambert enjoyed a high profile, showing a range of stunning Art Deco cut glass—the Arts Décoratifs de Paris series—that won the Grand Prix. All were in Art Deco style, with designs by Ledru and Joseph Simon (1874–1960). The latter designed transparent cased glass vases with dramatic intaglio cutting of slashes and patterns. These carry both the factory mark and the initial "S" for "Simon."

The major designer of the interwar years, however, was Charles Graffart (1893–1967). A master engraver, Graffart also created imposing vases with deeply cut, abstract, geometric and faceted designs that exploited the superb quality and weight of the Val Saint-Lambert crystal.

Above: Orange and yellow bowl cased in red on the outside and yellow on the inside. *c. 1905. 4 in (10 cm) high* **$10,000–12,000 MAL**

ART DECO GEOMETRIC DESIGN

Under the influence of the Modernist movement, the early Art Deco curves became straight lines, and naturalistic motifs became increasingly abstract. Forms became thicker and heavier as glass-cutting became deeper, and both became increasingly linear, angular, and geometric. Designers played with the eye-catching and fashionable contrasting combination of clear and black glass, as seen on the dramatic vase on the right, with its characteristic straight-edged foot, geometric cutting, and bold, highly stylized design.

Pink cut glass rectangular vase cut on both sides, which looks forward to the Modern style, designed by Léon Ledru. *c. 1900. 7 in (18 cm) high* **$10,000–15,000 MAL**

Clear and black cut glass vase with six vertical cutaway panels of black glass interspersed with a hexagonal geometric motif. *c. 1930. 9 in (23 cm) high* **$1,800–2,500 MAL**

Vase cased in apple green over clear glass designed for Val Saint-Lambert by Charles Graffart. *1947*

10 in (25.5 cm) high

$1,200–1,500 **MAL**

Vase on clear pedestal foot cased in blue on the outside and red on the inside, and cut to reveal the colors. *1930s*

8 in (20.5 cm) high

$15,000–20,000 **MAL**

Cut clear and very dark amethyst glass vase with four vertical panels of geometric patterns. *c. 1930*

10 in (25.5 cm) high

$1,800–2,500 **MAL**

Straw-colored glass vase cased in amber. It has a small pedestal base. *1930s*

14 in (35.5 cm) high

$9,000–10,000 **MAL**

Vase cased in amethyst over pale uranium straw-colored glass. The vase is cut to leave areas of straw glass. *1930s*

6 in (15 cm) high

$1,800–2,400 **MAL**

Footed tazza of clear glass cased with red. The cut design of the plate is mirrored on the rim. *c. 1910*

15¼ in (38.5 cm) wide

$1,500–2,000 **AL**

Vase cased in red over clear glass. It is cut with asymmetrical arches and features an undulating design at the base. *1930s*

12 in (30.5 cm) high

$5,000–8,000 **MAL**

Squat vase cased in amethyst over pale uranium straw-colored glass. The cutting leaves a ring of lozenges and broad panels. *1930s*

5 in (12.5 cm) high

$1,500–1,800 **MAL**

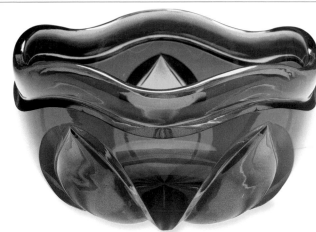

Red cut glass bowl with an undulating rim and deep cutting. *c. 1905*

4½ in (11.5 cm) high

$3,000–5,000 **MAL**

KEY FACTORIES

John Walsh Walsh, Birmingham (1851–1951).

Royal Brierley, Stourbridge (est. 1847 as Stevens & Williams); still active.

Stuart & Sons, Wordsley, near Stourbridge (est. 1885); still active.

Thomas Webb & Sons, Stourbridge (1859–1990).

Webb Corbett (est. 1897 as Thomas Webb & Corbett, Stourbridge); taken over by Royal Doulton 1969.

Whitefriars (est. 1834 as James Powell & Sons, Whitefriars, London); closed 1980.

BRITISH ENGRAVED & CUT

Cut glass was the mainstay of many British glassworks in the interwar years. Inexpensive glass from Czechoslovakia was flooding the lower end of the market, and British factories focused on the higher end of the market with ranges of luxury glass that combined cutting and engraving. Many designs were conservative; they looked back to the heavy, prickly, traditional 19th-century cut-glass patterns and the Art Nouveau style, using the sinuous line and organic plant and flower motifs associated with it. More forward-looking designers were eager to experiment with new stylized Art Deco motifs and shapes and the designs coming from Scandinavia (*see p.174*).

commissioned to design glass tableware that was made by Stuart & Sons (*see p.166*). The designers included Eric Ravilious, Dame Laura Knight, Ernest and Dod Procter, Graham Sutherland, Paul Nash, Vanessa Bell, and Duncan Grant.

Although a critical success, and avidly collected, these pieces were not particularly commercially successful, and many glassworks simply carried on with traditional designs or produced an uneasy mixture of traditional and modern, or ran the two styles in tandem.

MODERN BRITISH STYLES

Ironically, the two designers who played a large part in introducing modern British styles were Ludwig Kny, son of a Bohemian glasscutter, and Keith Murray, a New Zealand architect. Kny was a prolific, versatile, and highly talented designer whose technical accomplishments included a pioneering combination of intaglio and traditional miter cutting (*see p.166*). He created a host of modern designs for Stuart & Sons, which took the company forward into the Art Deco style. Murray produced a truly Modernist range of designs for Royal Brierley (*see p.169*).

Other designers were commissioned to create new modern lines for other established glassworks. W. Clyne Farquharson used a combination of

THE HARRODS EXHIBITION

One of the major showcases for glass design was the 1934 Modern Art for the Table exhibition held at Harrods department store, London. As part of a government initiative to improve design standards, a group of leading artists was

Webb cut and acid-etched vase with a single casing. *1930s. 8 in (20.5 cm) high* **$350–500 JH**

KEY STYLES

Colored glass in traditional shapes with Art Nouveau-inspired cut and engraved motifs of flora and fauna. *Thick-walled clear glass* with subtle, restrained, and cut and engraved decoration or dramatic deep-cut Art Deco motifs such as sunbursts, waves, and fish. *Clear glass* combined with black.

Sapphire bowl by Whitefriars, designed by William Wilson, with square cut base of four facets. The minimal cuts produce an optical effect at the base. *1935-37. 9¾ in (24.5 cm) high* **$600–800 JH**

Demonstrating the wheel-engraving technique, a glassworker holds a clear glass vase to a rapidly spinning disc that cuts into the glass. A design is built up by turning the piece and varying the length of time it is held to the wheel.

cutting and engraving for his range of Art Deco glass for the Birmingham-based glassworks of John Walsh Walsh; and at Whitefriars (*see p.52*) William Wilson designed stylized abstract cut patterns for the company's distinctive colored glass vases.

POSTWAR CUT AND ENGRAVED GLASS

After World War II, a truly British style emerged, as designers such as Geoffrey Baxter (*see p.55*), John Luxton (*see p.166*), and Irene Stevens (*see p.168*) absorbed the influences of the Harrods exhibition, the 1951 Festival of Britain, and the

Scandinavian style. Motifs became increasingly abstract and geometric, using deeply cut lines combined with lighter motifs, such as polished circles or star cuts. Patterns became more restrained and were used to complement the shape of the form rather than overwhelm it. Increasingly, however, British glassworks reverted to more traditional styles, which they had continued to produce alongside their modern glass ranges.

Geometrically cut yellow vase by William Wilson for Whitefriars. *1935–37. 11¾ in (30 cm) high* **$700–1,200 JH**

Cut glass bowl by Stuart, designed by legendary engraver Ludwig Kny. The 1930s design echoes the historical "star-cut base" style. *Mid-1930s 11¾ in (30 cm) wide* **$700–1,200 JH**

KEY DATES

1885 Frederick Stuart establishes Stuart & Sons at the Red House Glass Works at Wordsley, near Stourbridge, England.

1900 Frederick Stuart dies and his sons take over the glassworks, with Robert Stuart (1857–1946) as principal designer.

1918 Ludwig Kny (1869–1937) becomes chief designer.

1934 Stuart takes part in the Modern Art for the Table exhibition at Harrods department store, London, in which leading fine artists are invited to design glassware.

1949 John Luxton (b. 1920) joins Stuart as designer and produces an important range of glassware.

1995 Stuart is taken over by Waterford Wedgwood plc.

Stuart

A combination of talented technicians and designers willing to embrace new styles helped bring Stuart to the forefront of British cut glass in the 1920s and 1930s, producing some of the finest examples of British Art Deco glass.

Strong forms, original designs, and highly skilled cutting all resulted in a superb range of Stuart clear-cut glass in a distinctive British Art Deco style. Stuart glass had a high lead content, and in the 1920s the company introduced a final acid polish that gave the thick glass a brilliant finish. Ludwig Kny, the son of a Bohemian glass engraver and chief designer at Stuart from 1918, exploited these qualities even further with a wide range of modern designs that often included curving intaglio cutting to outline the straight deep cuts.

Most designs were in clear glass, but from the 1930s amber and green glass were reintroduced. The crisscross cutting and

lighter, more delicate engraved patterns of the 1920s gave way in the 1930s to designs with abstract or geometric, deep Art Deco designs with broad fluted cuts. By the late 1930s, Stuart was using ever-heavier blanks to accommodate the deeper cutting.

John Luxton played a key role in establishing the style of Stuart's cut glass after World War II. Like Kny, he designed in a variety of styles, from lightly cut tableware with arched, looping, and rhythmic linear patterns, to thicker pieces with deeply cut abstract patterns with polished lenses.

Above: Flared vase cut and engraved with a stylized seascape, designed by L. Kny, with provenance. Marked "Stuarts England." *1935–36. 7 in (17.75 cm) high* **$1,000–1,500 JH**

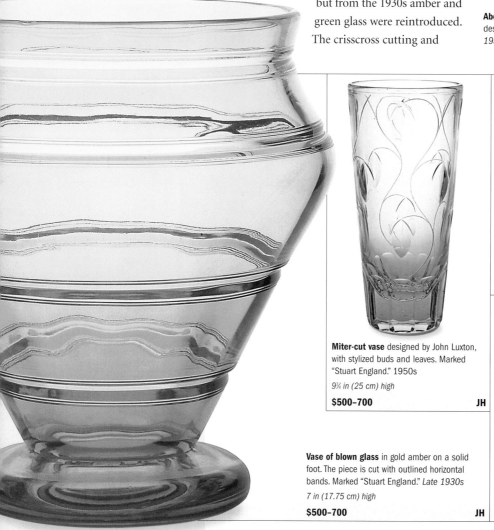

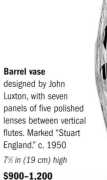

Miter-cut vase designed by John Luxton, with stylized buds and leaves. Marked "Stuart England." 1950s
9¾ in (25 cm) high
$500–700   **JH**

Vase of blown glass in gold amber on a solid foot. The piece is cut with outlined horizontal bands. Marked "Stuart England." *Late 1930s*
7 in (17.75 cm) high
$500–700   **JH**

Jug and two tumblers with gold/amber feet, cut with outlined horizontal bands. Marked "Stuart England." *Late 1930s*
Tumbler: 4½ in (11.5 cm) high
$700–900 (the set)   **JH**

Barrel vase designed by John Luxton, with seven panels of five polished lenses between vertical flutes. Marked "Stuart England." c. 1950
7½ in (19 cm) high
$900–1,200   **JH**

Thomas Webb

In the 1930s, Sven Fogelberg created the conditions under which Webb, known for its top-quality craftsmen in the 19th century, was once again able to take its place as one of the leading producers of British cut glass.

The talented glass-blowers whom Fogelberg recruited from a number of different countries introduced new glass-blowing techniques at Webb. These techniques were in turn employed by new designers, including, briefly, Fogelberg's wife Anna, architect Homery Folkes (b. 1906), and Thomas Pitchford.

Both Anna Fogelberg and Pitchford used a stylish Art Deco combination of black and clear crystal for a series of prestigious modern designs for the Rembrandt Guild, Birmingham (marked "Made for the Rembrandt Guild"). Pitchford was adept at working in a number of styles. His successful luxury Gay glass range of colored and cut glass, with four different patterns,

introduced in 1933 was more Art Nouveau in style, a marked contrast to his 1940s series of heavily cut pieces (*see below right*).

David Hammond, the leading postwar designer at Webb, had been apprenticed to Pitchford. He, too, worked in a variety of styles, both traditional and modern, and his pieces often combine different techniques, such as intaglio with engraving, and intaglio with deep cutting.

Above: Art Deco cut vase by Thomas Webb, made exclusively for the Rembrandt Art Guild England. *c. 1935. 7 in (17.5 cm) high* **$350–500 JH**

KEY DATES

1855 After being associated with various glassworks, Thomas Webb (1804–69) moves his company to the Dennis Glass Works, Amblecote, England, where, by 1859, it becomes known as Thomas Webb & Sons.

1920 Thomas Webb & Sons joins with the Edinburgh and Leith Flint Glass Co. and becomes Webb's Crystal Glass Co.

1932 Sven Fogelberg (d. 1971) joins Webb from the Kosta glassworks and modernizes the plant and designs.

1947 David Hammond (b. 1931) joins Webb and becomes its most important postwar designer.

1990 The glassworks closes after the parent company, Coloroll, goes bankrupt.

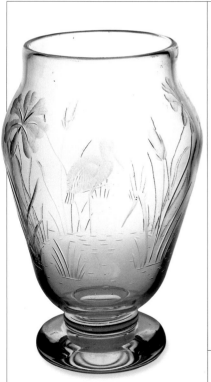

Vase engraved with cacti designed by Anna Fogelberg (the wife of the managing director of Thomas Webb). *1930s*
8 in (20.5 cm) high
$3,000–4,000   **JH**

Footed cut-glass vase designed by David Hammond for Thomas Webb. *1950s*
9¾ in (25 cm) high
$500–700   **JH**

Heavy cut vase designed by Tom Pitchford, with horizontal linear cuts, crossed by slanting, leaflike forms. *Late 1940s*
9¾ in (25 cm) wide
$700–1.000   **JH**

KEY DATES

1897 Thomas Webb & Corbett Ltd. is founded at the White House Glass Works, near Stourbridge, England.

1935 Webb Corbett shows its new modern designs in the British Art in Industry Exhibition at Burlington House, London.

1946 Irene Stevens is appointed chief designer.

1964 David Queensberry's Webb Corbett patterns win the Duke of Edinburgh's Award for Elegant Design.

1969 Royal Doulton takes over Webb Corbett. From 1986, glass is marketed as Royal Doulton Crystal.

Webb Corbett

In the 1920s and 1930s, in tandem with its traditional richly cut and engraved patterns, Webb Corbett introduced a series of modern cut glass in new shapes and patterns that now form part of an increasingly popular range of British Art Deco glass.

Many of the new designs by Webb Corbett were provided by managing director Herbert Webb (1871–1946). They included a distinctive tableware range of the mid-1930s with miter-cut, horizontal wavy lines, typically on clear glass. Webb Corbett motifs, similar to those used by other British glassworks, exploited the optical quality of clear glass, focusing on wavy lines, fish, stylized leaves and plants, and rhythmic linear patterns.

Irene Stevens (b. 1917) joined the company in 1946 and shaped its modern glass designs over the next two decades. Some of her patterns relied on a single style of cutting, such as spiraling miter cuts, while others employed combinations of styles and techniques, such as polished circles and horizontal cuts, matt elements with miter cutting, and sandblasting to add texture and contrast.

Under Stevens's influence, in 1963, David Queensberry, then professor of ceramics and glass at the Royal College of Art in London, was commissioned to design a series of highly acclaimed geometric patterns applied to a basic cylinder shape. Queensberry's patterns managed to combine modern and traditional appeal, but from the late 1960s the emphasis on the traditional led to the company's takeover.

Above: Decanter with flat stopper and cut leaf design, probably by Herbert Webb. *Mid-1930s. 11¾ in (30 cm) high* **$500–700 JH**

Small vase with cut lenses by David Queensberry. The design is known as "Queensway"; acid-stamped. *1960s*
4¼ in (11 cm) high
$350–500 JH

Footed vase with the slice neck above panels of stylized leaves and flutes. Designed by Freda M. Coleborn. Pattern number 15344; marked "Webb Corbett." *1938*
10 in (25.5 cm) high
$500–700 JH

Barrel vase with polished circles between triple horizontal cuts. Designed by Irene Stevens; marked with "Webb & Corbett England" and a star in the middle. *1947–49*
8¾ in (22.25 cm) high
$800–1,000 JH

Royal Brierley

Cutting, engraving, and acid-etching were among the many techniques in which Royal Brierley excelled. In the 1930s, Keith Murray exploited these techniques to produce a range of timeless glass designs that are now eagerly collected.

Royal Brierley's expertise in cutting and engraving was developed by some of the leading British glassmakers of the 19th century, among them John Northwood (1836–1902), the outstanding British cameo worker. So, when New Zealand architect Keith Murray was invited to develop a range of modern glass for Royal Brierley, he had huge reserves of expertise on which to draw.

From 1932, Murray was responsible for more than 1,000 designs for art glass and tableware, mostly in clear glass. Murray's designs, marked with his etched or stamped initials, were marketed separately. His passion for Modernism and the machine aesthetic was reflected in his formal, abstract cut-glass designs, while his

engraved motifs ranged from animals and plants (the cactus motif was, and still is, particularly popular) to airplanes.

From about 1946 to 1956, Deanne Meanley continued Murray's pioneering role, with cut-glass designs that ranged from powerful repeat patterns to intaglio cutting. While Murray's designs brought Royal Brierley to the forefront of modern glass design, the company also continued to produce a more traditional range of clear glass that combined miter, lens, and flute cutting. Royal Brierley is still making traditional cut-glass patterns today.

Above: Cut bowl with miter, lens, and flute cutting; pattern number 68449 and 50. *1937–38. 9 in (23 cm) high* **$500–700 JH**

KEY DATES

1847 The Moor Lane Glasshouse at Briar Lea Hill, Stourbridge, England, is renamed Stevens & Williams by Joseph Silvers (1779–1854).

1882 John Northwood, an outstanding glass technician, joins Stevens & Williams and introduces the cameo range.

1931 Stevens & Williams is renamed Royal Brierley Crystal, a name it patented after a visit from King George V.

1932 Keith Murray (1892–1981) becomes a freelance designer and creates an important range of modern glass.

1998 The company is acquired by Epsom Activities but continues to produce Royal Brierley glass.

Small glass jug with the body cut in a horizontal zigzag pattern in five rows. *1930s*
7 in (17.5 cm) high
$150–200   **JH**

Rectangular Keith Murray decanter with flat stopper, cut with rows of wavy lines. One of a pair. *c. 1935*
8¼ in (21 cm) high
$1,200–1,500 (the pair)   **JH**

Barrel vase cut with swirling leaf design between lenses. Marked "Royal Brierley." *c. 1940*
8½ in (21.5 cm) high
$700–1,000   **JH**

British Engraved & Cut

The high lead content of British glass made it particularly suitable for cut designs. Many Stourbridge-based glassworks, including Stourbridge (trade name Tudor Crystal), H.G. Richardson, and Harbridge Crystal, produced collectible ranges in the interwar years, as did Tutbury Glassworks in Gloucester and the Edinburgh and Leith Flint Glass Co. Some factories began to add acid-etched marks in the 1920s to distinguish their glass from imitations.

William Wilson combined color with cutting for Whitefriars (*see pp.52-55*), creating distinctive Art Deco designs, and Stevens & Williams produced cut, cased, and colored glass.

Gold amber glass vase by Whitefriars, designed by William Wilson. Provenance: Cargin Morley Collection. *1935-37*
7½ in (19 cm)
$600-900   JH

Whitefriars clear glass bottle-shaped vase decorated with two horizontal groups of bands; pattern number 9136. *Late 1930s*
8½ in (21.5 cm)
$500-700   JH

Unmarked shallow bowl by Keith Murray, the clear glass decorated with diagonal wavy lines. *1930s*
10 in (25.5 cm) wide
$500-700   JH

Stourbridge cut glass vase with floral design of stylized clover and grass, designed by Harry Cuneen for Tudor England. *c. 1950*
10 in (25.5 cm) high
$800-1,000   JH

Intaglio and engraved decanter (one of a pair) for Crystal, designed by Jack Lloyd. *1950s*
13¾ in (35 cm) high
$500-900 (the pair)   JH

Whitefriars footed vase with diagonal cut lenses and waves, pattern number C3 or C4, probably designed by William Wilson. *1940*
7¾ in (19 cm) high
$700-1,000   JH

Scottish cut glass vase with panels of miter-cut stylized grasses, marked "E & L." *Late 1940s*

6½ in (16.5 cm) high

$300–500   JH

Deeply cut vase with three elaborate panels between vertical flutes, marked "Richardson." *c. 1930*

8 in (20.5 cm) high

$300–500   JH

Stevens and Williams carved green and clear glass vase, decorated with grapes and floral motifs. *c. 1935*

5½ in (13 cm) high

$200–300   JH

Tutbury Glassworks lopsided jug allegedly made by the six directors of the company. *1934*

8 in (20 cm) high

$300–500   JH

John Walsh Walsh

Established in Birmingham in 1851, the John Walsh Walsh glassworks exploited the high quality of its lead crystal with a traditional range of cut and engraved decorated tableware and ornamental glass. In the 1930s, the company updated its image with a range of colored cut glass with shallow-cut floral patterns alongside a range of modern cut and engraved glass designed by William Clyne Farquharson (1906–92), whose name is now virtually synonymous with the company's Art Deco range. A draftsman turned engraver, Clyne Farquharson designed cut glass and engraved glass before combining the two in such popular designs as Kendal, Leaf, and Albany (*near right*), which were used both for tableware and vases.

John Walsh Walsh Albany vase designed by Clyne Farquharson, with staggered elliptical panels; signed "Clyne Farquharson, NRD 40." *1940s*

10 in (24.5 cm) high

$600–900   DN

John Walsh Walsh cut-glass bucket vase with geometric patterns of ovals and flutes, marked "Walsh Birmingham." *1930s*

6½ in (16.5 cm) high

$400–500   JH

John Walsh Gay Ware bowl, intaglio cut and engraved with flowing leaves. *c. 1935*

10 in (25 cm) wide

$200–250   JH

171

Central European Engraved & Cut

Bohemian glassmakers combined color and virtuoso cutting in their cased and stained glass in the mid-19th century and into the 20th century. Glassworks in Haida and Zwiesel used the technique to produce pieces designed by members of the Wiener Werkstätte, such as Otto Prutscher (1880–1949) and Bruno Mauder (1877–1948).

Forms and cutting reflected the different styles of the 20th century, becoming more geometric and angular in the 1930s, when Art Deco-style Czech cut glass was widely exported. In the 1950s, Czech glassmakers in the state-owned glassworks were able to reveal the continuity of their expertise in cutting and engraving.

Czechoslovakian display plate in clear glass, diamond-cut with a dynamic and stylized image of a rooster, and additionally engraved for shading. *1950s*

14 in (36 cm) wide

$1,800–2,500   JH

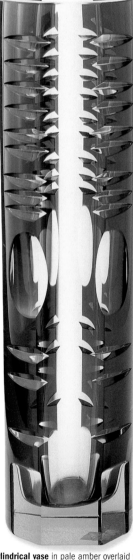

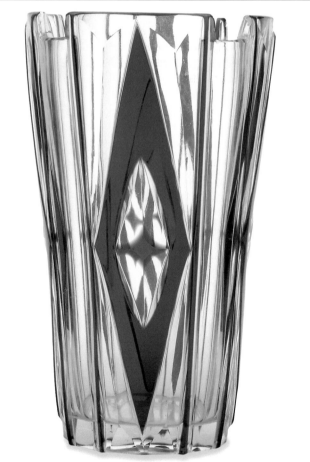

Bohemian clear glass vase of tubular form, molded and engraved with a partially obscured female torso. *1905*

10½ in (26.5 cm) high

$200–350   MW

Cylindrical vase in pale amber overlaid with blue glass, cut with vertical and horizontal fluting. Probably Czechoslovakian. *1930s*

12 in (30.5 cm) high

$150–250   DN

Czechoslovakian mold-blown tumbler with a folded and stepped rim, in clear-over-blue cased glass. Cut on four sides with diamond motifs. *1930s*

9¾ in (25 cm) high

$400–500   JH

Waisted, beaker-form glass by Johann Oertel & Co. of Haida, in clear glass cut with petal and leaf motifs, enameled in black, yellow, and blue, and with a gilded rim. *c. 1920*

5½ in (13.5 cm) high

$600–800 QU

Trumpet-shaped vase made in Haida, in the style of Otto Prutscher. Its body is molded and cut with a vertically and horizontally ribbed geometric pattern. *c. 1910*

8 in (20 cm) high

$400–600 QU

Zwiesel-school footed vase designed by Bruno Mauder, in clear glass overlaid with blue glass, and cut with a repeat geometric pattern of circular and oval shapes. *c. 1910*

6¾ in (17 cm) high

$150–250 FIS

Moser of Karlsbad

By the 1920s, the decorating workshop established by the glass engraver Ludwig Moser (1833–1916) in 1857 in Karlsbad had become one of the most prolific Bohemian glassworks. It produced glass in a variety of styles but was particularly known for its skillful carving, engraving, and painting. Faceted cutting became a Moser specialty, as did oroplastic decoration. This technique produced acid-etched, gilded, and polished patterns that were typically applied to dark blue and purple glass as a frieze. The classical effect was heightened by the use of motifs such as maidens, centaurs, and battle scenes. Through takeovers of other leading glassworks, Moser built up contacts with the Wiener Werkstätte and went on to collaborate with other leading designers.

Ludwig Moser & Söhne of Karlsbad baluster-shaped vase with cut floral decoration, two etched busts of a young girl, and a gilded neck. *1920s*

9¼ in (23.5 cm) high

$300–400 BMN

Ludwig Moser & Söhne of Karlsbad decagonal-shafted vase in purple glass with a band of fighting Amazons and centaurs around the shoulder. *1920s*

9½ in (24 cm) high

$500–600 FIS

Ludwig Moser & Söhne of Karlsbad faceted vase with a band of engraved and gilded flowers between gilding on the rim and base. *1920s*

16¾ in (42.5 cm) high

$500–700 BMN

Ludwig Moser & Söhne of Karlsbad purple glass goblet with a long, hexagonal-faceted stem and an engraved and gilded frieze of Amazonian figures among foliage. *1920s*

7½ in (19 cm) high

$200–300 FIS

SCANDINAVIAN ENGRAVED & CUT

Freelance Scandinavian designers translated their skills as draftsmen, painters, and sculptors into a distinctive style for cutting and engraving, which developed steadily from the 1920s and reached its peak in the 1950s and 60s.

The Orrefors glassworks pioneered both engraving and complex techniques based on cutting and engraving, such as Graal and Ariel (*see p.177*). In 1925, Swedish designers Simon Gate and Edvard Hald (*see p.176*) enjoyed much critical success at the Art Deco exhibition in Paris with pieces that showcased both the quality of the Orrefors glass and the skill of its engravers. Their styles were very different: Gate's exuberant figurative designs often depicted well-muscled naked forms; Hald, an ardent Modernist, created simplified stylized designs.

Edvard Hald and Gustaf Bergqvist, who helped Hald develop Ariel glass, were among the technical and artistic innovators at Orrefors.

Modernist credo to pieces with thicker walls and a selective use of decoration.

Designers started to use a combination of cut and engraved decoration in a new way. They let the shape determine the style of the decoration and played with illusion and perspective with a subtle combination of clear and engraved, etched matt and polished glass that created perspective and atmosphere. Vicke Lindstrand (*see p.42*), for example, often divided the design between the front and the back of the piece, or scattered lightly cut motifs over its surface to create the feeling of wind or movement. Motifs ranged from stylized, humorous, and realistic figures—

THE ART DECO ERA

The 1920s style of thin-walled clear glass with complex all-over engraved decoration gradually gave way in the 1930s under the influence of the "less is more"

Rounded rectangular glass vase designed by Strömbergshyttan, with shaped, typically square-cut rim and front surface engraved with a lizard; with original factory label. *1950s. 9¾ in (25 cm) high* **$600–900 JH**

KEY STYLES

Thin-walled clear glass vessels with all-over engraved decoration.
Thick-walled clear glass vessels with plant designs combining engraved and clear glass.
Thick-walled clear glass vessels with deep abstract patterns.
Clear glass vessels with shallow cutting.
Cased and colored glass in the Ariel and Graal techniques.

Ariel cased glass vase designed by Ingeborg Lundin for Orrefors, with trapped air bubbles trailed to form a series of irregular squares in shaded transparent blue and yellow glass; engraved and dated. *1972 5½ in (14 cm) high* **$1,000–1,500 BONBAY**

often Art Deco maidens, flora and fauna, and animals (fish were especially popular)—to abstract, geometric designs.

Scandinavian designers were swift to respond to the new Art Deco style, using combinations of black and clear glass and exploiting the reflective and refractive qualities of clear glass with cut designs. Simon Gate at Orrefors produced a series of vases with deep cutting and polished circles cut into thick clear glass. Scandinavian

designers showed typical control and restraint with their cut designs and, through judicious placing and restrained use of abstract decoration, maintained their reputation for harmonious, understated elegance that epitomized the influential Scandinavian Modern style.

POSTWAR DESIGNS

Finnish designers Tapio Wirkkala and Timo Sarpaneva, who swept the board at the Milan Triennale Design Fairs of the 1950s, used cutting and engraving as an integral part of the form rather than as surface decoration (*see p.182*). So did designers at the Swedish Orrefors glassworks, where Ernest Gordon (b. 1926) used simple asymmetrical line-cutting to transform standard clear glass shapes. Ingeborg Lundin (1921–92) similarly transformed elegant but unexceptional forms by carefully positioned abstract engraving. She incorporated circular motifs and abstract cross-cutting, and used contrasting polished and unpolished details. Her engraved designs included abstract patterns as well as witty, humorous designs with stylized figures and animals. Both Lundin and Eva Englund (b. 1937) went on to develop their own personal interpretations of the Ariel and Graal techniques in distinctive modernist styles.

The 1925 Art Deco exhibition in Paris was a landmark for Scandinavian glass, especially for Orrefors designers Gate and Hald.

Tapering clear glass vase with heavy foot and surface with deeply engraved spiraling lines, designed by Tapio Wirkkala for Iittala and signed on the base "Tapio Wirkkala – Iittala." *c. 1950* *6½ in (16 cm) high* **$700–900 BK**

Vingård footed vase designed by Eva Englund for Orrefors, with sycamore leaf design using the Graal technique. Signed on the base "Orrefors 909030 Eva Englund Graal Gallery 7-87." *1987. 12¼ in (30.5 cm) wide* **$1,500–2,000 BK**

Orrefors

The Orrefors glassworks blazed a technical and artistic trail in Sweden, playing a seminal role in establishing the Scandinavian style and bringing it to the forefront of glass design in the 20th century.

Orrefors rapidly established its position as one of the two giants of Swedish glass. Its success resulted from collaboration between a dedicated and highly skilled workforce and a series of talented designers from many different artistic backgrounds and different glass factories. The technical expertise of glass-blower Knut Bergqvist (1873–1953) helped pioneer the groundbreaking Graal technique, which dominated production until the 1920s, when wheel-engraving became a specialty.

In 1925, Orrefors wheel-engraved glass designed by Simon Gate and Edvard Hald received international acclaim at the Art Deco exhibition in Paris, where their style was dubbed "Swedish Grace."

From the 1930s, it was Vicke Lindstrand (*see p.42*) who took the company forward with a remarkable series of designs for thick-walled clear glass vessels with selective and carefully placed copper wheel-engraving in the new Art Deco style. He, together with glass-blower Gustaf Bergqvist and sculptor (Karl) Edvin Öhrström, was also instrumental in developing another technical breakthrough: Ariel glass.

Technical and artistic development continued to go hand in hand with designers who had trained at the Orrefors glass-engraving school. They included Sven Palmqvist (1906–84), who developed Kraka and Ravenna glass (*see p.178*),

Above: Clear glass bowl designed in 1953 by Edvard Hald. The oval body has a pronounced rim and is engraved with a wavy feather pattern. *1954. 5 in (13 cm) high* **$900–1,200 JH**

HALD AND GATE

Simon Gate (1883–1945) and Edvard Hald (1883–1980) launched Orrefors onto the international scene. The two men were very different. The exuberant extrovert Gate had a penchant for neo-classical engraved designs, which provided a useful bridge between the 19th- and 20th-century styles. Hald's talent for the drawn line resulted in a light, pictorial style and simplified elegant forms that reflected the emergent Art Deco designs. Hald and Gate's complementary styles resulted in both classic functional tableware and the engraved presentation vases that won such acclaim for Orrefors at the 1925 Paris Art Deco exhibition.

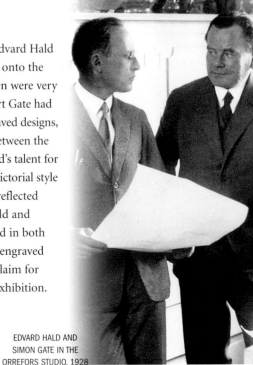

Rectangular Orrefors jug by Simon Gate engraved with a lady dancer on a plinth within a border surrounded by scrolling foliate forms. *1927 8½ in (22 cm) high* **$2,000–3,500 LN**

EDVARD HALD AND SIMON GATE IN THE ORREFORS STUDIO, 1928

GRAAL AND ARIEL

The Graal technique developed at Orrefors in 1916 was named after the apocryphal chalice—the Holy Grail—that held the blood of Christ. In Graal glass, the colored decoration is suspended between two layers of clear glass. The process requires a gather of clear crystal and a separate one of colored glass. The glass-blower draws the layer of colored glass over the layer of clear glass and then shapes the cased glass into a bullet-shaped blank. When it is cool, the colored layer is engraved or etched with the design, leaving the image in relief.

Graal vase designed by Simon Gate and made by Knut Bergqvist and Heinrich Wollmann. The inside is decorated with flowers; signed. *1919*
6½ in (15.5 cm) high
$7,000–10,000 BK

Ariel vase designed by Ingeborg Lundin, with internal bands of repeated circular, square, and triangular patterns, signed. *1976*
6½ in (15.5 cm) high
$700–900 BK

When the blank is reheated, the decoration softens and flattens and is cased in another layer of clear crystal and then reheated and blown to the final shape. This leaves the original design, now enlarged and distorted, floating between layers of clear glass.

The Ariel technique, named after the character in Shakespeare's *The Tempest*, supposedly came about by accident in 1937. Again the process begins by casing a layer of clear glass with a layer of colored glass. However, part of the design is made by sandblasting, which creates channels or holes that trap air when the outer layer of clear glass is applied. These trapped air bubbles then form an integral part of the design.

while also designing practical but classic tableware, and engraver Nils Landberg (1907–91). Landberg bridged the gap between technical expertise and creative design with his elegant stemware. He also developed the iconic Tulpaenglas range, whose attenuated shapes reflected Christian Dior's curvaceous "New Look."

Ingeborg Lundin (1921–92), the first woman designer at Orrefors, was equally versatile. Her designs ranged from beautifully simple blown forms such as the Apple vase (1955, *see p.44*), to designs for figurative and humorous engraved decoration, abstract cut designs, and her own interpretation of the Ariel technique (*see above*).

Orrefors has maintained its collaboration with designers from a wide range of disciplines who, in turn, have continued to contribute designs for art glass and tableware and, like Eva Englund (b. 1937, *see p.202*), to explore and reinterpret some of Orrefors' early groundbreaking techniques, such as Graal and Ariel.

INSPIRATIONS

The differences in background and temperament of the leading Orrefors designers made for a rich variety of inspiration and designs. Hald, for example, had trained with Matisse in Paris and was inspired by the Fauvist painting style; Gate looked to mythology and early Italian painters. Vicke Lindstrand embraced the modern world, using contemporary motifs, while Sven Palmqvist developed both the Kraka technique and a series of engraved designs based on fishing nets from Norse legend.

UNDERWATER THEMES

Designers exploited the depth and clarity of the Orrefors glass in a series of famous watery designs. Edvard Hald designed a magical series of Fish Graal patterns, in which fish and underwater plants drift suspended in time and space. Vicke Lindstrand's designs combined optical blowing that created a rippling watery effect with engraving in a series of vases with underwater themes.

Orrefors Graal vase with internal aquarium design featuring pond weed and a fish, designed in 1937. The reflections in the cased glass body give the effect of many fish and more pond weed. *c. 1950*
7¾ in (20 cm) high **$1,000–1,500 JH**

Engraved dish designed by Simon Gate and engraved by Thure Löfgren. The flared form is decorated with a frieze of stylized dancers with ribbons amid foliage; signed "Orrefors. S.Gate. Th. L." *1929*

14¾ in (37.5 cm) high

$4,000–6,000 BK

Cut-glass footed bowl. The body is divided into vertical sections, each cut with semicircles. *1930s*

5¼ in (13 cm) high

$250–350 JH

Cut glass bowl with heavily cut panels to the hemispherical form. It is signed "Orrefors LA355" and dated. *1931*

4¾ in (12 cm) wide

$180–300 JH

Bottle and stopper designed by Edvard Hald. The clear glass body is wheel-engraved with figures and a wall. With original rectangular stopper. *c. 1970*

9½ in (24 cm) high

$700–1,000 BONBAY

Ariel glass vase designed by Edvin Öhrström. The internal decoration consists of bubbles, a guitar-playing gondolier, a bust of a woman, waves, and blossoms; signed. *1940–60s*

6¾ in (17 cm) high

$4,000–6,000 QU

Ariel vase designed by Edvin Öhrström. The oval form has a heavy clear glass foot and an internal pattern of a reclining woman. *1930s*

6¾ in (17 cm) high

$6,000–8,000 LN

Orrefors engraved vase designed by Sven Palmqvist. The cylindrical body is delicately engraved with a figure looking at a bird flying overhead. *1950s*

8¾ in (22.5 cm) high

$150–200 JH

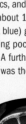

Orrefors Mermaid vase designed by Vicke Lindstrand. *1930s*

8½ in (22 cm) high

$1,800–2,400 LN

RAVENNA TECHNIQUE

Sven Palmqvist built on the Orrefors tradition of virtuoso decoration with his Ravenna glass. It was named after and inspired by the richly colored Italian mosaics, and also by stained glass. Palmqvist developed the demanding technique from about 1948. A layer of clear glass was cased with a layer of colored (often cobalt blue) glass. The design was sandblasted through the top colored layer, and the resulting pockets and channels in the clear glass were filled with crushed colored glass. A further layer of clear glass was added to seal in the decoration, and the blank was then reheated and the piece shaped.

Ravenna bowl designed by Sven Palmqvist, of oval dishlike form with thick wavy rim and decorated internally with a repeated square pattern; signed "Orrefors Ravenna Nr: 1864 Sven Palmqvist." *1961. 10 in (25.5 cm) long* **$900–1,200** BK

Ariel vase by Edvin Öhrström, of squat square form with heavy clear glass casing over internal green glass with bubbles. *1944*

4¼ in (11 cm) high

$2,500–3,500   **BONBAY**

Ariel vase by Ingeborg Lundin, with a heavy base and internal decoration of vertically trailed shapes; signed. *1964*

6 in (15.5 cm) high

$700–1,000   **BK**

Oval Ariel vase designed by Edvin Öhrström, with a thick rim and internal decoration of bubbles; signed. *1944*

5½ in (14 cm) high

$4,000–6,000   **BK**

Ansikten Ariel vase designed by Ingeborg Lundin. The cylindrical form with flared rim is decorated internally with blue forms; signed. *1969*

6¾ in (17 cm) high

$2,500–4,500   **BK**

Graal vase designed by Edvard Hald, of waisted cylindrical form with internal aquarium scene of fish and pond weed. It is signed on the base. *1944*

7¼ in (18.5 cm) high

$900–1,200   **FIS**

Graal vase by Edvard Hald, of near-spherical form with aquarium scene of fish swimming in pond weed; signed. *1938*

5 in (12.5 cm) high

$4,000–6,000   **VS**

Slipgraal vase designed by Edvard Hald, with thick rim and foot. The dishlike form is decorated internally with cream dots on a gray ground; signed. *1953*

8 in (20.5 cm) high

$350–450   **BK**

Kosta Boda

The Kosta glassworks (*see p.42*) emerged from the shadow of its famous rival Orrefors (*see p.176*) when first Elis Bergh (art director 1929–50) and then Vicke Lindstrand (art director 1950–73) joined the company. Under their influence, cut, engraved, and acid-etched glass in the distinctive Scandinavian Modern style flourished, with Lindstrand producing a wealth of figurative and abstract designs for cut and engraved art glass. Kosta glass is usually marked, and designs by Lindstrand are particularly popular, provided the engraving is in perfect condition.

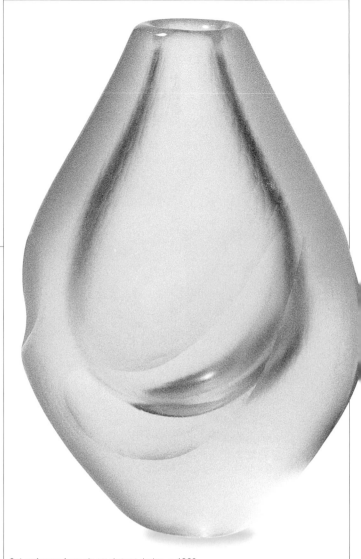

Triangular clear-glass display piece with stylized dancing figures, designed by Vicke Lindstrand. Wooden base. *Late 20th century*

14¾ in (37.5 cm) high

$900–1,500   DRA

The Bath clear-glass vase with shaped sides, designed by Vicke Lindstrand. Engraved with a curving figure entering the water. *1950s*

8¼ in (21 cm) high

$300–400   JH

Cut and carved vase in an abstract design. *c. 1960*

6 in (15.5 cm) high

$300–450   JH

Triangular clear-glass display piece designed by Vicke Lindstrand, with stylized dancing figures and a wooden base. *Late 20th century*

14¾ in (37.5 cm) high

$500–700   DRA

Bowl with rock-textured surface designed by Vicke Lindstrand. It is engraved with primitive hunting figures in the style of prehistoric cave paintings. Signed on the base "Kosta LS 502." *1950s*

10¼ in (26 cm) wide

$1,200–1,500   BK

LARS KJELLANDER

Although little is known about Lars Kjellander, he left behind a distinctive body of work that is becoming increasingly collectable. He worked at Kosta from 1881 to 1925, possibly as workshop manager, before setting up on his own and working in a variety of styles, but mostly using figurative designs. He was particularly adept at creating the sense of movement, either with stylized figures or, on thicker glass, by decorating both sides of the vase using a combination of deep engraving and soft matt surfaces. Although not a major name, Kjellander's designs (usually signed) epitomize the two broad strands of Scandinavian design and have a vitality and distinct personality that make them extremely attractive.

Vase with heavy base designed by Vicke Lindstrand. The surface is textured like rock and engraved with primitive figures in the style of prehistoric cave paintings. Signed "Kosta LS 503." *c. 1950*

8 in (20.5 cm) high

$3,000–5,000　　　　**VS**

Mermaid engraved heavy rectangular vase designed by Lars Kjellander, who worked at Kosta before setting up his own factory. *1930s*

6½ in (16.5 cm) high

$500–600　　　　**JH**

Clear-glass bowl with flared rim designed by Ernest Gordon. The ruby-red glass casing is cut back to reveal the clear glass in circles and the central band of triangular shapes, which has then been sandblasted. *1954*

4¼ in (11 cm) high

$700–900　　　　**JH**

Scandinavian Engraved & Cut Glass

Two styles operated in tandem in the interwar and postwar years in Scandinavian engraved and cut glass: engraved figurative images, often including contemporary motifs; and a restrained abstract style inspired by the shapes and textures of the landscape. As designers moved freely between glassworks and countries, a cohesive Scandinavian style could be seen in the clear glass produced by the Swedish giants Orrefors and Kosta, and other Swedish firms such as Åfors (est. 1876), Johansfors (1889–1990; reopened 1992), and Strömbergshyttan (1933–79); and also by Iittala, Nuutajärvi, and Riihimäki glassworks in Finland, the Danish Holmegaard (*see p.46*), and Hadeland (est. 1762) in Norway.

Leaf dish designed by Tapio Wirkkala for Iittala, in clear glass. The surface is cut with very fine lines; signed "Tapio Wirkkala – Iittala." *1950s*

7 in (18 cm) wide

$600–900 JH

IITTALA ENGRAVED & CUT

In the late 1940s, the Finnish Iittala factory (*see p.49*) came to the forefront of Scandinavian design. When it swept the board at the Milan Triennale exhibitions of 1951 and 1954, the company became globally renowned. This was largely due to the work of two designers: Tapio Wirkkala (1915–85) and Timo Sarpaneva (b. 1926), who designed clear glass organic forms inspired by the Finnish landscape. These were decorated with abstract cut and engraved designs that were an integral part of the form.

Wirkkala had trained as a sculptor and wood-carver and used the cut line on glass as one would use the grain in a piece of wood to complement or highlight a form and give added surface interest. Thus Wirkkala's iconic Kantarelli vase (1946), and the variations it inspired, were cut with fine lines that echoed the sculptural shape and gentle curves of the form and the natural ribbing of a chanterelle mushroom. Similarly, his leaf-shaped matt and polished bowls were cut with lines that replicated the veining found in nature.

Cutting was also used to create abstract texture and surface effects. Smooth-turn mold-blown pieces were given comb-cut decoration. Many vessels were decorated with shallow, unpolished lines cut with a copper wheel on the outside. These created a subtle surface texture that softened the form and contrasted with a shiny interior to give a soft diffused effect like mist or rain.

Cylindrical clear glass bottle produced by Iittala. It is engraved with a sailboat on a lake; with original stopper. *1930s*

10¼ in (26 cm) high

$300–400 JH

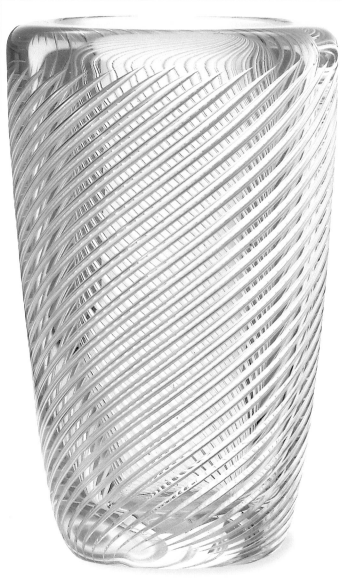

Clear glass vase with thick glass body wheel-engraved with a series of parallel diagonal lines. Designed by Kaj Franck for Nuutajärvi-Notsjö and engraved and dated on the base. *1953*

3¼ in (8 cm) high

$180–240 JH

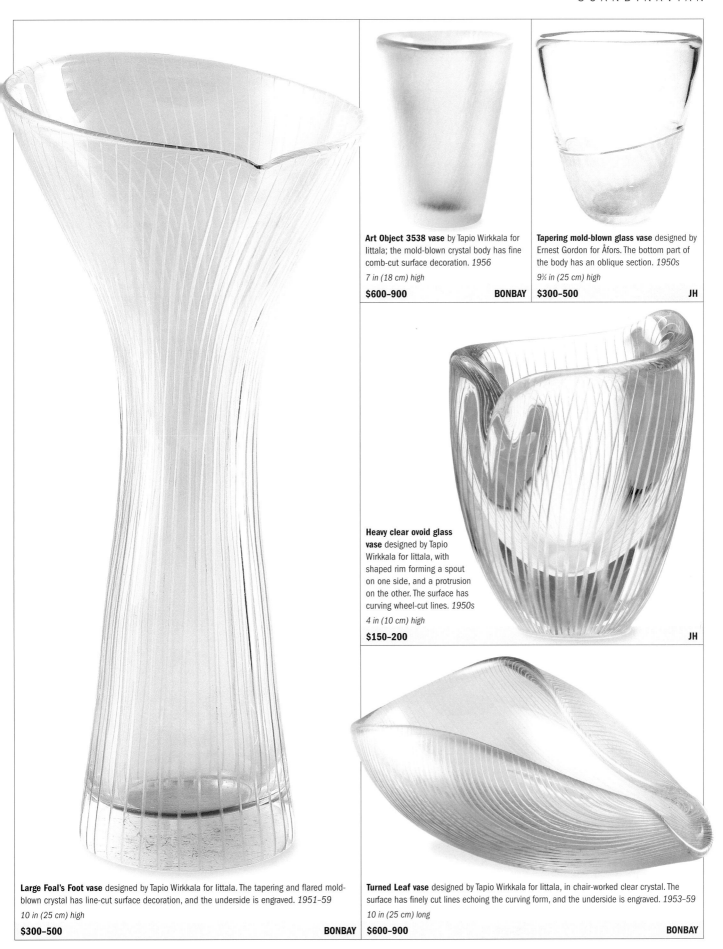

Art Object 3538 vase by Tapio Wirkkala for Iittala; the mold-blown crystal body has fine comb-cut surface decoration. *1956*

7 in (18 cm) high

$600–900   **BONBAY**

Tapering mold-blown glass vase designed by Ernest Gordon for Åfors. The bottom part of the body has an oblique section. *1950s*

9¾ in (25 cm) high

$300–500   **JH**

Heavy clear ovoid glass vase designed by Tapio Wirkkala for Iittala, with shaped rim forming a spout on one side, and a protrusion on the other. The surface has curving wheel-cut lines. *1950s*

4 in (10 cm) high

$150–200   **JH**

Large Foal's Foot vase designed by Tapio Wirkkala for Iittala. The tapering and flared mold-blown crystal has line-cut surface decoration, and the underside is engraved. *1951–59*

10 in (25 cm) high

$300–500   **BONBAY**

Turned Leaf vase designed by Tapio Wirkkala for Iittala, in chair-worked clear crystal. The surface has finely cut lines echoing the curving form, and the underside is engraved. *1953–59*

10 in (25 cm) long

$600–900   **BONBAY**

Steuben

With the development of a new lead crystal in 1932, the Steuben glassworks (*see p.122*) developed a range of superb engraved clear glass that reinvented the company image. The thick-walled pieces, with matt copper wheel-engraving set against the brilliant metal, reflected the Scandinavian influence. The sculptor Sidney Waugh (1904–63) set the high standard, and other talented fine artists were commissioned for designs, often in sets of limited editions, such as those that made up the Twenty-Seven Artists in Crystal exhibition in 1940. This included designs by Henri Matisse, Georgia O'Keeffe, and the Russian-born painter and designer Pavel Tchelitchew.

Vase with Acrobats designed by Pavel Tchelitchew. The bowl of the goblet-like vase depicts an acrobat balancing another acrobat and a ball on a plank on his feet. *1939*

13 in (33 cm) high

NPA   **CMG**

Fountain in Spain vase designed by Sir Muirhead Bone. The mold-blown body shows a crowd around a fountain. *1939*

11½ in (29 cm) high

NPA   **CMG**

Barnyard Scene vase with a heavy foot designed by Grant Wood for Steuben. The body is engraved with a scene of a lady feeding some ducks from a bowl. *1939*

13 in (33 cm) high

NPA   **CMG**

Gazelle Art Deco-style bowl designed by Sidney Waugh. The near-spherical form is engraved with a frieze of leaping gazelles and linear borders. It is mounted on a four-part stand. *1935*

7 in (18 cm) high

$18,000–24,000   **LN**

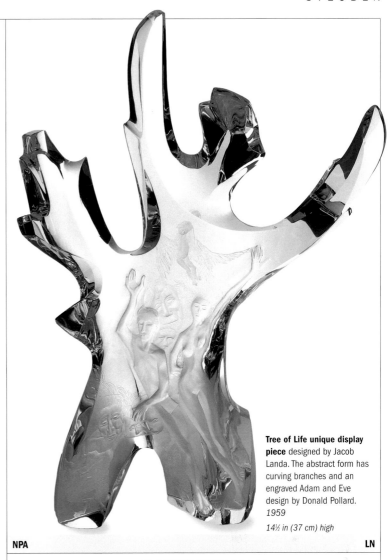

Tree of Life unique display piece designed by Jacob Landa. The abstract form has curving branches and an engraved Adam and Eve design by Donald Pollard. *1959*

14½ in (37 cm) high

NPA   LN

Adam and Eve footed jar with cover designed by Sidney Waugh. The tapering body is engraved with Adam and Eve standing either side of a stylized plant. *1938*

16 in (40.5 cm) high

$9,000–15,000   LN

Vase with Centaur and Unicorn designed by Jean Hugo. The mold-blown shaped bowl has two handles and features an engraved scene of a centaur with a spear, a unicorn, and a tree. *1939*

11½ in (29 cm) high

NPA   CMG

Perfume bottles

In the 20th century, the perfume industry became increasingly commercial, and famous glassworks were commissioned to produce luxurious, inventive bottles that would help perfume companies establish their brands in the competitive market.

French perfumiers led the way, while manufacturers of other nationalities, wishing to attain similar kudos, adopted Gallic names for their products and even commissioned the French to create their bottles. Designs reflected contemporary fashions and the styles of the glassworks, so Gallé (*see p.76*) created stylish production-line cameo bottles with organic Art Nouveau motifs, and Baccarat (est. 1764) made cut-glass bottles for perfumiers such as Guerlain, Caron, and Jean Patou.

In the 1920s and 1930s—the golden age of perfume bottles—French glassworks produced luxurious bottles that epitomized the hedonism of the jazz age. Lalique bottles, in clear, opalescent, and frosted glass, were highly stylized and made inventive use of a dramatic crescent-shaped stopper. Lalique produced press-molded bottles for some 60 different perfumiers.

Czech glassmakers made elaborate cut-glass Art Deco-style bottles, usually in clear or pastel-pink glass (turquoise blue and browns are rarer) with large, elaborate stoppers. Many were exported to the United States, where they proved popular as gifts.

Bottle shapes became ever more inventive, and couture houses launched their own brands. In 1927, the Russian Prince Matchabelli patented a crown-shaped bottle for his "royalty" perfumes, and Mae West's curvaceous silhouette was one of the surreal shapes that fashion designer Elsa Schiaparelli used for her perfume range.

From the late 1930s, wartime restrictions and the use of mass production and plastics changed the design of the perfume bottle. Notable exceptions in the 1950s were the French couture houses, with Christian Dior (1905–57) and Balenciaga (1895–1972) among others commissioning elegant cut-glass bottles.

Original boxes are part of the appeal and value to collectors, as is an unopened bottle complete with tags or ribbons.

Lalique *Au Coeur des Calices* perfume bottle for Coty. Molded and impressed "LALIQUE." *c. 1915. 2¼ in (6 cm) high* **$7,000–10,000 RDL**

Princess Maria perfume bottle for Prince Matchabelli, in opaque white glass with gold detail and paper label. Stenciled "France." *1920s. 2½ in (6.25 cm) high* **$500–700 RDL**

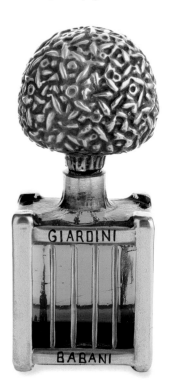

Giardini perfume bottle for Babani, in green glass with gilded and enameled detail. *c. 1920. 4¼ in (11 cm) high* **$1,800–3,600 RDL**

Gallé perfume bottle with cameo decoration of flower-blossom leaves. *Early 20th century. 6 in (15 cm) high* **$1,500–1,800 JDJ**

Lucien Gaillard *Pourpre d'Automne* **perfume bottle** for Violet, in clear glass with painted detail. *c. 1920. 3¼ in (8.5 cm) high* **$800–1,000 RDL**

Lalique *Leurs Ames* **perfume bottle** for D'Orsay, in clear and frosted glass with a sepia patina. *c. 1915. 5 in (12.5 cm) high* **$8,000–10,000 RDL**

Ingrid perfume bottle in clear and frosted amber crystal. With stenciled oval "Made in Czechoslovakia" mark. *1920s 5¾ in (14.5 cm) high* **$2,000–2,500 RDL**

Czechoslovakian tiara perfume bottle in turquoise crystal. With stenciled circle "Made in Czechoslovakia." *1930s. 5¾ in (14.5 cm) high* **$600–800 RDL**

Caron perfume bottle for *Les Pois de Senteur de Chez Moi.* *1927. 4½ in (11.5 cm) high* **$200–300 LB**

Shocking perfume bottle for Schiaparelli, with pearlized glass flowers. Sealed in a glass dome and box. *1940s. 4¾ in (12 cm) high* **$400–600 RDL**

Lalique *Deux Figurines, Bouchon Figurines* perfume bottle, in clear and frosted glass with sepia patina. *c. 1910. 5½ in (13.5 cm) high* **$8,000–12,000 RDL**

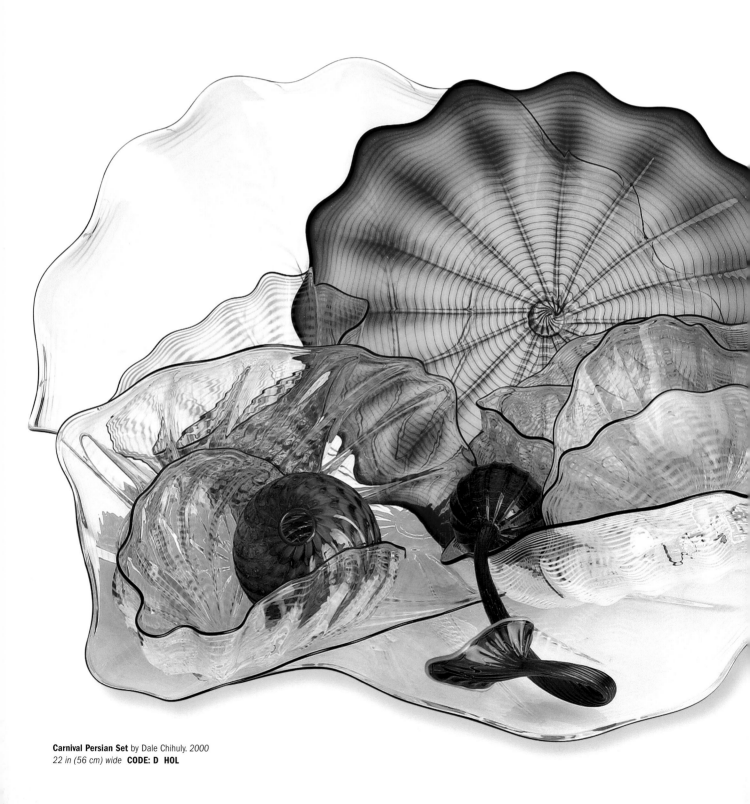

Carnival Persian Set by Dale Chihuly. *2000*
22 in (56 cm) wide **CODE: D HOL**

Contemporary & Studio Glass

The 20th century had seen dynamic and powerful changes in terms of style, form, and technique, but it was the studio movement of the 1960s that caused an explosion in the way glass was made, collected, and considered. As well as allowing thousands of creative and artistic minds and personalities to work directly with the material, it freed glass from the confines of the factory and led to unprecedented levels of creativity and expression. From the 1980s, modern studio glass was considered a true art form and began to appear in public collections and at auction. With a rapidly growing base of collectors, a varied, energized, and truly vibrant market has grown— one that is sure to continue growing into the 21st century and beyond.

The pieces in this chapter are coded by price band:

A	Over $80,000	**D**	$30,000–50,000	**G**	$3,000–7,000
B	$60,000–80,000	**E**	$20,000–30,000	**H**	$1,500–3,000
C	$50,000–60,000	**F**	$7,000–20,000	**I**	Under $1,500

ART FORM OVER CRAFT

Before the 1960s, practically all glass was made in a factory environment, and training could be gained only by working in these factories because glassmaking was not taught anywhere else. Ceramics were already being explored by individual makers, and people were beginning to consider their limited production as an art form rather than pure craft. Glass could not enjoy this liberty, since it could not be produced outside factories. However, a few artists experimented with working glass at low temperatures, and there were others, including American potter and teacher Harvey Littleton, who were convinced that this could be taken further.

NEW GLASS THEORIES

Littleton put his theories into practice at a seminar at the Toledo [Ohio] Museum of Art in 1962, when he was able to design and build a small furnace to melt glass. However, errors in the formula meant the glass did not melt properly. A breakthrough came when scientist Dominick Labino worked on the formula, and at a second meeting in the same year there were further successes. Thanks to these "Toledo Seminars," the studio-glass movement was born.

By 1963, Littleton was teaching the first of a new generation of glass artists at the University of Wisconsin, with the now world-famous Dale Chihuly and Marvin Lipofsky among them. In 1967, fellow student Sam Herman took the techniques to Great Britain, where a hot-glass workshop was held at the Royal College of Art in London. By 1971, Chihuly had studied in Venice and opened the influential Pilchuck Glass School near Seattle. This institution has dominated the development of the studio glass movement ever since.

Much of the glass produced at the time tends to be simply, and often crudely, blown or formed, as the new artists felt their way with the medium. Applied, trailed, and pulled decoration on thickly rendered bodies were common, and colors tended to be dull or simple, limited to variations of colored and clear glass. As experience was gained and techniques learned throughout the late 1960s and 70s, the artists became more creative, producing glass in a dazzling rainbow of colors and an array of abstract, natural, or figural forms.

INCREASED VARIETY

Despite a growing base of private collectors, the art world was slow to accept glass as a new art form, deeming it to be craft combined with new technology. However, by the early 1980s,

Sam Herman studio glass vase. The freeform, near-baluster form is decorated with multicolored random swirls, dots, and streaks and has areas of iridescence. It is signed on the base "Samuel Herman." *1980s 10½ in (27 cm) high* **CODE: I DN**

COLLECTORS' TIPS

Studio glass from the 1960s–80s by the pioneers in each country may reach high levels of desirability, with values to match.
Signatures and dates are often the only means of identifying a piece but can easily be faked.
Handle as many pieces as possible and learn to recognize their qualities.
New artists are constantly emerging; those who produce attractive, appealing works probably hold the best potential.

Goblet-like vase designed and made by Erwin Eisch, decorated with pulled ruby trails and iridescence. Signed on the base "Eisch 78." *1978 10 in (25 cm) high* **CODE: I VZ**

Colomba vase designed by Pablo Picasso and made on Murano by the La Fucina degli Angeli design studio. Of abstract birdlike form with a bulbous red body, which has applied opaque dark purple trails representing the feathers, eye, feet, and beak. *1962. 12¼ in (31 cm) high* **CODE: F FIS**

World-famous glass artist Dale Chihuly in front of two of his unique chandeliers that comprise many components assembled on a metal frame. Chihuly wears an eye patch after losing an eye in a car crash in 1979.

public collections began to take interest and studios were run professionally, with artists striving to manage successful businesses as well as promote their work and ideas.

The 1980s and 90s saw increased variety and vibrancy in a rapidly developing market, with thousands of artists constantly pushing the boundaries of glass art to new limits. The range of techniques mushroomed, and the growing experience and skill in blowing glass led to an ever-increasing range of extravagant forms. Glass has been engraved, cut, laminated, stained with enamels to look like substances such as rock, and combined with materials such as metal and granite. The optical properties of glass have also been fully explored, with a growing number of artists using fine-quality clear optical glass.

MODERN WORKING PRACTICES

Few artists now work alone in their studios, preferring to work as part of a team, and a considerable number of glass designers take their designs to studios for professional glassmakers to create. Many of these works show a dominant feeling for the modern and innovative, even though techniques and inspiration are often the same as those used by the glassmasters of the early 20th century. Contemporary glass produced today represents the result of a fine balance between technique, skill, and creative ability.

The works of art shown on the following pages represent the production of a selection of the world's leading glass artists working today. Although many were created in the early years of the 21st century, all are considered fine examples of the art today. As with masters throughout history, styles are never static: they change frequently as new avenues in inspiration, form, color, or technique are explored.

Upward Undulation by Harvey K. Littleton, in transparent light-yellow glass and kiln-formed sheet glass; aluminum base. *1974 63½ in (161.5 cm) high* **NPA CMG**

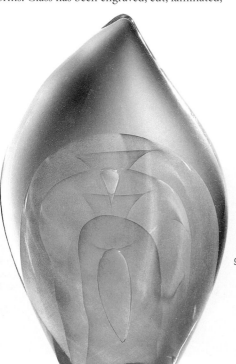

Emergence XV from the Emergence series, designed and made by Dominick Labino. Of teardrop-shaped form with internal rose-pink "veils." *1973 9¾ in (24.5 cm) high* **NPA V&A**

Amsel

Galia Amsel (b. 1967, London) trained at the Royal College of Art, London. She has been commissioned by ABSA Awards, Coopers & Lybrand PLC Awards, and Royal Caribbean Cruise Lines. Her work appears in the Victoria and Albert Museum, London, and the Ulster Museum, Northern Ireland.

Passage V by Galia Amsel. *2002*
8 in (20.5 cm) high

CODE: H   CG

Balgavý

Miloš Balgavý. 1955, Bratislava, Slovakia) trained at the École des Arts Appliqués de Bratislava. His work can be seen in collections at the Musée de Design et d'Arts Appliqués, Lausanne, Switzerland; the Glasmuseet Ebeltoft, Denmark; and the Jan van der Togt Museum, Amsterdam, The Netherlands.

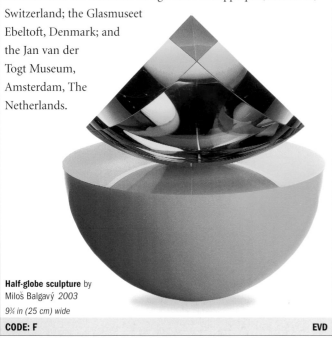

Half-globe sculpture by Miloš Balgavý *2003*
9¾ in (25 cm) wide

CODE: F   EVD

Baldwin & Guggisberg

Philip Baldwin (b. 1947, New York) works in partnership with Monica Guggisberg (b. 1955, Bern, Switzerland). They trained at Orrefors in Sweden, and their work features in public collections at the Musée des Arts Décoratifs, Paris, and the Corning Museum of Glass, New York. Their work has featured in many exhibitions across the world.

Vase by Philip Baldwin & Monica Guggisberg. *2004*
18½ in (47 cm) high

CODE: G   EVD

Bohus

Zoltan Bohus (b. 1941, Endröd, Hungary) trained at the Hungarian Academy of Applied Arts, Budapest, where he is now head professor of the glass department. Exhibitions include shows at the Habatat Galleries and the Heller Gallery, both in the US. He has pieces in collections at the Corning Museum of Glass, New York; the Musée des Beaux Arts, France; and the Yokohama Museum, Japan.

Borowski

Stanislaw Borowski (b. 1944, Moutiers, France) trained at the Krosno Glass Factory in Poland. He founded Glasstudio Borowski in Germany. His son Pawel (b. 1969) is the creative director of the German studio and the Polish branch in Krosno. Stanislaw's work is featured at the Corning Museum of Glass, New York, and the Glasmuseum Frauenau, Germany.

Meet the Bird by Pawel Borowski. *1999*
25½ in (65 cm) high

CODE: G | EVD

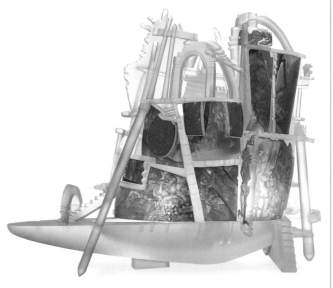

The Swimming Tower of Babylon by Stanislaw Borowski. *1995*
13¾ in (35 cm) high

CODE: E | EVD

Sculpture by Zoltan Bohus. *1992*
17 in (43 cm) high

CODE: E | EVD

Boyadjiev

Latchezar Boyadjiev (b. 1959, Sofia, Bulgaria) trained at the Academy of Arts, Sofia, and at the Academy of Applied Arts, Prague. He has exhibited his work at the Christy Taylor Gallery, Florida; Rachael Collection, Colorado; Sandra Ainsley Gallery, Canada; Art Glass Center International, Netherlands; and Gallerie L, Germany. He has pieces at the Museum of Applied Arts, Prague; the White House, Washington, D.C.; the Glasmuseet Ebeltoft, Denmark; and the Glasmuseum der Ernsting Stiftung, Germany.

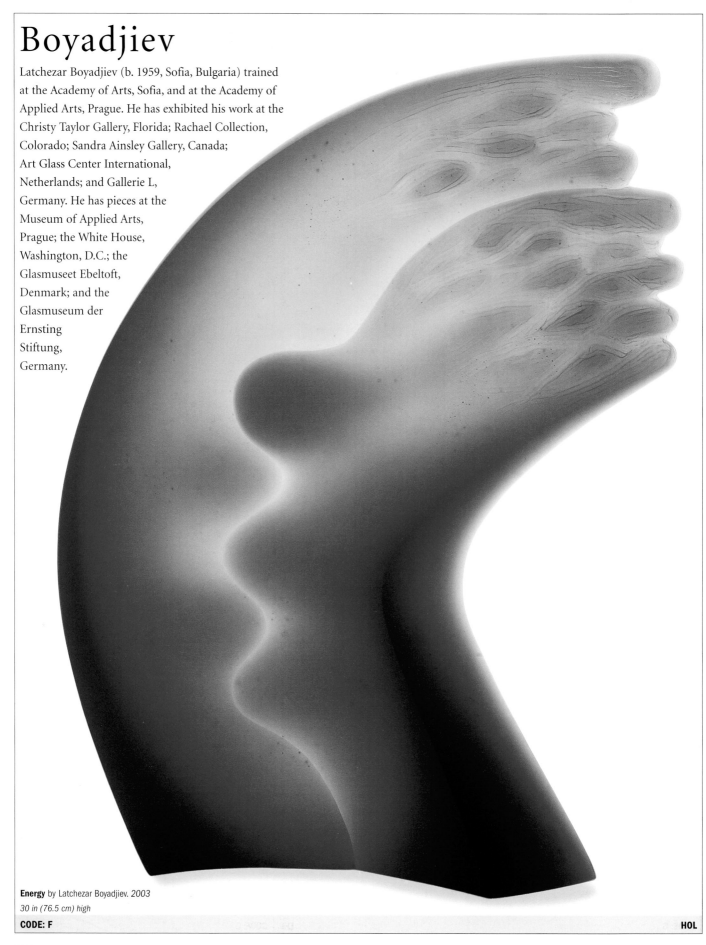

Energy by Latchezar Boyadjiev. *2003*
30 in (76.5 cm) high

CODE: F   HOL

194

Bremers

Peter Bremers (b. 1957, Maastricht, Netherlands) trained at the University of Fine Arts and at the Jan van Eyck Akademie, Maastricht. He has exhibited his work across the world. His commissions have included the National Glass Museum, Leerdam, Netherlands, and What Pha Nanachat monastery in Thailand.

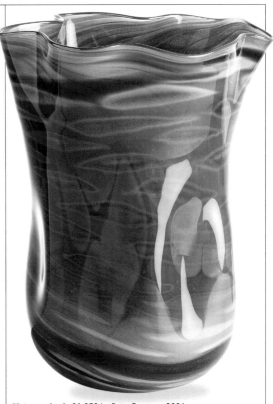

Metamorphosis 01-056 by Peter Bremers. *2001*

16½ in (42 cm) high

CODE: F   **EVD**

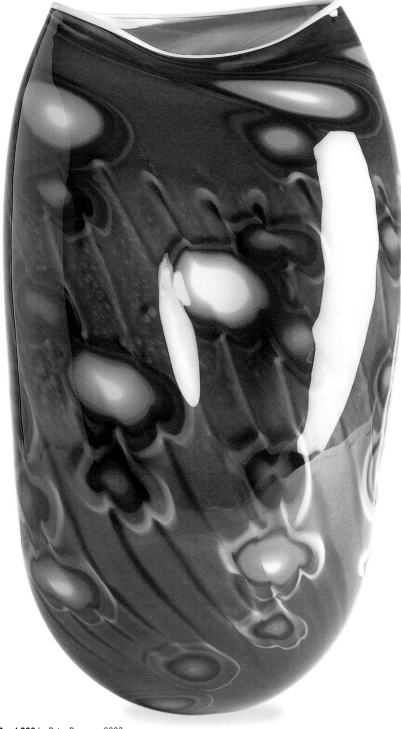

Graal 306 by Peter Bremers. *2003*

17¼ in (44 cm) high

CODE: G   **EVD**

Graal 318 by Peter Bremers. *2003*

11½ in (29 cm) high

CODE: G   **EVD**

Carrère

Xavier Carrère (b. 1966, Draguignan, France) trained at the Photography Academy, Orthez, and at l'ADAC, Paris. He has exhibited worldwide. Public collection work features the Millennium Monument, Ville de Soustons, and the House of Region, Montpellier.

From the Links series by Xavier Carrère. *2003*

21¾ in (55 cm) wide

CODE: G   **GMD**

From the Links series by Xavier Carrère. *2003*

21¼ in (54 cm) high

CODE: G   **GMD**

Chabrier

Gilles Chabrier (b. 1959, Riom-és-Montagnes, France) began training with his grandfather in his Paris studio. He has exhibited at the Miller Gallery, New York, and the Sordello Gallery, Paris. Some of his work is on display at the Musée National de Céramique, Sèvres.

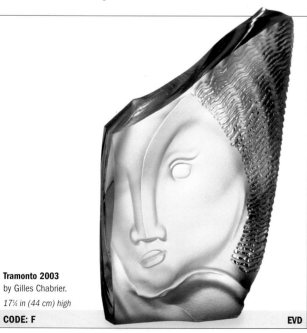

Tramonto 2003
by Gilles Chabrier.

17¼ in (44 cm) high

CODE: F   **EVD**

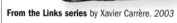

Cube with faces by Gilles Chabrier. *2002*

11 in (28 cm) high

CODE: G   **EVD**

Chardiet

José Chardiet (b. 1956, Havana, Cuba) trained at the Southern Connecticut State University and Kent State University, Ohio. He has exhibited worldwide. Some of his pieces are in public collections in the United States, Japan, and Switzerland.

Timbal by José Chardiet. *2003*

32 in (81.5 cm) high

CODE: F   **LKM**

Chaseling

Scott Chaseling (b. 1962, Tamworth, Australia) trained at the Canberra School of Art. He has had commissions from the South Australian Film Corporation and the Canberra Arts Patrons Organization. His work is in collections in the United States and Australia.

REVERSE OF PIECE

Pilgrimage by Scott Chaseling. *2003*

20 in (51 cm) high

CODE: F   **LKM**

Dale Chihuly

Dale Chihuly (b. 1941, Tacoma, WA), co-founder of the Pilchuck Glass School, trained at the University of Wisconsin (working with Harvey Littleton, *see p.190*) and the Rhode Island School of Design, where he also taught. His work appears in many public collections, including the Metropolitan Museum of Art, New York; the Smithsonian American Art Museum, Washington, D.C.; the Musée des Arts Décoratifs, Paris; and the Corning Glass Museum, New York. Over the years, his many exhibitions have included the National Gallery of Australia, Canberra; the Corcoran Gallery of Art, Washington, D.C.; and the Victoria and Albert Museum, London.

Carnival Pheasant Macchia by Dale Chihuly. *2002*
21 in (53.5 cm) wide

CODE: D   **HOL**

Persian set (blue) by Dale Chihuly. *1999*
27½ in (70 cm) wide

CODE: C   **EVD**

Harrison Red Basket Set by Dale Chihuly. *2003*
11 in (28 cm) high

CODE: E   **HOL**

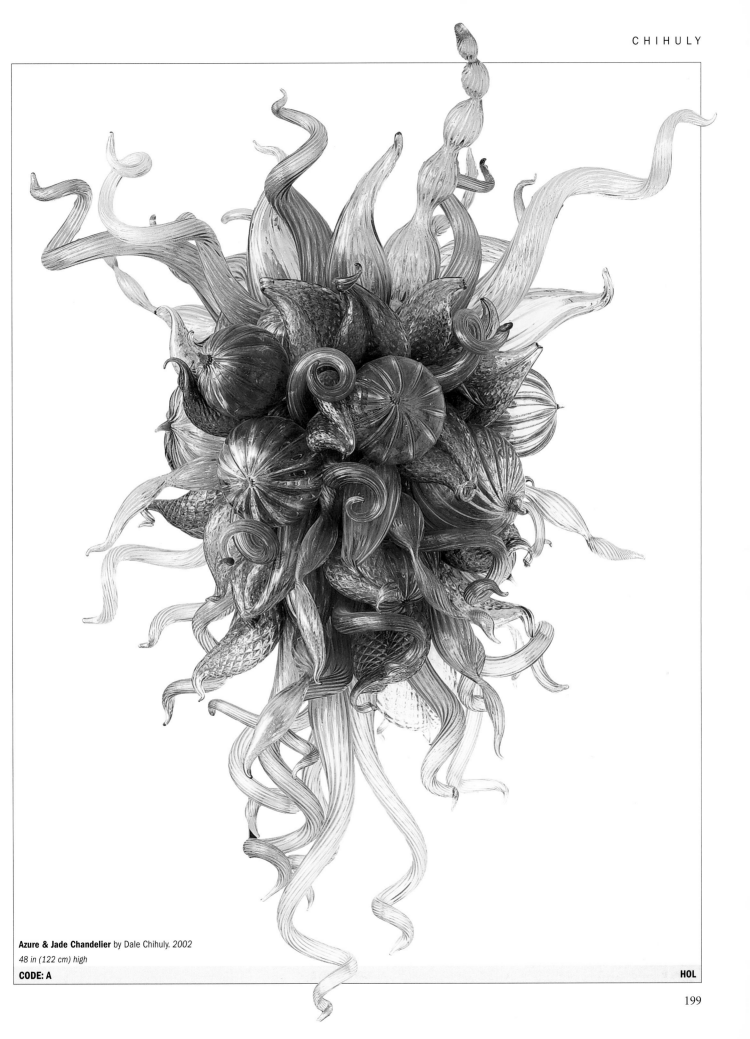

Azure & Jade Chandelier by Dale Chihuly. *2002*
48 in (122 cm) high

CODE: A

HOL

Cigler

Václav Cigler (b. 1929, Vsetin, Czech Republic) trained at the School of Glassmaking in Novy Bor and the Prague Academy of Arts, Architecture, and Design. His work can be seen at the American Craft Museum, New York, and the Museum of Applied Arts, Prague.

Tower 2003 by Václav Cigler.
19¼ in (49 cm) high

CODE: D   **EVD**

Clegg

Tessa Clegg (b. 1946, London) trained at the Stourbridge College of Art, UK. Her exhibitions include the Glasmuseet Ebeltoft, Denmark, and some of her pieces are part of public collections at the Hokkaido Museum of Modern Art, Japan; the Corning Museum of Glass, New York; the Musée des Arts Décoratifs, Paris; and the Victoria and Albert Museum, London.

Window Box by Tessa Clegg. *2001*
10¾ in (27.5 cm) high

CODE: H   **CG**

Cribbs

Kéké Cribbs (b. 1951, Colorado Springs) is largely self-taught but also attended the Pilchuck Glass School, Seattle. She has exhibited worldwide. Her work is in public collections including the Corning Museum of Glass, New York.

Sleeping Beauty by Kéké Cribbs. *2001*
13½ in (34.5 cm) high

CODE: F   **LKM**

Cummings

Keith Cummings (b. 1940, London) trained at the University of Durham, and became professor of art and design at the University of Wolverhampton. He has exhibited across the world. Public collections include the Victoria and Albert Museum, London, and the Musée des Arts Décoratifs, Paris.

Alfred's Mirror by Keith Cummings. *2003*
14½ in (37 cm) long
CODE: G   CG

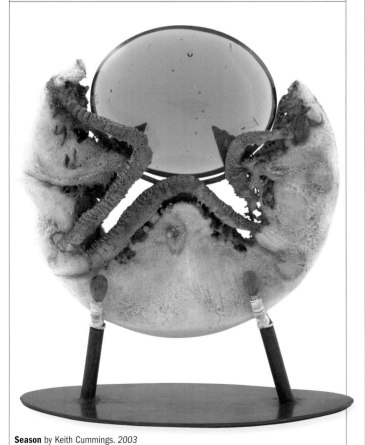

Season by Keith Cummings. *2003*
5½ in (13 cm) wide
CODE: H   CG

Dailey

Dan Dailey (b. 1947, Philadelphia) trained at the Rhode Island School of Design and the Philadelphia College of Art. Among his many commissions is the Rainbow Room at the Rockefeller Center, New York. Public collections include the Musée des Arts Décoratifs, Paris, and the Metropolitan Museum of Art, New York.

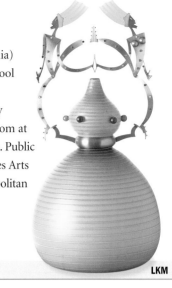

Sparklers by Dan Dailey. *2003*
30 in (76.5 cm) high
CODE: B   LKM

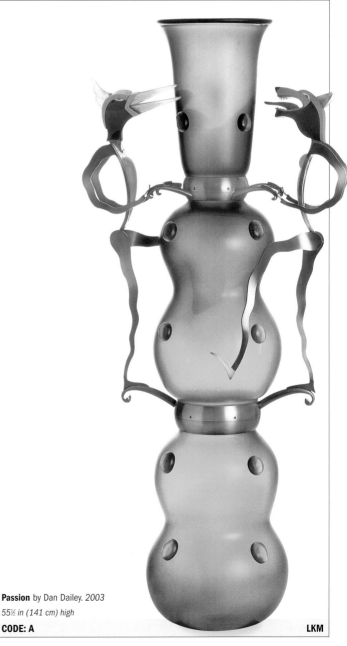

Passion by Dan Dailey. *2003*
55½ in (141 cm) high
CODE: A   LKM

Englund

Eva Englund (1937–98) trained at SAC, Gothenburg; the Art Academy, Munich; and Schliess Keramik, Austria. After graduating, she joined Pukeberg in 1964 and stayed until 1973. She then went on to design for the Swedish firm Orrefors.

Graal vase by Eva Englund for Orrefors. *1987*

7 in (17.5 cm) high

CODE: G　　　　　　　　　　　　　　　　**BK**

Mötet by Eva Englund for Orrefors. *1988*

14¼ in (36 cm) high

CODE: G　　　　　　　　　　　　　　　　**BK**

Ferro

Vittorio Ferro (b. 1932, Murano, Italy) is the son of AVEM co-founder Giuseppe Ferro. He trained as a glassmaster with his uncles, Armando and Amleto Zuffi, co-owners and glassmasters at Fratelli Toso. The Corning Museum of Glass, New York, has a piece of his work in its collection.

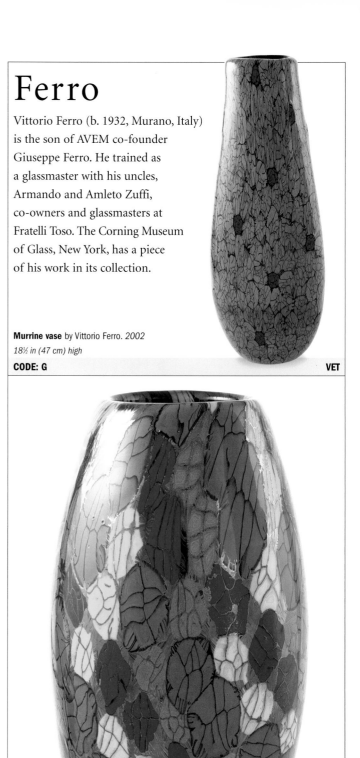

Murrine vase by Vittorio Ferro. *2002*

18½ in (47 cm) high

CODE: G　　　　　　　　　　　　　　　　**VET**

Murrine vase by Vittorio Ferro. *2002*

14½ in (37 cm) high

CODE: G　　　　　　　　　　　　　　　　**VET**

Frijns

Bert Frijns (b. 1953, Ubach over Worms, Netherlands) studied Sculpture and Glass at the Gerrit Rietveld Academie, Amsterdam. He has exhibited at the Corning Glass Museum, New York, and the European Fine Art Fair, Maastricht. He has items in public collections at the National Glass Museum, Leerdam, Netherlands, and the Hokkaido Museum of Modern Art, Japan.

Vase on stand by Bert Frijns. *2001*
Vase: 20 in (51 cm) high
CODE: F   **EVD**

Groot

Mieke Groot (b. 1949, Alkmaar, Netherlands) trained at the Gerrit Rietveld Academie, Amsterdam. Her many Dutch exhibitions include the National Glass Museum, Leerdam, and the Braggiotti Gallery, Amsterdam. Some of her creations are in public collections at the Corning Museum of Glass, New York, and the Pilchuck Collection, Seattle.

Vase by Mieke Groot. *2002*
15 in (38 cm) high
CODE: H   **EVD**

Frydrych

Jan Frydrych (b. 1953, Sumperk, Czech Republic) trained at the Novy Bor Glass School. His work has been exhibited in solo shows at Novy Bor. Major commissions have included metro stations in Prague; the Wurzburg New Church, Germany; the Castle Schloss Berg, Germany; and the Renaissance House, Florence.

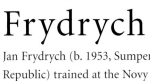

Triangle with ball, 2002 by Jan Frydrych.
15 in (38 cm) high
CODE: F   **EVD**

Rhomboid by Jan Frydrych. *2002*
5 in (12.75 cm) wide
CODE: F   **EVD**

Hafner

Dorothy Hafner (b. 1952, Connecticut) trained at the Skidmore College, Saratoga Springs, New York. Her work is in public collections at the Corning Museum of Glass, New York; Victoria and Albert Museum, London; and the Museum Voor Hedendaagse Kunst, Belgium. She has exhibited at the Tampa Museum of Art, Florida; the Heller Gallery, New York; and the Sanske Gallerie, Zurich.

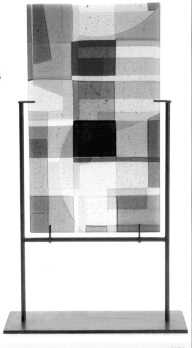

On Call by Dorothy Hafner. *2003*
25 in (63.5 cm) high
CODE: F   **HOL**

Harcuba

Jiri Harcuba (b. 1928, Harrachov, Czech Republic) trained at the Harrachov Glass Factory, the Novy Bor Glass School, and the Palackeho University, Olomouc, Czech Republic. His exhibitions have been held at the Brussels World Exhibition and the Pittsburgh Glass Center, Pennsylvania.

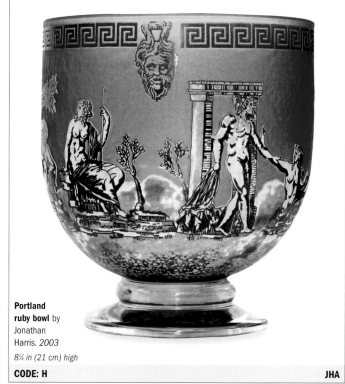

Franz Kafka's portrait by Jiri Harcuba. *1991*
8½ in (21.5 cm) wide

CODE: H   FIS

Young and old portraits of Rainer Maria Rilke by Jiri Harcuba. *1988*
5 in (12.5 cm) wide

CODE: I   FIS

Harris

Jonathan Harris (b. 1965, London) trained at the Stourbridge College of Art, UK. He has pieces in public collections at the Victoria and Albert Museum, London; the British Museum, London; and the Broadfield House Glass Museum, West Midlands.

Portland ruby bowl by Jonathan Harris. *2003*
8¼ in (21 cm) high

CODE: H   JHA

Hlôska

Pavol Hlôska (b. 1953, Banska-Stiavnica, Slovakia) trained at the Bratislava Academy of Fine Arts. Some of his pieces are featured in public collections at the National Gallery of Slovakia, Bratislava; the National Glass Museum, Leerdam; and the Jan van der Togt Museum, Amsterdam. He has exhibited at the Plateaux Gallery, London, and the Galerie L'Éclat du Verre, Paris.

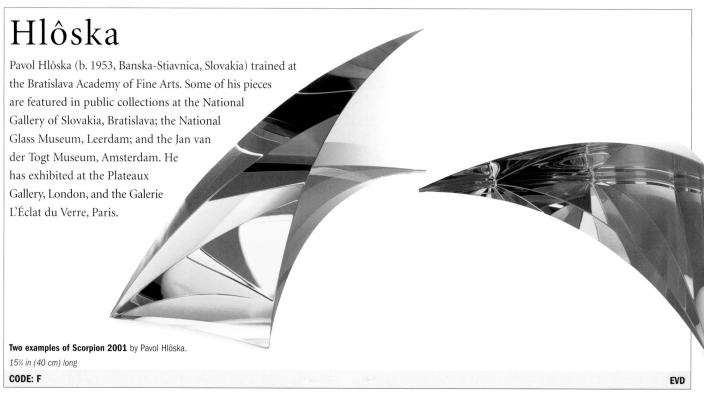

Two examples of Scorpion 2001 by Pavol Hlôska.
15¾ in (40 cm) long

CODE: F   EVD

Huchthausen

David Huchthausen (b. 1952, Wisconsin) trained at the universities of Wisconsin and Illinois, and the University of Applied Arts, Vienna. He has exhibited at the Habatat Galleries, Michigan; the Heller Gallery, New York; and the Corning Museum of Glass, New York. Public collections include the Smithsonian, Washington, D.C.; the Metropolitan Museum of Art, New York; and the Musée de Verre de Liege, Belgium.

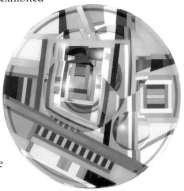

FRONT VIEW

Disc Five by David Huchthausen. *2003*
11 in (28 cm) wide

CODE: C   **LKM**

Hutter

Sidney Hutter (b. 1954, Champaign, Illinois) trained at the Massachusetts College of Art and Illinois State University, as well as at the Pilchuck Glass School, Seattle. Some of his pieces feature in public collections at the Corning Museum of Glass, New York; the Metropolitan Museum of Art, New York; and the White House Collection, Washington, D.C.

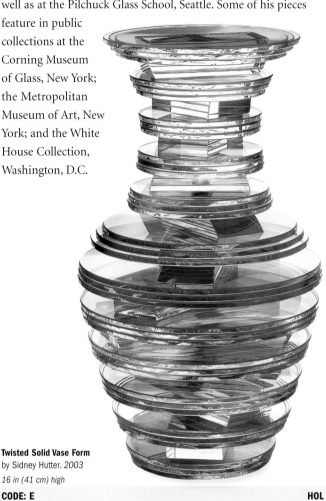

Twisted Solid Vase Form
by Sidney Hutter. *2003*
16 in (41 cm) high

CODE: E   **HOL**

Ink

Jack Ink (b. 1944, Canton, Ohio) trained at Kent State University, Ohio, and the University of Wisconsin with Harvey Littleton (*see p. 190*). He was artist in residence at J. & L. Lobmeyr, Vienna, and has been commissioned by the Natural History Museum, Vienna.

Shell with 2 parts 1416B, 2001 by Jack Ink.
20½ in (52 cm) long

CODE: F   **EVD**

Jakab

Andrej Jakab (b. 1950, Bratislava, Slovakia) began working with glassmakers in 1974. His exhibitions include the Studio Glass Gallery, London; the Art Point Gallery, Vienna; and the Galerie L'Éclat du Verre, Paris. Some of his pieces are at the Corning Glass Museum, New York, and the NGB/Netherlandische Glasbond/Gouda, Netherlands.

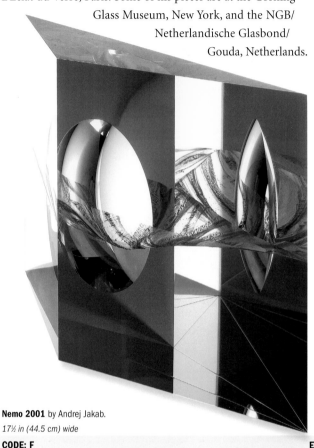

Nemo 2001 by Andrej Jakab.
17½ in (44.5 cm) wide

CODE: F   **EVD**

Kallenberger

Kreg Kallenberger (b. 1950, Austin, Texas) trained at the University of Tulsa, Oklahoma. His collections include the Corning Museum of Glass, New York; the Musée des Arts Décoratifs, Paris; and the Hokkaido Museum of Modern Art, Japan. He has exhibited at the Habatat Galleries, Michigan, and the Heller Gallery, New York.

View at Kelly's Peak
by Kreg Kallenberger. *2003*
23 in (58.5 cm) wide

CODE: F   **HOL**

Jolley

Richard Jolley (b. 1952, Kansas) trained at Vanderbilt University and the Penland School, North Carolina. He has exhibited at the Knoxville Museum of Art, Tennessee, and the Carnegie Museum of Art, Pittsburgh. His pieces can be seen at the Corning Museum of Glass, New York; the Glasmuseet Ebeltoft, Denmark; and the Museum of Contemporary Arts and Design, New York.

Quietude by Richard Jolley. *2003*
19 in (48.5 cm) high

CODE: E   **LKM**

Suspended male and female figures (Aqua) by Richard Jolley. *2003*
34 in (86.5 cm) high

CODE: F (each)   **LKM**

Karbler & David

Kit Karbler (b. 1954, Sandusky, Ohio) and Michael David (b. 1952, White Plains, New York) work as a team. Kit trained at Ohio University and at UCLA, California, while Michael trained at the University of Colorado, Goddard College, Vermont, and Cornell University, New York.

Their work features at the Kjarvalsstadir Museum, Iceland, and the Corning Museum of Glass, New York.

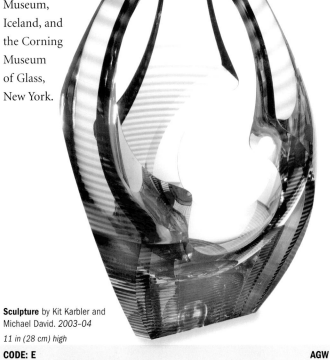

Sculpture by Kit Karbler and Michael David. *2003–04*
11 in (28 cm) high

CODE: E   **AGW**

Kinnaird

Alison Kinnaird (b. 1949, Edinburgh) trained at Edinburgh University. Her work can be seen at the Royal Museum of Scotland, Edinburgh; the Victoria and Albert Museum, London; and the Corning Museum of Glass, New York. Commissions include Broadfield House Glass Museum, West Midlands.

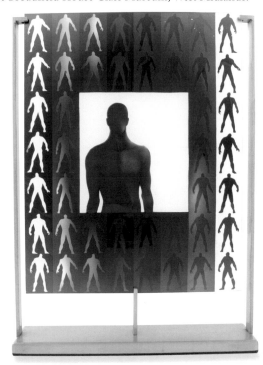

Eclipse by Alison Kinnaird. *2001*
Panel: 11½ in (29.5 cm) high

CODE: G   **CG**

Lauwers

Inge Lauwers (b. 1970, Lubumbashi, Zaire) trained at the Surrey Institute of Art and Design, UK, later completing an apprenticeship under glassmaster Koen Vanderstukken. Her exhibitions include the Mariska Dirkx Gallery, Netherlands; the Galleri Kvinnelist and the Galleri Gardenia, both in Norway.

Horse's head by Inge Lauwers. *2002*
25¼ in (64 cm) high

CODE: G   **GMD**

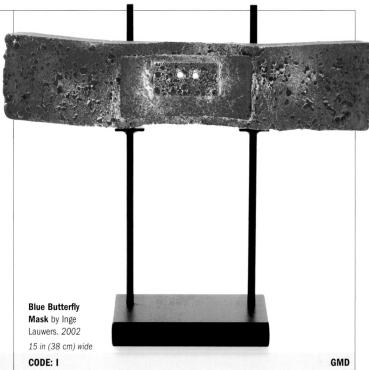

Blue Butterfly Mask by Inge Lauwers. *2002*
15 in (38 cm) wide

CODE: I   **GMD**

Layton

Peter Layton (b. 1937, Prague, Czech Republic) trained at the Central School of Art and Design, London. He has had many exhibitions worldwide. He has pieces in collections at the Fitzwilliam Museum, Cambridge, UK; the Victoria and Albert Museum, London; and the National Gallery, Prague. He also produces large architectural and sculptural works.

Ariel Stone Form vase by Peter Layton. *2004*
8 in (20.5 cm) high

CODE: H   PL

Mirage Stone Form vase by Peter Layton. *2004*
13½ in (34 cm) wide

CODE: G   PL

Leperlier

Etienne Leperlier (b. 1952, Evreux, France) is the grandson of glass artist François Décorchemont (1881–1971). Exhibitions include the Heller Gallery and the Habatat Galleries, in the US. His work is at the Museum of Contemporary Glass, Germany; the Kurokabe Glass Museum, Japan; and the Musée des Arts Décoratifs, Paris.

Sculpture by Etienne Leperlier. *1998*
23½ in (60 cm) high

CODE: F   EVD

Lewis

John Lewis (b. 1942, California) studied at the University of California, Berkeley. He has exhibited worldwide. Some of his pieces are included in public collections at the American Craft Museum, New York; the Metropolitan Museum of Art, New York; and the Corning Museum of Glass, New York.

Gold Glacier vessel by John Lewis. *2003*
25½ in (65 cm) high

CODE: F   LKM

Lintzen

Sabine Lintzen (b. 1956, Aachen, Germany) trained at AKB Maastricht and the Berlin Art Academy. Her work has been exhibited at the Van Tetterode Glass Studio, Amsterdam, and the Mariska Dirkx Gallery, Roermond, Netherlands. Some of her items are in Dutch collections at the National Glass Museum, Leerdam; the Jan van der Togt Museum, Amsterdam; and the Museum Het Domein, Sittard.

Bells by Sabine Lintzen. *2004*
27½ in (70 cm) high

CODE: G   GMD

Lipofsky

Marvin Lipofsky (b. 1938, Illinois) trained in industrial design at the University of Illinois, and in sculpture at the University of Wisconsin, where he worked with Harvey Littleton (*see p.190*). He has exhibited worldwide, and has pieces at the National Museum of Modern Art, Japan; the Corning Museum of Glass, New York; the Museo del Vidrio, Spain; and the Metropolitan Museum of Art, New York.

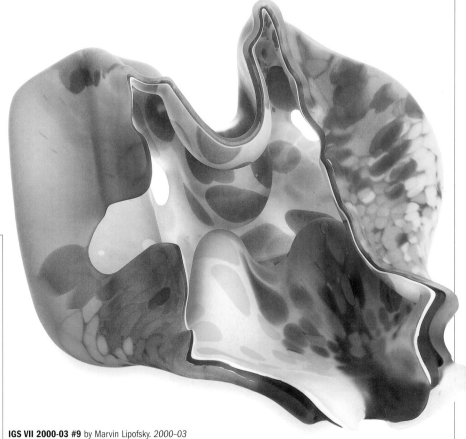

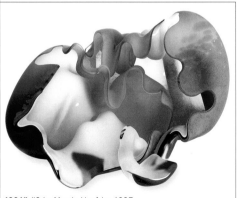

IGS VI #3 by Marvin Lipofsky. *1997*
24 in (61 cm) wide

CODE: D   HOL

IGS VII 2000-03 #9 by Marvin Lipofsky. *2000-03*
16 in (40.5 cm) wide

CODE: E   HOL

Lugossy

Maria Lugossy (b. 1950, Budapest, Hungary) trained at the Hungarian Academy of Applied Arts. She has exhibited all over the world. Her work is in public collections at the Corning Museum of Glass, New York; the Hungarian National Gallery, Budapest; the Musée des Beaux Arts, Rouen; and the British Museum, London.

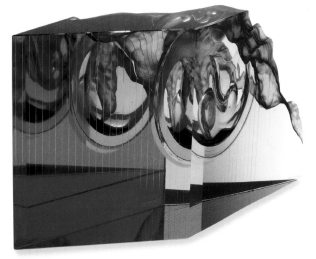

Green glass sculpture by Maria Lugossy. *1988*
9¾ in (25 cm) high
CODE: F   **EVD**

Martinuzzi

Gian Paolo Martinuzzi (b. 1933, Friuli, Italy) is a self-taught artist. He has exhibited across the world. Public collections include the Hokkaido Museum, Sapporo, Japan; the Musée-Château d'Annecy, France; the Musées Royaux d'Art et d'Histoire, Belgium; and the Kunstmuseum, Düsseldorf, Germany.

Engraved panel by Gian Paolo Martinuzzi. *1969*
11¾ in (30 cm) long
CODE: F   **EVD**

Marioni

Dante Marioni (b. 1964, California) trained at the Pilchuck Glass School, Seattle, and the Penland School of Craft, North Carolina. He has exhibited at the Marx Saunders Gallery, Chicago, and the William Traver Gallery, Seattle. Some of his pieces are in public collections at the Japanese National Museum of Craft, Tokyo; the White House Crafts Collection, Washington, D.C.; and the Glasmuseet Ebeltoft, Denmark.

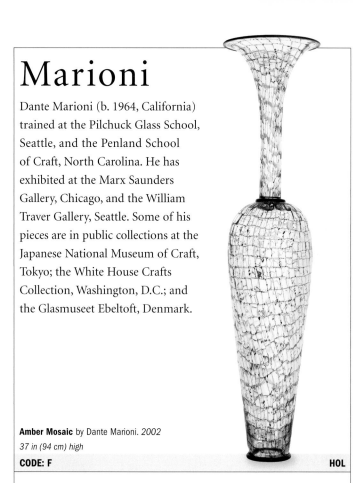

Amber Mosaic by Dante Marioni. *2002*
37 in (94 cm) high
CODE: F   **HOL**

Green Trio by Dante Marioni. *2001*
Tallest: 29 in (74 cm) high
CODE: F   **HOL**

Miner

Charles Miner (b. 1947, California) trained at the Pilchuck Glass School, Seattle. He has exhibited at the Portia Gallery, Chicago, and the Heller Gallery, New York. Some of his pieces are at the Renwick Gallery of the Smithsonian American Art Museum, Washington, D.C., and the New Mexico Museum of Fine Arts.

Cleo by Charles Miner. *2003*
17 in (43 cm) high
CODE: G HOL

Morris

William Morris (b. 1957, California) trained at California State University and Central Washington University and has had many exhibitions. He has pieces in public collections at the American Craft Museum, New York; the Chrysler Museum of Art, Virginia; and the Corning Museum of Glass, New York.

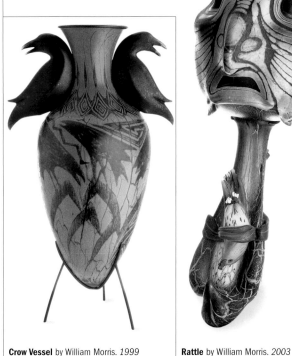

Crow Vessel by William Morris. *1999*
20½ in (52 cm) high
CODE: A HOL

Rattle by William Morris. *2003*
20½ in (52 cm) high
CODE: B HOL

Mukaide

Keiko Mukaide (b. 1954, Tokyo, Japan) trained at the Musashino Art University, Tokyo; the Pilchuck Glass School, Seattle; and the Royal College of Art, London. Her work can be seen at the Victoria and Albert Museum, London.

Stream Bowl by Keiko Mukaide. *2003*
12¼ in (31.5 cm) wide
CODE: H CG

Musler

Jay Musler (b. 1949, California) trained at the California College of Arts and Crafts. Collections include the Corning Museum of Glass, New York, and the Kitano Museum, Kobe, Japan.

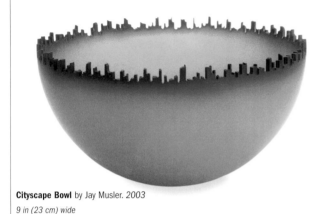

Cityscape Bowl by Jay Musler. *2003*
9 in (23 cm) wide

CODE: F	HOL

Najean

Aristide Najean (b. 1959, France) studied in Paris, Munich, and Florence. Exhibitions of his work have been held all over Europe. He has pieces in public collections at the Mairie de Paris XVI, France.

Maternity II by Aristide Najean. *2002*
16½ in (41 cm) high

CODE: H	VET

Mother & Child by Aristide Najean. *2002*
20¼ in (51.5 cm) high

CODE: G	VET

Patti

Tom Patti (b. 1943, Massachusetts) trained at the New School for Social Research, New York; the Pratt Institute, New York; and the Boston Museum School. He has been involved with many exhibitions. Public collections include the Metropolitan Museum of Art and the American Craft Museum, New York; the Carnegie Museum, Pittsburgh; the Philadelphia Museum of Art; and the Victoria and Albert Museum, London.

Compacted Solarized Blue with Dual Ring and Orange Pinstripes by Tom Patti. *1989–91*
6 in (15.5 cm) wide

CODE: B	HOL

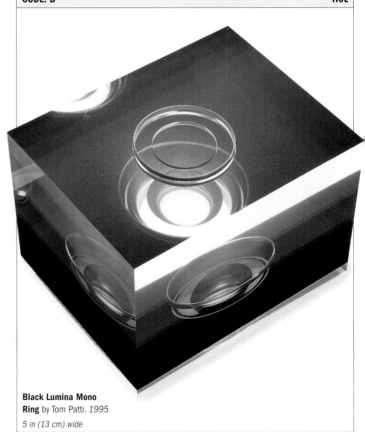

Black Lumina Mono Ring by Tom Patti. *1995*
5 in (13 cm) wide

CODE: C	HOL

Pedrosa

Bruno Pedrosa (b. 1950, Cedro, Brazil) studied at the Rio de Janeiro School of Fine Arts. He began working with glass in 1995. Exhibitions include the Brazilian-American Cultural Institute, Washington, D.C.

Pieces in public collections include the Museum of Modern Art, Rio de Janeiro, and the Corning Museum of Glass, New York.

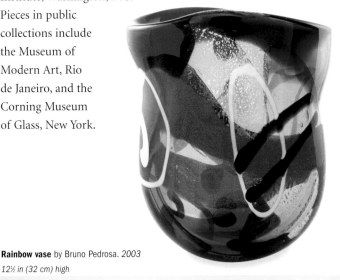

Rainbow vase by Bruno Pedrosa. *2003*
12½ in (32 cm) high

CODE: G   **VET**

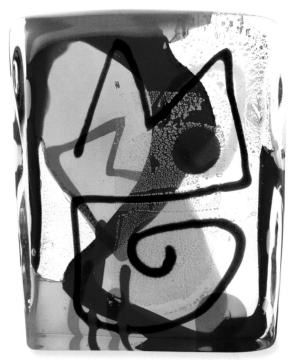

Por do Sol em Bozios by Bruno Pedrosa. *2003*
11¼ in (28.5 cm) high

CODE: H   **VET**

Pennell

Ronald Pennell (b. 1935, Birmingham, UK) trained at the Birmingham College of Art. His work has been exhibited worldwide. Public collections include the Crafts Council, the Victoria and Albert Museum, and the British Museum, all in London, and the Corning Museum of Glass, New York.

Dog Days by Ronald Pennell. *2003*
8 in (20.5 cm) high

CODE: G   **CG**

Powell

Stephen Powell (b. 1951, Alabama) studied at Louisiana State University and is currently professor of art at Centre College, Kentucky. His work has been on display at the Masterworks Gallery, New Zealand; the Habatat Galleries, Florida; and the Marx-Saunders Gallery, Chicago. He has contributed pieces to public collections of the Huntsville Museum of Art, Alabama, and the Corning Museum of Glass, New York.

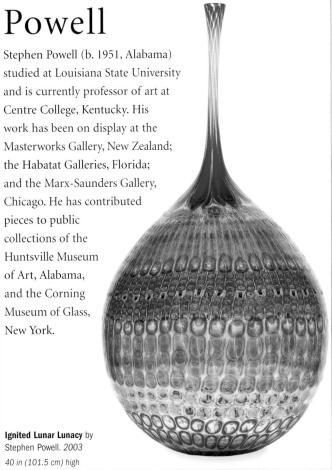

Ignited Lunar Lunacy by Stephen Powell. *2003*
40 in (101.5 cm) high

CODE: E   **HOL**

Price

Richard Price (b. 1959, Aldershot, UK) trained at the School of Art and Design, North Staffordshire, and the Rietveld Academy in Amsterdam. He has held exhibitions in the Netherlands at the Willem Baars Art Consultancy, the Bianca Landgraaf Gallery, the Mariska Dirkx Gallery, the Carla Koch Gallery, and the Wildevuur Gallery. His work has been featured at the Glass Museum, Hoogeveen, Netherlands.

The Body by Richard Price. 2004
34¼ in (87 cm) high

CODE: G   GMD

Reekie

David Reekie (b. 1947, London) trained at the Stourbridge College of Art, UK. He has exhibited worldwide. He has work in British public collections at the Manchester City Art Galleries; the Broadfield House Glass Museum; the Crafts Council Collection, and the Victoria and Albert Museum; as well as in the Glasmuseet Ebeltoft, Denmark.

Greek Head VIII by David Reekie. *1994*
16¾ in (42.5 cm) high

CODE: G   CG

Raymond

Jean-Paul Raymond (b. 1948, Brive, France) completed an apprenticeship under glassmaster Walter Couffini. He has exhibited throughout Europe and has objects in collections at the Musée des Arts Décoratifs, Paris, and at the Museo del Vidrio, Spain.

La Ronde by Jean-Paul Raymond. *2003*
29¼ in (74 cm) wide

CODE: G   GMD

Reid

Colin Reid (b. 1953, Cheshire, UK) trained in the UK at the Stourbridge School of Art and the St. Martins School of Art. His work has been exhibited at the Galerie International de Verre, France, and the Habatat Galleries in Michigan. Public collections include the Victoria and Albert Museum, London; the Corning Museum of Glass, New York; and the Museum of Decorative Arts, Prague.

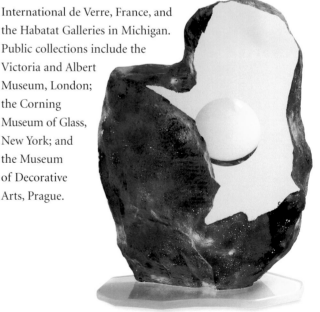

Untitled R1144 by Colin Reid. *2003*
19¾ in (50 cm) high

CODE: F   COL

Mindless Technology by David Reekie. *2003*
27¼ in (69 cm) wide

CODE: E TRR

Ries

Christopher Ries (b. 1952, Columbus, Ohio) trained at Ohio State University and at the University of Wisconsin with Harvey Littleton (*see p.190*). Public collections include the Carnegie Museum of Art and the Columbus Museum of Art, New York, and the Museum of American Glass, New Jersey.

Wild Orchid by Christopher Ries. *2001*
20½ in (52 cm) high

CODE: D HOL

Rosol

Martin Rosol (b. 1956, Prague, Czech Republic) trained at the School of Arts and Crafts, Prague, and later assisted at the Corning Museum of Glass, New York. His work is in public collections at the American Craft Museum, New York; the Kanazawa Museum, Japan; and the Moravian National Gallery, Czech Republic.

Radius VI by Martin Rosol. *2003*
11 in (28 cm) high

CODE: F HOL

Royal

Richard Royal (b. 1952, US) started his studies in glass-blowing in 1971 and began working at the Pilchuck Glass School, Seattle, in 1978. Exhibitions of his work have been held at the LewAllen Gallery, New Mexico; the Jerald Melberg Gallery, North Carolina; and the William Traver Gallery, Seattle. His pieces are part of public and corporate collections including the Daiichi Museum, Japan; the New Orleans Museum of Art; and the IBM Collection, New York.

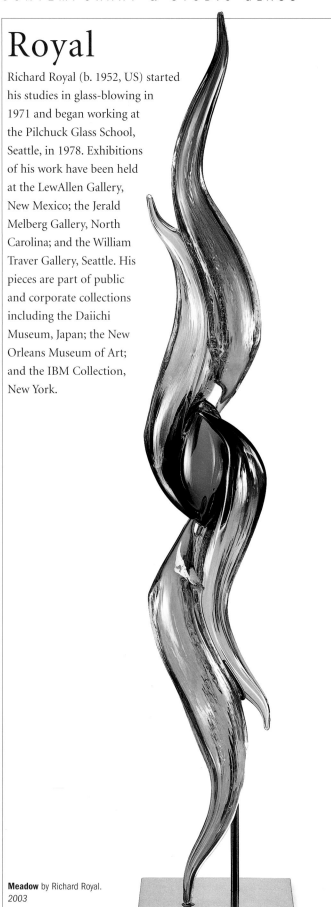

Meadow by Richard Royal. *2003*
50 in (127 cm) high

CODE: F   HOL

Seide

Paul Seide (b. 1949, New York) trained at the Egani Neon Glassblowing School, New York, and the University of Wisconsin. He has been commissioned by Swarovski World of Crystal, Australia. Public collections include the Corning Museum of Glass, New York, and the National Museum of Modern Art, Kyoto, Japan.

Fractacality by Paul Seide. *1998*
51cm (20in) high

CODE: F   LKM

Sellner

Theodor Sellner (b. 1947, Zwiesel, Germany) trained at the Specialized Glass School, Zwiesel, and the Corning Glass Center, New York. He has exhibited at the SM Gallery, Frankfurt, and the Corning Museum of Glass, New York. Public collections include the Musée des Arts Décoratifs, Paris; the Art Gallery, Immenhausen and the Glasmuseum Frauenau, both in Germany.

CLOSE-UP OF HEAD

Friedenswächter (The Peacekeeper) by Theodor Sellner. *2002*
39¼ in (100 cm) high

CODE: G   GMD

Solven

Pauline Solven (b. 1943, London) trained at the Stourbridge College of Art and the Royal College of Art, London. She has exhibited in the UK at the Crafts Council, the Oxford Gallery, and the National Glass Center. Public collections include the Victoria and Albert Museum, London; the Broadfield House Glass Museum, West Midlands; the Corning Museum of Glass, New York; and the Museum of Decorative Arts, Prague.

Emerging Sun by Pauline Solven. *2000*
14 in (35.5 cm) high

CODE: H   CG

Sterling

Lisabeth Sterling (b. 1958, Chicago) trained at the Pilchuck Glass School, Seattle; the University of Minnesota; and the Pennsylvania Academy of Fine Arts. Exhibitions include the Riley Hawk Galleries, New York; the Marx-Saunders Gallery, Chicago; and the William Traver Gallery, Washington. Public collections include the Wheaton Museum of American Glass, New Jersey, and the American Interfaith Institute, Philadelphia.

Susie Homemaker & Her Carnivorous Plants by Lisabeth Sterling. *2003*
17 in (43.5 cm) high

CODE: F   HOL

Stahl

Georges (b. 1951, Nancy, France) and Monique (b. 1946, Reims, France) Stahl are a husband-and-wife team. Their exhibitions include the Contemporary Art Fair in Strasbourg. Public collections include the Hsinchu Municipal Glass Museum, Taiwan; Caisse d'Eparange, Vierzon; and Roundabout, Bedarieux, France.

Splash by Georges & Monique Stahl. *2004*
15¾ in (40 cm) wide

CODE: H   GMD

Desir d'Ailes by Georges & Monique Stahl. *2003*
19¾ in (50 cm) high

CODE: H   GMD

Stern

Anthony Stern (b. 1944, Cambridge, UK) completed a BA in Architecture and Fine Art at St. John's College, Cambridge, and then studied at the Royal College of Art, where he got an MA in Glass. His work is represented in major glass museums. His London studio is open to visitors by appointment.

Seascape bowl by Anthony Stern. *2003*
8½ in (22 cm) high

CODE: H   ASG

Tagliapietra

Lino Tagliapietra (b. 1934, Murano, Italy) was an apprentice to Archimede Seguso in Murano and became a maestro at the age of 21. He has collaborated with artists such as Dale Chihuly and Dan Dailey. His pieces can be seen at the Detroit Institute of Arts, Michigan; the Corning Museum of Glass, New York; the Hokkaido Museum of Modern Art, Japan; and the Musée des Arts Décoratifs, Paris.

Hopi by Lino Tagliapietra. *2003*
15 in (38 cm) high
CODE: D   **HOL**

Dinosaur by Lino Tagliapietra. *2003*
15 in (38 cm) high
CODE: D   **HOL**

Bilbao by Lino Tagliapietra. *2003*
18½ in (47 cm) high
CODE: D   **HOL**

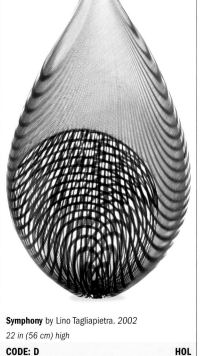

Symphony by Lino Tagliapietra. *2002*
22 in (56 cm) high
CODE: D   **HOL**

Traub

David Traub (b. 1949, New York) trained at East Texas State University and the Royal College of Art, London. His work can be seen at the Broadfield House Glass Museum, West Midlands; the Museum of Art, São Paolo, Brazil; and the Glasmuseet Ebeltoft, Denmark.

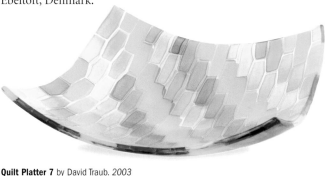

Quilt Platter 7 by David Traub. *2003*
17¼ in (44 cm) square
CODE: G   **CG**

Van Wijk

Dick van Wijk (b. 1943, Leiden, Netherlands) trained at the Art Academy and the Jan Van Eyck Academy, Maastricht. His exhibitions in the Netherlands include the Smelik & Stokking Galleries, the De Kliuw Gallery, and the Mariska Dirkx Gallery. Some of his pieces are at the Stedelijk Museum, Amsterdam, and he also has sculptural work in a number of public spaces.

Zonnewind (Solarwind) by Dick van Wijk (glass made by Jan Willen van Zijst). *2004*
43¼ in (110 cm) long
CODE: G   **GMD**

Van Cline

Mary Van Cline (b. 1954, Texas) began studying glass at the Penland School of Craft, North Carolina. Her work can be seen at The Smithsonian, Washington, D.C., and the Corning Museum of Glass, New York.

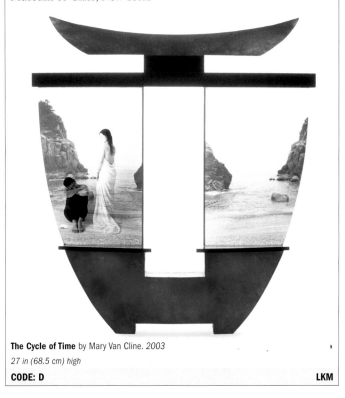

The Cycle of Time by Mary Van Cline. *2003*
27 in (68.5 cm) high
CODE: D   **LKM**

Vanderstukken

Koen Vanderstukken (b. 1964, Wilrijk, Belgium) studied Industrial Chemistry and Lampworking under Dieter Dornheim, and went to the State Institute of Art Crafts in Mechelen, Belgium. His work features at the Glasmuseet Ebeltoft, Denmark; the National Glass Museum, Leerdam, Netherlands; and is in the Royal Collection of Queen Fabiola in Belgium.

From the Faces series by Koen Vanderstukken. *2003*
17 in (43 cm) wide
CODE: H   **GMD**

Vigliaturo

Silvio Vigliaturo (b. 1949, Acri, Italy) trained at the Fine Arts Academy in Turin. He has exhibited across Europe. Some of his pieces are in collections at the Glass Museum, Altare, Italy, and the Salon International de l'Art Contemporain, Marseille.

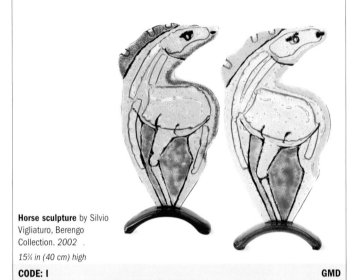

Horse sculpture by Silvio Vigliaturo, Berengo Collection. *2002*
15¾ in (40 cm) high

CODE: I GMD

Vízner

Frantisek Vízner (b. 1936, Prague, Czechoslovakia) trained at the Glassmaking School, Novy Bor, and the Prague Academy of Applied Arts. He has exhibited works at the Corning Museum of Glass, New York.

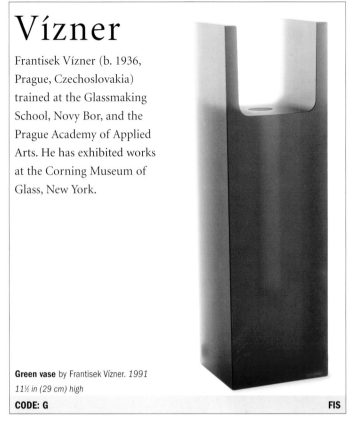

Green vase by Frantisek Vízner. *1991*
11½ in (29 cm) high

CODE: G FIS

Weinberg

Steven Weinberg (b. 1954, New York) trained at the Rhode Island School of Design and the New York State College of Ceramics at Alfred University. Public collections include the Los Angeles County Museum; the Corning Museum of Glass, New York; and The Smithsonian, Washington, D.C.

Blue Cube by Steven Weinberg. *1996*
8¼ in (21 cm) square

CODE: C HOL

Wilkin

Neil Wilkin (b. 1959, Portsmouth, UK) trained at the Portsmouth College of Art and the North Staffordshire Polytechnic. Public collections in London include the Crafts Council Collection and the Victoria and Albert Museum.

Blue Wild Flower by Neil Wilkin. *1998*
23½ in (60 cm) wide

CODE: G NW

Yamamoto

Koichiro Yamamoto (b. 1969, Japan) trained at Tsukuba University, Japan, and the Royal College of Art, London. His work is part of the public collections at the Victoria and Albert Museum, London; the Manchester City Art Gallery, UK; and the Glasmuseet Ebeltoft, Denmark.

Jug & Cup by Koichiro Yamamoto. *2001*
6 in (15.5 cm) high
CODE: H   **CG**

Yamano

Hiroshi Yamano (b. 1956, Fukuoka, Japan) trained at Chuo University, Japan; the California College of Arts and Crafts; and the Tokyo Glass Art Institute. His work has been exhibited in the United States and Japan. Public collections include the Corning Museum of Glass, New York, and the Wheaton Glass Museum, New Jersey.

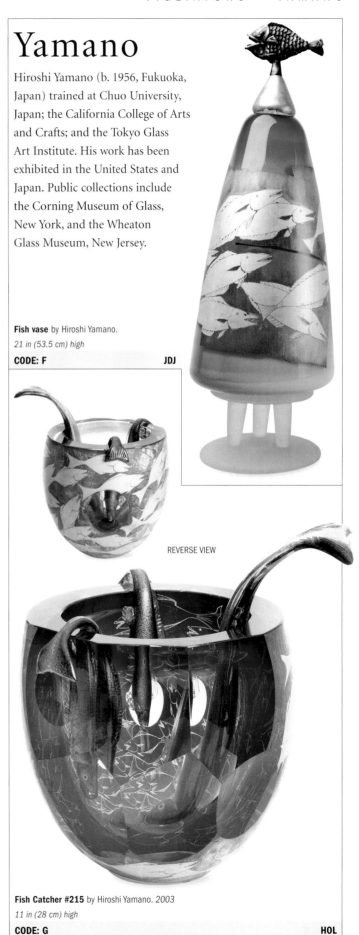

Fish vase by Hiroshi Yamano.
21 in (53.5 cm) high
CODE: F   **JDJ**

REVERSE VIEW

Zbynovsky

Vladimir Zbynovsky (b. 1964, Bratislava, Slovakia) trained at the Institute of Decorative Arts, Bratislava, and the Institute of Fine Arts and School of Applied Arts, Paris. His exhibitions have been shown throughout the world. His work is featured in collections at the Meisenthal Museum, France, and the XXI Century Museum, Kanazawa, Japan.

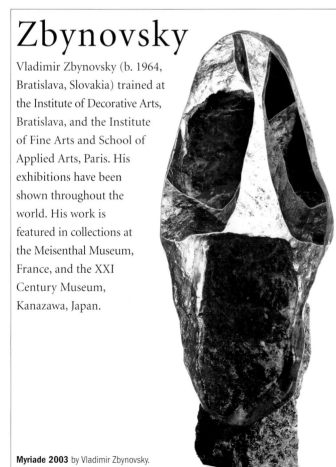

Myriade 2003 by Vladimir Zbynovsky.
17¼ in (44 cm) high
CODE: F   **EVD**

Fish Catcher #215 by Hiroshi Yamano. *2003*
11 in (28 cm) high
CODE: G   **HOL**

Zilio

Andrea Zilio (b. 1966, Venice, Italy) received no formal training but completed an apprenticeship in 1989. His work has been exhibited at the Murano Museum of Glass, Venice; the International Biennale of Glass in Venice; and the Contemporary Glass Exhibition of Young Artists, Milan. He has instructed at the Pilchuck Glass School, Seattle.

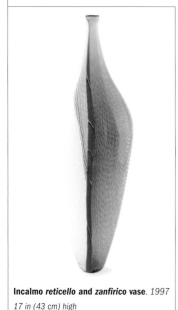

Incalmo *reticello* and *zanfirico* vase. 1997
17 in (43 cm) high

CODE: G   **ANF**

Incalmo vase by Andrea Zilio. 1999
19¾ in (50 cm) high

CODE: G   **ANF**

Zimmermann

Jörg Zimmermann (b. 1940, Uhingen, Germany) trained at the College of Applied Art and Design in Schwäbisch Gmünd, Germany. Some of his pieces are on display in Germany at the Museum of Art, Veste Coburg; the Glass Museum, Frauenau; and the Museum of Art, Hamburg.

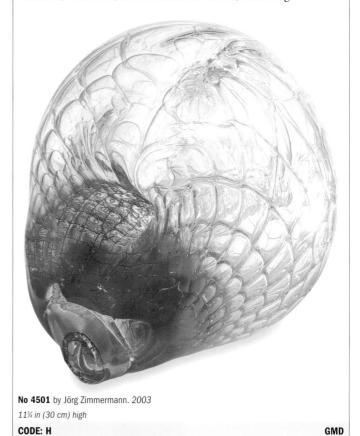

No 4501 by Jörg Zimmermann. 2003
11¾ in (30 cm) high

CODE: H   **GMD**

Zynsky

Mary Ann "Toots" Zynsky (b. 1951, Boston) was one of the founders of the Pilchuck Glass School, Seattle, in 1971. She has had many exhibitions worldwide. Public collections include the White House Collection of American Craft, Washington, D.C.; the Metropolitan Museum of Art, New York; and the American Craft Museum, New York.

Green and blue bowl by Mary Ann "Toots" Zynsky. c. 1990
15¾ in (40 cm) wide

CODE: G   **QU**

Zoritchak

Yan Zoritchak (b. 1944, Zdiar, Slovakia) trained at the Institute of Applied Glass, Zelezny Brod, and the School of Applied Arts, Prague. Exhibitions of his work were held at Citia, Conservatory of Art and History, Annecy, France. Some of his works are in public collections at the Art Museum, Düsseldorf; the Museum of Glass, Belgium; the Hsinchu Municipal Glass Museum, Taiwan; and the Glasmuseet Ebeltoft, Denmark.

Jardin Celeste by Yan Zoritchak. *1998*
17¾ in (45 cm) long
CODE: F   **EVD**

Messager de l'Espace by Yan Zoritchak. *2003*
18 in (46 cm) long
CODE: F   **EVD**

Loetz iridescent glass vase with a bulbous body and an elongated neck. It is decorated with a "pulled" or "feathered" technique popular with Art Nouveau glassmakers, but dating back to the Romans in style. *1900–10 11¾ in (30 cm) high* **$3,600–4,500 LN**

Appendices
& index

This section of the book contains a wealth of essential, practical information for keen glass collectors. An extensive glossary of materials and techniques explains all the specialist terms used in the book, and this is followed by a key to the suppliers' codes used in the price guides. The directory of other dealers, auction houses, and museums provides not only the addresses of useful specialists who may be able to help you in your search for certain pieces, but also lists the museums that have good collections of glass, an invaluable source of further background information.

Glossary

A canne A striped *filigrana* pattern (*see p.227*) comprising a row of colored canes.

Acid-etching A technique originally developed to create a matt or frosted finish on glass by immersion in hydrofluoric acid. Areas not to be etched are protected with wax or varnish. Also used to remove areas of overlaid glass, to create designs in relief on cameo glass vessels.

Annealing The slow cooling of a completed glass object to avoid straining and breaking through a sudden drop in temperature.

Ariel A technique developed at Orrefors around 1930 in which a pattern is sandblasted in relief on a clear or colored vessel. The vessel is then reheated and cased in clear glass to enclose the pattern in trails of air bubbles.

Art Deco An art movement of the 1920s and 30s. The name derives from the 1925 Paris exhibition called *Exposition Internationale des Arts Décoratifs et Industriels Modernes*. Elements of the style include geometric patterns and strong use of color.

Art Nouveau An art movement that emerged in the late 1880s and continued into the first decade of the 20th century. Art Nouveau style is characterized by flowing plant forms and whiplash motifs. Also known as Jugendstil (*see p.227*).

At-the-fire A technique of reheating glass before blowing or other decorative procedures.

Aurene ware A trade name for Steuben's iridescent glass developed by Frederick Carder in the United States. The name derives from the Latin for gold.

Aventurine A translucent glass given a sparkling appearance by the incorporation of golden or copper flecks of oxidized metal. Can also be used as a glaze. The name probably derives from a quartz, known as *avventurina* in Italian, that has a similar appearance. Also known as *avventurina*.

Batch The mixture of raw materials such as sand, fluxing agents, and coloring agents, melted in a pot or tank to make glass. Cullet (*see below*) is also added to aid the melting process.

Blank A piece of glass that has been formed but will have further decorative and/or structural working.

Blown glass A technique where the glassmaker literally blows air through a hollow, tubular rod or blowpipe, shaping a gather of molten glass. The glass can be either free-blown or blown into a mold to create a more uniform shape.

Blowpipe
See Pontil

Cameo glass Glass made up of two or more separate, colored glass layers. The top layers are wheel-carved or acid-etched to produce a relief image and reveal the different-colored layer(s) beneath.

Cane
See Rod

Carnival glass A pressed glass with an iridescent surface. It was produced in the United States in the early part of the 20th century and was reputedly given away as a prize at funfairs and carnivals.

Carving A method of decorating a glass surface by the controlled and systematic removal of areas of glass with handheld tools or mechanical means.

Casing Where a piece of glass is covered with an additional layer of glass, often of a contrasting color. In some instances, the casing will be further worked with cutting or etching to reveal the layer beneath.

Casting Creating a product by pouring molten glass into a preformed mold.

Chipped ice A technique used by Handel & Co. to give a frosted effect on the surface of glass. It is achieved by applying glue to the surface and heating it. When dry, the glue flakes off and creates a textured surface.

Cire perdue
See Lost wax casting

Cluthra glass Developed in the 1920s by Frederick Carder at Steuben Glassworks in Corning, New York.

Cold enameling The application of colored enamels (*see Enameling*), but without a subsequent firing to enhance durability.

Cold-worked Glass that is decorated—for example, by cutting—once it has cooled down and is solid.

Crackle glass Type of glass, also known as *craquelé* or ice glass, with a crackled surface produced by plunging a hot gather into cold water. Can also be simulated in a textured mold.

Cullet Pieces of previously discarded waste glass. It melts faster than the new batch to which it is added, reducing fuel costs.

Cutting Where glass is removed from the surface of a piece to create a motif or pattern. Glass can be ground with a rotating stone, wood, or metal wheel, and an abrasive suspended in liquid. *See also Carving; Wheel-carving*

Depression glass Pressed glass produced inexpensively during the Depression years (1920s and 30s) in the United States. It was often offered free as a promotional gift to customers in shops and is now highly collectible.

Dichroic glass Glass that changes color, with a slight iridescence, depending on how the light hits it and how it is viewed.

Enameling Painting with a mixture of powdered colored glass bound in an oil medium, then reheating the vessel to fuse the design and enhance durability.

Engraved Where the surface of a piece of glass is cut with a wheel and abrasive, or scratched, sometimes with a diamond-tipped tool.

Facet-cut A piece cut with adjoining flat planes, in the style of gemstone cutting.

Favrile A term referring to the iridescent glass developed by Louis Comfort Tiffany, patented in 1894. The name derives from the German "fabrile," meaning handmade.

Fazzoletto The Italian word used to describe a handkerchief vase—that is, a vase that takes the form of a falling handkerchief.

Filigrana A general term for the technique where decorative threads of colored glass or rods are incorporated into the body of a piece.

Filigrana a retortoli See Zanfirico

Fire-polished A process in which a piece of glass is reheated to reduce any imperfections in manufacture, giving it a bright, lustrous finish.

Fluogravure A technique devised by Müller Frères where a piece of glass is partly enameled and partly acid-etched, producing contrasting opaque and transparent elements.

Gaffer The lead or master glassmaker, who orchestrates the movements of the team.

Gather (of glass) A mass of molten glass (sometimes called a gob) that is collected on the end of a blowpipe, pontil, or gathering iron.

Gilding Glass decoration using gold leaf, paint, or dust. It can be applied in hot or cold techniques.

Glory hole A small hole in the glass furnace near the main aperture where glass is gathered. Pieces are often reheated here quickly for further work or finishing such as fire-polishing.

Graal Technique developed around 1916 at Orrefors in which a small colored glass vessel is cut, engraved, or acid-etched with a pattern, then reheated, cased in clear glass, and blown to a final form.

Grisaille Monochromatic, gray paintwork. Sometimes this paintwork is used to imitate the effect of relief sculpture.

Hot-worked Molten glass that is worked on or decorated in heat, such as the creation of internal bubbles in the liquefied glass.

Incalmo In this technique, two or more blown pieces are heated, "opened out," and carefully joined together to create distinct bands of color. The name refers to the calm, careful work required of the glassmaker to complete this complex process.

Inciso The Italian term for incised glass, which was developed by

Venini. The technique creates many shallow, horizontal cuts across the glass surface.

Inlay The application and fusion of a prepared piece of glass into the surface of a glass vessel for decorative effect. See Marqueterie-sur-verre

Intaglio A technique in which a motif or pattern is engraved or wheel-cut in relief, leaving its background above it on the surface of the vessel.

Intercalaire A term for a decoration that is between layers of glass.

Iridescence A surface effect that creates the appearance of rainbow colors caused by differential refraction of light waves, similar to light catching an oil spill on a wet surface. It is mostly produced by spraying a mist of metalic salts on to the hot glass vessel.

Jack in the Pulpit The name given to a vessel resembling the North American plant Arisaema triphyllum.

Jugendstil Literally "youth style," this is the German term for Art Nouveau. It is derived from Jugend, the name of a German contemporary-art magazine first published in 1896.

Knop A protruding shape found on the stem of a drinking glass, often spherical or oval, but it can be cut.

Lamp work Delicate, ornamental technique used to make pieces fashioned from thin rods. The rods are shaped, bent, and attached to each other by being heated over a small burner. These designs are often embedded in paperweights and spheres.

Latticinio From the Italian for milk (latte), this is a term for the white threads resembling spaghetti used for decoration in clear glass.

Lava glass Also known as volcanic glass, this is an iridescent gold glass often with a rough surface and dripping, lavalike decoration. It was developed in the United States by Louis Comfort Tiffany.

Lost wax casting (or cire perdue) A technique adopted from metal-working and used for pieces too detailed for conventional casting. A model of the piece is made in wax. The wax template is encased in clay or plaster to create a mold of the design. When heated, the wax melts away from the ceramic mold and drains out through "gates." Finally, molten glass is poured into the ceramic mold through these gates. Powdered glass can also be used and fired. After cooling, the mold is broken away to reveal the glass object inside.

Luster A surface effect that has similar properties to an iridescent surface. See Iridescence

Marqueterie-sur-verre A technique developed by Emile Gallé in which pieces of hot glass are pressed into a hot body to a predetermined design.

Martelé A French term meaning hammer-textured. It was used on silver by Gorham in the United States. The effect is also created on glass through cutting, and was used on some Daum cameo pieces.

Millefili Italian term, referring to a thousand threads, meaning a type of glass that is made up of very fine canes.

Millefiori Italian for a thousand flowers. In this technique, tile-like cross-sections of brightly colored canes are arranged in patterns known as "set-ups" and embedded in clear glass. *Millefiori* is often used in paperweights.

Miter The beveled end or edge of a piece where a joint is made by cutting two sections at an angle.

Mold-blown A technique where glass is blown into a mold to create a uniform shape, either by hand or as part of a mechanized process.

Murrine Slices of transparent or opaque colored glass canes. Usually patterned, from floral to abstract, they can be pressed together into a form or, more often, picked up on a glass gather that is then blown into a vessel.

Opalescence An effect in glass that emulates opals, having a milky-blue appearance by reflected light and an amber tint by transmitted light.

Overlay A glass layer over the main glass body that can be decorated by various techniques, such as carving, acid-etching, or painting with enamels.

Paperweight glass A magnifying dome of clear, faceted, or cased glass (usually lead glass), with a *millefiori* or lamp-work design at or near its base.

Pâte-de-verre From the French for paste of glass. A technique where ground glass is mixed with a liquid to form a paste. It is then pressed into a mold and slowly heated to form the required shape.

Pezzato Italian technique creating "patched" glass. Generally, square pieces of colored glass are fused together to create a sheet of glass resembling a patchwork quilt. This sheet is then used to form a vessel.

Pontil An iron rod that is used when the final shaping or finishing of a piece is required. The object would be attached to the rod at its base when handles were attached, for example.

Pontil mark A rough scar left when the pontil is removed from the base of a piece; often polished away in further finishing.

Pressed glass Developed in the United States in the 1820s and formed by pouring molten glass into a metal mold before pressing it home with a plunger. Resulting pieces have patterned exteriors and smooth interiors and can be finished by hand.

Pulegoso From the Murano dialect for bubbly. The term describes a piece with a rough surface and tiny bubbles. The technique is typical of the 1920s and was developed by Napoleone Martinuzzi.

Ravenna A technique developed around 1948 by Sven Palmqvist in which a pattern is sandblasted into colored glass. The resulting cavities are filled with crushed glass in other colors. The piece is then covered with a further layer of clear glass and heated to create the shape.

Reverse-painting Painting an image in reverse on the inner surface of glass, especially on lamps. This technique was popular on Art Nouveau lamps in the United States.

Rod Generally a thin shaft of glass, possibly colored, created by pulling a gather of glass in opposite directions into a narrow thread. The thread can be cut to size for specific use and fused with other rods. Also known as a cane.

Sandblasting An etching process that involves firing an abrasive material at a section of a piece.

Seeds Air bubbles caught in glass, often in groups.

Sommerso Technique developed in Murano in the 1930s. The term translates as "submerged" and involves casing one or more layers of transparent colored glass within a layer of thick, colorless glass.

Tesserae The small squares of colored glass used to create a mosaic pattern. The word derives from the Greek *tesseres*, meaning four-sided.

Tessuto Describes a design in glass that gives a woven appearance, as if threads or strips of glass have been woven together over the body.

Vaseline glass An opalescent glass with a greasy appearance, made by adding tiny amounts of uranium and metal oxides to the glass.

Verre de soie From the French for silk glass, this refers to glass with a silky finish.

Wheel-carving A decorative technique in which a piece is carved by a series of wheels varying in size, each giving a different fineness of detail to the finished piece. Decoration of great subtlety can be achieved by this technique.

Zanfirico rods Refers to the technique *Filigrana a retortoli*. This is where white and colored threads or ribbons are twisted together in a filigree within clear glass. It is commonly found in Murano glass. The term is a corruption of the name of early 19th-century Venetian art dealer Antonio Sanquirico.

Key to Source Codes

Each piece of glass shown in this book has an accompanying letter code that identifies the dealer or auction house that either is selling or has sold it, or the museum or picture agency where the piece or image is held. It should be noted that inclusion in this book in no way constitutes or implies a contract or a binding offer on the part of any contributing dealer or auction house to supply or sell the pieces illustrated, or similar items, at the price stated.

AAC
Sanford Alderfer Auction Company
501 Fairgrounds Road
Hatfield, PA 19440
Tel: 215 393 3000
Fax: 215 368 9055
E-mail: info@alderferauction.com
www.alderferauction.com

AG
Antique Glass
@ Frank Dux Antiques
33 Belvedere, Lansdown Road
Bath BA1 5HR, UK
Tel/Fax: +44(0)1225 312 367
E-mail: m.hopkins@
antique-glass.co.uk
www.antique-glass.co.uk

AGW
American Art
Glass Works Inc
41 Wooster Street, 1st floor
New York, NY 10013
Tel: 212 625 0783
Fax: 212 625 0217
E-mail: artglassgallery@aol.com
www.americanartglassgallery.com

AL
Andrew Lineham Fine Glass
Stand G19, The Mall Antiques Arcade
359 Upper Street,
London N1 8ED, UK
Tel: +44(0)20 7704 0195
Fax: +44(0)1243 576 241
www.antiquecoloredglass.co.uk

ANA
Ancient Art
85 The Vale
London N14 6AT, UK
Tel: +44(0)20 8882 1509
Fax: +44(0)20 8886 5235
www.ancientart.co.uk

ANF
Vetreria Anfora
Sacca Serenella 10
Murano 30141, Venice
Italy
Tel: +39 041 736 669

AOY
All Our Yesterdays
6 Park Road, Kelvin Bridge
Glasgow G4 9JG, Scotland
Tel: +44(0)141 334 7788
Fax: +44(0)141 339 8994
E-mail: antiques@
allouryesterdays.fsnet.co.uk

AS&S
Andrew Smith & Son Auctions
The Auction Room
Manor Farm
Itchen Stoke
Nr Winchester, UK
Tel: +44(0)1962 735 988
Fax: +44(0)1962 738 879
E-mail: auctions@andrew
smithandson.com

ASG
Anthony Stern Glass
Unit 205
Avro House
Havelock Terrace
London SW8 4AL, UK
Tel: +44(0)20 7622 9463
Fax: +44(0)20 7738 8100
E-mail:
anthony@anthonysternglass.com
www.anthonysternglass.com

BA
Branksome Antiques
370 Poole Road
Branksome
Poole, Dorset BH12 1AW, UK
Tel: +44(0)1202 763 324

BAD
Beth Adams
Unit GO43/4, Alfie's Antique Market, 13–25 Church Street
Marylebone, London NW8 8DT, UK
Tel: +44(0)20 7723 5613
Fax: +44(0)20 7262 1576
E-mail: badams@alfies.clara.net

BB
Barbara Blau
South Street Antiques Market
615 South 6th Street
Philadelphia, PA 19147-2128
Tel: 215 739 4995/
215 592 0256
E-mail: bbjools@msm.com

BGL
Block Glass Ltd
E-mail: blockglss@aol.com
www.blockglass.com

BHM
Broadfield House Glass Museum
See Museum listing

BK
Bukowskis
Arsenalsgatan 4, Box 1754
111 87 Stockholm
Sweden
Tel: +46 8 614 0800
Fax: +46 8 611 4674
E-mail: info@bukowskis.se
www.bukowskis.se

BMN
Auktionhaus Bergmann
Möhrendorferstrasse 4
D-91056 Erlangen, Germany
Tel: +49 (0)9 131 450 666
Fax: +49 (0)9 131 450 204
E-mail: kontact@auction-bergmann.de
www.auction-bergmann.de

BONBAY
Bonhams, Bayswater
10 Salem Road
London W2 4DL, UK
Tel: +44(0)20 7393 3900
Fax: +44(0)20 7313 2703
E-mail: info@bonhams.com
www.bonhams.com

BY
Bonny Yankauer
E-mail: bonnyy@aol.com

CA
Chiswick Auctions
1–5 Colville Road
London W3 8BL, UK
Tel: +44(0)20 8992 4442
Fax: +44(0)20 8896 0541
www.chiswickauctions.co.uk

CG
Cowdy Gallery
31 Culver Street, Newent
Gloucestershire GL18 1DB, UK
Tel: +44(0)1531 821 173
E-mail: info@cowdygallery.co.uk
www.cowdygallery.co.uk

CHAA
Cowan's Historic Americana Auctions
673 Wilmer Avenue
Cincinnati, OH 45226
Tel: 513 871 1670
Fax: 513 871 8670
E-mail: info@historicamericana.com
www.historicamericana.com

CHEF
Cheffins
Cheffins Fine Art Department, 1&2
Clifton Road, Cambridge CB1 7EA, UK
Tel: +44(0)1223 213 343
E-mail: fine.art@cheffins.co.uk
www.cheffins.co.uk

CMG
Corning Museum of Glass
See Museum listing

COL
Colin Reid Glass
New Mills
Slad Road, Stroud
Gloucestershire GL5 1RN, UK
Tel/Fax: +44(0)1453 751 421
E-mail: mail@colinreidglass.co.uk
www.colinreidglass.co.uk

CR
See code DRA

CRIS
Cristobal
G125–127, Alfie's Antique Market
13–25 Church Street
Marylebone
London NW8 8DT, UK
Tel/Fax: +44(0)20 7724 7230
E-mail: steven@cristobal.co.uk
www.cristobal.co.uk

CVS
**Cad van Swankster at
The Girl Can't Help It**
G100, Alfie's Antique Market
13–25 Church Street
Marylebone
London NW8 8DT, UK
Tel: +44(0)20 7724 8984

CW
**Christine Wildman
Collection**
E-mail: wild123@allstream.net

DCC
Dee Carlton Collection
E-mail: qnoscots@aol.com

DN
Dreweatt Neate
Donnington Priory Salerooms
Donnington
Newbury
Berkshire RG14 2JE, UK
Tel: +44(0)1635 553 553
Fax: +44(0)1635 553 599
E-mail: fineart@
dreweatt-neate.co.uk
www.auctions.dreweatt-neate.co.uk

DOR
Dorotheum
Palais Dorotheum
Dorotheergasse 17
A-1010 Vienna
Austria
Tel: +43 (0)1 515 600
Fax: +43 (0)1 515 60443
E-mail: kundendienst@
dorotheum.at
www.dorotheum.at

DRA
David Rago Auctions
333 North Main Street
Lambertville, NJ 08530
Tel: 609 397 9374
Fax: 609 397 9377
E-mail: info@ragoarts.com
www.ragoarts.com

DTC
Design20c
Tel: 07946 092 138
E-mail: sales@design20c.com
www.design20c.com

EOH
The End of History
548 1/2 Hudson Street
New York, NY 10014
Tel: 212 647 7598
Fax: 212 647 7634

EVD
**Etienne & Van den Doel,
Expressive Glass Art**
De Lind 38
NL-5061 HX Oisterwijk
The Netherlands
Tel: +31 (0)13 5299599
Fax: +31 (0)13 5299590
E-mail: info@etienne
vandendoel.com
www.etiennevandendoel.com

FIS
Auktionshaus Dr Fischer
Trappensee-Schößchen
D-74074 Heilbronn
Germany
Tel: +49 (0)71 31 15 55 70
Fax: +49 (0)71 31 15 55 720
E-mail: info@auctions-fischer.de
www.auctions-fischer.de

FM
Francesca Martire
F131–137, Alfie's Antique Market
13–25 Church Street
Marylebone
London NW8 8DT, UK
Tel: +44(0)20 7724 4802
Fax: +44(0)20 7586 0292
E-mail: mare@ukf.net

FRE
Freeman's
1808 Chestnut Street
Philadelphia, PA 19103
Tel: 215 563 9275
Fax: 215 563 8236
E-mail: info@
freemansauction.com
www.freemansauction.com

GAZE
Thos. Wm. Gaze & Son
Diss Auction Rooms
Roydon Road, Diss
Norfolk IP22 4LN, UK
Tel: +44(0)1379 650 306
Fax: +44(0)1379 644 313
E-mail: sales@
dissauctionrooms.co.uk
www.twgaze.com

GC
Graham Cooley
Tel: 07968 722 269
E-mail: graham.cooley@
metalysis.com

GMD
Galerie Mariska Dirkx
Wilhelminasingel 67
NL-6041 CH Roermond
The Netherlands
Tel/Fax: +31 (0)475 317137
E-mail: galerie.dirkx@wxs.nl
www.galeriemariskadirkx.nl

GORL
Gorringes, Lewes
15 North Street, Lewes
East Sussex BN7 2PD
Tel: +44(0)1273 472 503
Fax: +44(0)1273 479 559
E-mail: clientservices@
gorringes.co.uk
www.gorringes.co.uk

HBK
Hall-Bakker @ Heritage
Heritage, 6 Market Place
Woodstock, Oxon OX20 1TA, UK
Tel: +44(0)1993 811 332
E-mail: info@hallbakker.co.uk
www.hallbakker.co.uk

HERR
Auktionshaus WG Herr
Friesenwall 35
D-50672 Cologne, Germany
Tel: +49 (0)221 25 45 48
Fax: +49 (0)221 270 6742
E-mail: kunst@herr-auktionen.de
www.herr-auktionen.de

HOL
Holsten Galleries
3 Elm Street, Stockbridge
MA 01262
Tel: 413 298 3044
Fax: 413 298 3275
E-mail: artglass@
holstengalleries.com
www.holstengalleries.com

JDJ
James D. Julia Inc.
PO Box 830
Fairfield, ME 04937
Tel: 207 453 7125
Fax: 207 453 2502
E-mail: lampnglass@
juliaauctions.com
www.juliaauctions.com

JH
Jeanette Hayhurst Fine Glass
32a Kensington Church Street
London W8 4HA, UK
Tel: +44(0)20 7938 1539
www.antiqueglasslondon.com

JHA
**Jonathan Harris
Studio Glass Ltd**
Woodland House
24 Peregrine Way
Apley Castle, Telford TF1 6TH, UK
Tel: +44(0)1952 246 381
Fax: +44(0)1952 248 555
E-mail: jonathan@
jhstudioglass.com
www.jhstudioglass.com

L&T
Lyon & Turnbull Ltd
33 Broughton Place
Edinburgh EH1 3RR, Scotland
Tel: +44(0)131 557 8844
Fax: +44(0)131 557 8668
E-mail: info@
lyonandturnbull.com
www.lyonandturnbull.com

LB
Linda Bee
Grays Antique Markets
Stand L18–21
The Mews
58 Davies Street
London W1Y 2LP, UK
Tel/Fax: +44(0)20 7629 5921
www.graysantiques.com

LKM
Leo Kaplan Modern
41 East 57th Street
7th Floor
New York, NY 10021
Tel: 212 872 1616
Fax: 212 872 1617
E-mail: info@lkmodern.com
www.lkmodern.com

LN
Lillian Nassau Ltd
220 East 57th Street
New York, NY 10022
Tel: 212 759 6062
Fax: 212 832 9493

MAC
Mary Ann's Collectibles
c/o South Street Antiques Center
615 South 6th Street
Philadelphia
PA 19147-2128
Tel: 215 923 3247

MACK
Macklowe Gallery
667 Madison Avenue
New York
NY 10021
Tel: 212 644 6400
Fax: 212 755 6143
E-mail: email
@macklowegallery.com
www.macklowegallery.com

MAL
Mallett
141 New Bond Street
London W1S 2BS, UK
Tel: +44(0)20 7499 7411
Fax: +44(0)20 7495 3179
www.mallettantiques.com

MHC
Mark Hill Collection
Tel: 07798 915 474
E-mail: stylophile@btopenworld.com

MHT
Mum Had That
Tel: 01442 412 360
E-mail: gary@mumhadthat.com
www.mumhadthat.com

MW
Mike Weedon
7 Camden Passage
Islington, London N1 8EA, UK
Tel: +44(0)20 7226 5319
Fax: +44(0)20 7700 6387
E-mail: info@mikeweedonantiques.com
www.mikeweedonantiques.com

NA
Northeast Auctions
93 Pleasant Street
Portsmouth, NH 03801
Tel: 603 433 8400
Fax: 603 433 0415
E-mail: contact@northeastauctions.com
www.northeastauctions.com

NBEN
Nigel Benson
58–60 Kensington Church Street
London W8 4DB, UK
Tel: +44(0)20 7938 1137
Fax: +44(0)20 7729 9875
E-mail: nigelbenson@
20thcentury-glass.com
www.20thcentury-glass.com

NW
Neil Wilkin
Unit 3 Wallbridge Industrial Estate
Frome, Somerset
BA11 5JY, UK
Tel: +44(0)1373 452574
E mail: neil@neilwilkin.com
www.neilwilkin.com

OACC
Otford Antiques &
Collectors Centre
26–28 High Street
Otford, Kent TN14 5PQ, UK
Tel: +44(0)1959 522 025
Fax: +44(0)1959 525 858
E-mail: info@otfordantiques.co.uk
www.otfordantiques.co.uk

P&I
Paola & Iaia
Unit SO57–58
Alfie's Antiques Market
13–25 Church Street
London NW8 8DT, UK
Tel: 07751 084 135
E-mail: paolaeiaialondon@
hotmail.com

PAC
Port Antiques Center
289 Main Street
Port Washington
NY 11050
Tel: 516 767 3313
E-mail: visualedge2@aol.com

PC
Private Collection

PL
Peter Layton,
London Glassblowing
7 The Leather Market
Weston Street
London SE1 3ER, UK
Tel: +44(0)20 7403 2800
Fax: +44(0)20 7403 7778
E-mail: info@
londonglassblowing.co.uk
www.londonglassblowing.co.uk

POOK
Pook & Pook
PO Box 268
Downington, PA 19335
or 463 East Lancaster Avenue
Downington, PA 19335
Tel: 610 269 4040/
610 269 0695
Fax: 610 269 9274
E-mail: info@
pookandpook.com
www.pookandpook.com

PR
Paul Reichwein
2321 Hershey Avenue
East Petersburg
PA 17520
Tel: 717 569 7637
E-mail: paulrdg@aol.com

QU
Quittenbaum
Hohenstaufenstrasse 1
D-80801, Munich
Germany
Tel: +49 (0)89 33 00 756
Fax: +49 (0)89 33 00 7577
E-mail: dialog@quittenbaum.de
www.quittenbaum.de

RDL
David Rago/Nicholas Dawes
Lalique Auctions
333 North Main Street
Lambertville
NJ 08530
Tel: 609 397 9374
Fax: 609 397 9377
E-mail: info@ragoarts.com
www.ragoarts.com

RITZ
Ritzy
7 The Mall Antiques Arcade
359 Upper Street
London N1 0PD, UK
Tel: +44(0)20 7351 5353
Fax: +44(0)20 7351 5350

ROX
Roxanne Stuart
E-mail: gemfairy@aol.com

S&K
Sloans & Kenyon
4605 Bradley Boulevard
Bethesda
MD 20815
Tel: 301 634 2330
Fax: 301 656 7074
E-mail: info@
sloansandkenyon.com
www.sloansandkenyon.com

SL
Sloans
No longer trading

SUM
Sue Mautner
No longer trading

SWT
Swing Time
St. Apern-Strasse 66/68
D-50667 Cologne, Germany
Tel: +49 (0)221 257 3181
Fax: +49 (0)221 257 3184
E-mail: artdeco@
swing-time.com
www.swing-time.com

TA
333 Auctions LLC
333 North Main Street
Lambertville
NJ 08530
Tel: 609 397 9374
Fax: 609 397 9377
www.ragoarts.com

TAB
Take-A-Boo Emporium
1927 Avenue Road
Toronto, Ontario M5M 4A2
Canada
Tel: 416 785 4555
Fax: 416 785 4594
E-mail: swinton@takeaboo.com
www.takeaboo.com

TCS
The Country Seat
Huntercombe Manor Barn
Nr Henley on Thames
Oxon RG9 5RY, UK
Tel: +44(0)1491 641 349
Fax: +44(0)1491 641 533
E-mail: ferry-clegg@
thecountryseat.com
www.thecountryseat.com

TDC
Thomas Dreiling
Collection
Private Collection

TDG
The Design Gallery
5 The Green, Westerham
Kent TN16 1AS, UK
Tel: +44(0)1959 561 234
E-mail: sales@t
hedesigngallery.uk.com
www.thedesigngallery.uk.com

TEL
Galerie Telkamp
Maximilianstrasse 6
D-80539 Munich
Germany
Tel: +49 (0)89 226 283
Fax: +49 (0)89 242 14652

TGM
The Glass Merchant
Tel: 07775 683 961
E-mail: as@titan98.
freeserve.co.uk

TO
Titus Omega
Tel: +44(0)20 7688 1295
www.titusomega.com

TRR
Thomas R. Riley Galleries
642 North High Street
Columbus, OH 43215
Tel: 614 228 6554
www.rileygalleries.com

V
Ventesimo
G122, Alfie's Antique Market
13–25 Church Street
Marylebone,
London NW8 8DT, UK
Tel: 07767 498766

V&A
Victoria and
Albert Museum
See Museum listing

VET
Vetro & Arte Gallery in
Venice
V&A S.nc.
Calle del Cappeller 3212
Dorsoduro, 30123 Venice, Italy
Tel/Fax: +39 041 522 8525
E-mail: contact@
venicewebgallery.com
www.venicewebgallery.com

VGA
Village Green Antiques
Port Antiques Center
289 Main Street
Port Washington, NY 11050
Tel: 516 625 2946
E-mail: amysdish@optonline.net

VS
Von Speath
Tel/Fax: +49 (0)89 280 9132
E-mail: info@glasvonspaeth.com
www.glasvonspaeth.com

VZ
Von Zezschwitz
Friedrichstrasse 1a
D-80801 Munich
Germany
Tel: +49 (0)89 38 98 930
Fax: +49 (0)89 38 98 9325
E-mail: info@von-zezschwitz.de
www.von-zezschwitz.de

WAIN
William Wain at Antiquarius
Stand J6, Antiquarius
135 King's Road, Chelsea
London SW3 4PW, UK
Tel: +44(0)20 7351 4905
Fax: +44(0)20 8693 1814
E-mail: w.wain@btopenworld.com

WKA
Wiener Kunst Auktionen –
Palais Kinsky
Freyung 4
A-1010 Vienna
Austria
Tel: +43 (0)1 532 42 00
Fax: +43 (0)1 532 42 009
E-mail: office@imkinsky.com
www.palais-kinsky.com

WW
Woolley & Wallis
51–61 Castle Street, Salisbury
Wiltshire SP1 3SU, UK
Tel: +44(0)1722 424 500
Fax: +44(0)1722 424 508
E-mail: enquiries@woolley
andwallis.co.uk
www.woolleyandwallis.co.uk

Directory of Other Dealers, Auction Houses, and Museums

FRANCE

Eclat de Verre
Madame Elodie Bernard
Louvre des Antiquaires
2 Place du Palais Royal
75001 Paris
Tel: +33 (0)1 47 03 37 19
Fax: +33 (0)1 49 27 00 86
E-mail: 86galerie@
eclatduverre.com
www.eclatduverre.com

Galerie Capazza
Le Grenier de Villâtre
18330 Nançay
Tel: +33 (0)2 48 51 80 22
Fax: +33 (0)2 48 51 83 27
www.capazza-galerie.com

Galerie Daudet
10 Rue de la Trinité
31000 Toulouse
Tel: +33 (0)5 34 31 74 84
Fax: +33 (0)5 34 31 74 80
E-mail: galeriealaindaudet@
wanadoo.fr
www.galeriedaudet.com

Galerie
Place des Arts
Françoise et Rebecca Polack
8 Rue de l'Argenterie
34000 Montpellier
Tel: +33 (0)4 67 66 05 08
Fax: +33 (0)4 67 66 14 96
E-mail: place-des-arts@
wanadoo.fr
www.place-des-arts.fr

Galerie de Verre
Internationale
Chemin des Combes
06410 Biot
Tel: +33 (0)4 93 65 03 00
Fax: +33 (0)4 93 65 00 56
E-mail: verrerie@
verreriebiot.com
www.verreriebiot.com

Silice
115 Avenue Daumesnil
75012 Paris
Tel: +33 (0)1 43 43 36 00

GERMANY

CCAA Glasgalerie Köln GmbH
Auf dem Berlich 30
D-50667 Cologne
Tel: +49 (0)2 21 2 57 61 91
Fax: +49 (0)2 21 2 57 61 92
E-mail: info@ccaa.de
www.ccaa.de

Galerie Splinter
Sophie-Gips-Höfe
Sophienstrasse 20-21
D-10178 Berlin-Mitte
Tel: +49 (0)30 28 59 87 37
Fax: +49 (0)30 28 59 87 38
E-mail: splinter@glasgaleriesplinter.de
www.glasgaleriesplinter.de

Schürenberg Kunsthandel GbR
Annastrasse 17
D-52062 Aachen
Tel: +49 (0)241 30852
Fax: +49 (0)241 4012285
E-mail: mailbox@schuerenberg.com
www.schuerenberg.com

UK

Artizana
The Village, Prestbury
Cheshire SK10 4DG
Tel/Fax: +44(0)1625 827 582
E-mail: info@artizana.co.uk
www.artizana.co.uk

Mark J. West
39B High Street, Wimbledon Village
London SW19 5BY
Tel/Fax: +44(0)20 8946 2811
E-mail: mark@
markwest-glass.com
www.markwest-glass.com

The Studio Glass Gallery
63 Connaught Street
London W2 2AE
Tel: +44(0)20 7706 3013
Fax: +44(0)20 7706 3069
E-mail: mail@studioglass.co.uk
www.studioglass.co.uk

Themes & Variations
31 Westbourne Grove
London W11 2SE
Tel: +44(0)20 7727 5531
Fax: +44(0)20 7221 6378
E-mail:
go@themesandvariations.com
www.themesandvariations.com

Vessel
114 Kensington Park Road
London W11 2PW
Tel: +44(0)20 7727 8001
E-mail: info@vesselgallery.com
www.vesselgallery.com

Victor Arwas Gallery
Editions Graphiques Ltd
3 Clifford Street
London W1F 2LF
Tel: +44(0)20 7734 3944
Fax: +44(0)20 437 1859
E-mail: art@victorarwas.com
www.victorarwas.com

USA & CANADA

Chappell Gallery
14 Newbury Street
Boston, MA 02116
Tel: 617 236 2255
Fax: 617 236 5522
E-mail: amchappell@aol.com
www.chappellgallery.com

Glass Artists Gallery
2527 103rd Ave SE
Bellevue, Washington 98004
Tel: 425 454 0539
E-mail: info@GlassArtistsGallery.com
www.glassartistsgallery.com

Habatat Galleries
202 E Maple Rd
Birmingham, MI 48009
(plus other locations)
Tel: 248 554 0590
Fax: 248 554 0594
E-mail: info@habatat.com
www.habatat.com

Heller Gallery
420 West 14th Street
New York, NY 10014
Tel: 212 414 4014
Fax: 212 414 2636
E-mail: info@hellergallery.com
www.hellergallery.com

Leo Kaplan Ltd
114 East 57th Street
New York City, NY 10022-2601
Tel: 212 355 7212
E-mail: leokaplan@mindspring.com
www.leokaplan.com

Mark McDonald Ltd
555 Warren Street
Hudson, NY 12534
Tel: 518 828 6320
Fax: 518 828 9282
E-mail: 330@markmcdonald.biz
www.markmcdonald.biz

Marx-Saunders Gallery Ltd
230 West Superior Street
Chicago, IL 60610
Tel: 312 573 1400
Fax: 312 573 0575
E-mail: marxsaunders
@earthlink.net
www.marxsaunders.com

Ophir Gallery
33 Park Place
Englewood, NJ 07631
Tel: 201 871 0424
Fax: 201 871 7707
E-mail: gallerymail@
ophirgallery.com
www.ophirgallery.com

Primavera Gallery

808 Madison Avenue
(68th Street)
New York, NY 10021
Tel: 212 288 1569
Fax: 212 288 2102
E-mail:
info@primaveragallery.com
www.primaveragallery.com

Sarah Ainsley Gallery

55 Mill Street Building 32
Toronto, Ontario M5A 3C4
Tel: 416 214 9490
Fax: 416 214 9503
E-mail: contact@
sandraainsleygallery.com
www.sandraainsleygallery.com

www.planetglass.net

Laura Freidman
300 Brockmont Drive
Glendale, CA 91202
Tel: 818 241 2284
E-mail: Laura@PlanetGlass.net

MUSEUMS

AUSTRIA

**Vienna Glass Museum
(Lobmeyr)**

Kärntnerstrasse 26
1010 Vienna
Tel: +43 (0)1 5120508
Fax: +43 (0)1 5120508 85
E-mail: office@lobmeyr.at
www.lobmeyr.at

CZECH REPUBLIC

Museum of Decorative Arts

Ulice 1, Listopada 2
Staré Mesto, Prague 1
Tel: +42 (0)2 2481 1241
E-mail: direct@upm-praha.anet.cz

Sklárské Muzeum

CZ-473 01 Nový´ Bor
Nám.Míru 105
Tel: +42 424 32196

DENMARK

Glasmuseet Ebeltoft

Strandvejen 8
8400 Ebeltoft
Tel: +45 8634 1799
Fax: +45 8634 6060
E-mail: glasmuseet@glasmuseet.dk
www.glasmuseet.dk

FINLAND

Finnish Glass Museum

Tehtaankatu 23
FIN-11910 Riihimäki
Tel: +358 (0)20 758 4108
Fax: +358 (0)20 758 4110
E-mail: glass.museum@riihimaki.fi
http://kunta.riihimaki.fi/lasimus/

FRANCE

Musée de l'Ecole de Nancy

36–38 Rue du Sergent Blandan
54000 Nancy
Tel.: +33 3 83 40 14 86
Fax: +33 3 83 40 83 31
E-mail: men@mairie-nancy.fr
www.ot-nancy.fr

Musée des Arts Décoratifs

107 Rue de Rivoli, 75001 Paris
Tel: +33 (0)1 44 55 57 50
Fax: +33 (0)1 44 55 57 84
www.ucad.fr

Musée des Beaux-Arts

3 Place Stanislas
54000 Nancy
Tel: +33 3 83 85 30 72
Fax: +33 3 83 85 30 76
E-mail: mba@mairie-nancy.fr
www.ot-nancy.fr

**Musée du Verre Sars
Pottery**

1 Rue du Général de Gaulle
59216 Sars-Poteries
Tel: +33 (0)3 27 61 61 44
Fax: +33 (0)3 27 61 65 64
E-mail: museeduverre@cg59.fr
www.cg59.fr/SARSPOTERIES/
default.htm#

GERMANY

Glasmuseum Frauenau

Am Museumspark 1
D-94258 Frauenau
Tel: +49 (0)9926 940 035
Fax: +49 (0)9926 940 036
E-mail: info@
glasmuseum-frauenau.de
www.glasmuseum-frauenau.de

**Glasmuseum
Weißwasser**

Forster Strasse 12
D-02943 Weißwasser
Tel: +49 (0)3576 204 000
Fax: +49 (0)3576 212 9613
E-mail: info@
glasmuseum-weisswasser.de
www.glasmuseum-weisswasser.de

Passauer Glasmuseum

Am Rathausplatz
D-94032 Passau
Tel: +49 (0)851 35071
Fax: +49 (0)851 31712
www.glasmuseum.de

**Stiftung Museum Kunst
Palast**

Ehrenhof 4–5
40479 Düsseldorf
Tel: +49 (0)211 899 6241
Fax: +49 (0)211 892 9307
www.museum-kunst-palast.de

ITALY

Museo Correr

Piazza San Marco 52
30124 Venice
Tel: +39 041 240 5211
Fax: +39 041 520 0935
E-mail: mkt.musei@
comune.venezia.it
www.museiciviciveneziani.it

Museo Vetrario Murano

Fondamenta Giustinian 8
Murano 30141, Venice
Tel/Fax: +39 041 739 586
E-mail: mkt.musei@
comune.venezia.it
www.museiciviciveneziani.it

JAPAN

**Hokkaido Museum of
Modern Art**

Kita 1, Nishi 17, Chuo-ku,
Sapporo, Hokkaido 060-0001
Tel: +81 (0)11 644 6881
www.aurora-net.or.jp/art/dokinbi

Suntory Museum of Art

Tokyo Suntory Building
11th Floor , 1-2-3 Moto-akasaka
Minato-ku
Tokyo 107-8430
Tel: +81 (0)3 3470 1073
Fax: +81 (0)3 3470 9186
www.suntory.co.jp

Yokohama Museum of Art

3-4-1, Minatomirai
Nishi-ku
Yokohama-shi
Kanagawa 220-0012
Tel: +81 (0)45 221 0300
Fax: +81 (0)45 221 0317
www.art-museum.city.yokohama.jp

THE NETHERLANDS

Glasmuseum Hoogeveen

Brinkstraat 5
7902 AC Hoogeveen
Tel: +31 (0)528 220 999
Fax: +31 (0)528 220 981
E-mail: info@
glasmuseum.nl
www.glasmuseum.nl

Museum Jan van der Togt

Dorpsstraat 50
1182 JE Amstelveen
Tel: +31 (0)20 641 5754
Fax: +31 (0)20 645 2335
E-mail: jvdtogt@xs4all.nl
www.jvdtogt.nl

**Nationaal Glasmuseum
Leerdam**

Lingedijk 28
4142 LD Leerdam
Tel: +31 (0)345 612 714
Fax: +31 (0)345 613 662
E-mail: info@leerdamkristal.nl
www.leerdamkristal.nl

SWEDEN

Nationalmuseum, Stockholm

Södra Blasieholmshamnen
Postal address: Box 16176
103 24 Stockholm
Tel: +46 (0)8 5195 4300
Fax: +46 (0)8 5195 4450
E-mail: info@national
museum.se
www.nationalmuseum.se

Orrefors Exhibition Hall

SE-380 40 Orrefors
Tel: +46 (0)481 340 00
Fax: +46 (0)481 304 00
E-mail: info@orrefors.se
www.orrefors.se

Smålands Museum

Södra Järnvägsgatan 2
Box 102
SE-351 04 Växjö
Tel: +46 (0)470 704 200
E-mail: reception@s
malandsmuseum.se
www.smalandsmuseum.se

SWITZERLAND

Musée de Design et d'Arts Appliqués Contemporains

Place de la Cathédrale 6
1005 Lausanne
Tel: +41 (0)21 315 25 30
Fax: +41 (0)21 315 25 39
E-mail: mu.dac@lausanne.ch
www.lausanne.ch

UK

Brighton Museum & Art Gallery

The Royal Pavilion
Libraries & Museums
4/5 Pavilion Buildings
Brighton BN1 1EE
Tel: +44(0)1273 290 900
E-mail: museums@
brighton-hove.gov.uk
www.brighton.virtualmuseum.info

Broadfield House Glass Museum

Compton Drive
Kingswinford
West Midlands DY6 9NS
Tel: +44(0)1384 812 745
www.glassmuseum.org.uk

National Glass Centre

Liberty Way
Sunderland SR6 OGL
Tel: +44(0)191 515 5555
Fax: +44(0)191 515 5556
www.nationalglasscentre.com

The Stained Glass Museum

The South Triforium, Ely Cathedral
Ely, Cambridgeshire CB7 4DL
Tel: +44(0)1353 660347
Tel/Fax: +44(0)1353 665025
E-mail: admin@stainedglass
museum.com
www.sgm.abelgratis.com

Ulster Museum

Botanic Gardens, Belfast
Northern Ireland BT9 5AB
Tel: +44(0)28 9038 3000
www.ulstermuseum.org.uk

Victoria and Albert Museum

Cromwell Road
South Kensington
London SW7 2RL
Tel: +44(0)20 7942 2000
www.vam.ac.uk

UNITED STATES

The Blenko Museum of Seattle

Tel: 206 789 5786
E-mail: inquiries@
BlenkoMuseumOfSeattle.com
www.BlenkoMuseum.com

Chrysler Museum of Art

245 West Olney Road
(at Mowbray Arch)
Norfolk, VA 23510
Tel: 757 664 6200
Fax: 757 664 6201
E-mail: museum@chrysler.org
www.chrysler.org

Corning Museum of Glass

One Museum Way
Corning, NY 14830
Tel: 607 937 5371
www.cmog.org

The Metropolitan Museum of Art

1000 Fifth Avenue at 82nd Street
New York, NY 10028-0198
Tel: 212 535 7710
www.metmuseum.org

Museum of American Glass

Wheaton Village
1501 Glasstown Road
Millville, NJ 08332-1566
Tel: 856 825 6800
E-mail: mail@wheatonvillage.org
www.wheatonvillage.org

Museum of Arts and Design

40 West 53rd Street
New York, NY 10019
Tel: 212 956 3535
E-mail: info@madmuseum.org
www.americancraftmuseum.org

Museum of Glass

1801 East Dock Street
Tacoma, WA 98402-3217
Tel: 253 284 4750 (Pierce County
only)/1 866 4 MUSEUM
Fax: 253 396 1769
E-mail: info@museumofglass.org
www.museumofglass.org

Index (Page numbers in *italics* refer to illustrations)

Acknowledgments

PICTURE CREDITS

The publisher would like to thank the following for their kind permission to reproduce their photographs. (Abbreviations key: t=top, b=bottom, r=right, l=left, c=center.)

16: Judith Miller/DK/RDL/ADAGP, Paris and DACS, London 2004 (bl); **23:** Corbis/Bojan Brecelj (tl); **25:** The Corning Museum of Glass, Corning, NY (r); **25:** Foundation La Triennale di Milano (br); **41:** Alamy Images (tl); **42:** Orrefors Kosta Boda AB/John Selbing (br); **45:** Courtesy of the Trustees of the V&A (bcr); **52:** Corbis/ Burstein Collection (br); **53:** Hulton Archive/Getty Images (r); **70:** Alamy Images (br); **75:** Alamy Images (tl); **78:** Réunion Des Musées Nationaux Agence Photographique/Musee Des Beaux Arts, Nancy/Harry Brejat (br); **84:** Judith Miller/DK/RDL/ADAGP, Paris and DACS, London 2004; **86:** Judith Miller/DK/RDL/ADAGP, Paris and DACS, London 2004 (cl), (tr), (br); **87:** Judith Miller/DK/RDL/ADAGP, Paris and DACS, London 2004 (br); **88:** The Advertising Archive/ADAGP, Paris and DACS, London 2004 (br), Judith Miller/DK/RDL/ADAGP, Paris and DACS, London 2004 (bl), (tr); **89:** Judith Miller/DK/RDL/ADAGP, London 2004 (tl), (tc), (tr), (cl), (c), (cr), bl), (bcl), (bcr), (br); **90:** Alamy Images (br); **94:** Judith Miller/DK/Christine Wildman Collection/ADAGP, Paris and DACS, London 2004 (tr), Judith Miller/DK/Gorringes/ADAGP, Paris and DACS, London 2004 (cr); **95:** Judith Miller/DK/Gorringes/ADAGP, Paris and DACS, London 2004 (tc); **97:** Broadfield House Glass Museum, Kingswinford (bl), (r), (t); **98:** Science Photo Library/Lawrence Lawry (r), Judith Miller/DK/Drewatt Neate/ADAGP, Paris and DACS, London 2004 (bl); **99:** Judith Miller/DK/RDL/ ADAGP, Paris and DACS, London 2004 (r); **100:** Judith Miller/DK/RDL/ADAGP, Paris and DACS, London 2004 (tr), (cl), (cr), (bl), (br), Judith Miller/DK/Lyon and Turnbull Ltd/ADAGP, Paris and DACS, London 2004; **101:** Judith Miller/DK/RDL/ADAGP, Paris and DACS, London 2004 (tl), (tr), (cl), (c), (bl), (bcl), (bcr), (br); **104:** Judith Miller/DK/MACK/ADAGP, Paris and DACS, London 2004 (br); **105:** Judith Miller/DK/James D Julia Inc/ADAGP, Paris and DACS, London 2004 (tr); **109:** Mary Evans Picture Library (tl); **115:** Judith Miller/DK/Rago Modern Auctions/ADAGP, Paris and DACS, London 2004 (tcr); **118:** J. Alastair Duncan (tr); **119:** J. Alastair Duncan (l); **120:** Corbis: Mimmo Jodice (br); **122:** Corning Inc. Archives (br); **129:** Hulton Archive/Getty Images/A.E French/Archive Photos (tl); **137:** Corbis/Hulton-Deutsch Collection (tl); **146:** Corbis/Adam Woolfitt (br); **154:** Arcaid/Mark Fiennes (tr); **160:** Corbis/Peter Bakeley (tr); **165:** Corbis/E.O.Hoppe (tl); **174:** Orrefors Kosta Boda AB: John Selbing (tr); **175:** Corbis/Swim Ink (l); **176:** Orrefors Kosta Boda AB (br); **177:** Corbis/Mark M. Lawrence (r); **184:** The Corning Museum of Glass, Corning, NY/gift of Harry W. and Mary M Anderson in memory of Carl G. and Borghild M. Anderson and Paul E. and Louise Wheeler (bl); gift of Steuben Division of Corning Incorporated (cl), Courtesy of the Trustees of the V&A/Daniel McGrath (tr); **185:** The Corning Museum of Glass, Corning, NY (br); **186:** Judith Miller/DK/RDL/ADAGP, Paris and DACS, London 2004 (tr); **187:** Judith Miller/DK/RDL/ADAGP, Paris and DACS, London 2004 (tcr), (bl); **191:** The Corning Museum of Glass, Corning, NY (r), Corbis/Peter Yates (tl), Courtesy of the Trustees of the V&A (bl).

Jacket: Front: Judith Miller/DK/RDL/ ADAGP, Paris and DACS, London 2004.

All other images © Dorling Kindersley and The Price Guide Company For further information see: www.dkimages.com

AUTHOR'S ACKNOWLEDGMENTS

The Price Guide Company would like to thank the following people for their contributions to the production of this book:
Harry Cowdy and Pauline Solven at Cowdy Gallery, Newent, UK; Terry Davidson at Leo Kaplan Modern, New York, US; Nicholas Dawes at David Rago Auctions, Lambertville, New Jersey, US; Dr Graham Dry at Von Zezschwitz, Munich, Germany; Matisse P. Etienne at Etienne & Van den Doel, Oisterwijk, The Netherlands; Mr & Mrs Herr at W.G. Herr, Cologne, Germany; Peter Layton at London Glass Blowing, London, UK; John Mackie at Lyon & Turnbull, Edinburgh, UK; Stephen Saunders and Damon Crain at The End of History, New York, US; Jim Schantz and Mary Childs at Holsten Galleries, Massachusetts, US; Alvise Schiavon and Veronika Leibetseder at Vetro & Arte Gallery, Venice, Italy; Allan Shanks at American Art Glass Works, New York, US; Eric Silver at Lillian Nassau, New York, US; John Smith, Mallett, London, UK; Anthony Stern at Anthony Stern Glass, London, UK; Askan Quittenbaum at Quittenbaum Auctions, Munich, Germany; Horst Ungar at Dr Fischer, Heilbronn, Germany; Olivier van Wijk and Mariska Dirkx at Galerie Mariska Dirkx, Roermond, The Netherlands.
Thanks also to: Keith Baker, Dr Graham Cooley, Martina Franke, Wilfrid von Spaeth, and Nicolas Tricaud de Montonniere.

PUBLISHER'S ACKNOWLEDGMENTS

Dorling Kindersley would like to thank Paula Regan and Angela Wilkes for editorial assistance, Anna Plucinska for design assistance, Dorothy Frame for the index, and Scott Stickland and Jonathan Brooks for digital image coordination.